A ~~~~~~~~~
A PI~~~~~~~~~~~~~~~~~~~~~

With expert readings and forecasts, you can chart a course to romance, adventure, good health, or career opportunities while gaining valuable insight into yourself and others. Offering a daily outlook for 18 full months, this fascinating guide shows you:

- The important dates in your life
- What to expect from an astrological reading
- How the stars can help you stay healthy and fit
  And more!

Let this sound advice guide you through a year of heavenly possibilities—for today and for every day of 2009!

SYDNEY OMARR'S® DAY-BY-DAY ASTROLOGICAL GUIDE FOR

ARIES—March 21–April 19
TAURUS—April 20–May 20
GEMINI—May 21–June 20
CANCER—June 21–July 22
LEO—July 23–August 22
VIRGO—August 23–September 22
LIBRA—September 23–October 22
SCORPIO—October 23–November 21
SAGITTARIUS—November 22–December 21
CAPRICORN—December 22–January 19
AQUARIUS—January 20–February 18
PISCES—February 19–March 20

IN 2009

SYDNEY OMARR'S®

DAY-BY-DAY ASTROLOGICAL GUIDE FOR

LIBRA

SEPTEMBER 23–OCTOBER 22

2009

by Trish MacGregor
with Carol Tonsing

Ø
A SIGNET BOOK

Published by New American Library, a division of
Penguin Group (USA) Inc., 375 Hudson Street,
New York, New York 10014, USA
Penguin Group (Canada), 90 Eglinton Avenue East, Suite 700, Toronto,
Ontario M4P 2Y3, Canada (a division of Pearson Penguin Canada Inc.)
Penguin Books Ltd., 80 Strand, London WC2R 0RL, England
Penguin Ireland, 25 St. Stephen's Green, Dublin 2,
Ireland (a division of Penguin Books Ltd.)
Penguin Group (Australia), 250 Camberwell Road, Camberwell, Victoria 3124,
Australia (a division of Pearson Australia Group Pty. Ltd.)
Penguin Books India Pvt. Ltd., 11 Community Centre, Panchsheel Park,
New Delhi - 110 017, India
Penguin Group (NZ), 67 Apollo Drive, Rosedale, North Shore 0632,
New Zealand (a division of Pearson New Zealand Ltd.)
Penguin Books (South Africa) (Pty.) Ltd., 24 Sturdee Avenue,
Rosebank, Johannesburg 2196, South Africa

Penguin Books Ltd., Registered Offices:
80 Strand, London WC2R 0RL, England

First published by Signet, an imprint of New American Library,
a division of Penguin Group (USA) Inc.

First Printing, June 2008
10 9 8 7 6 5 4 3 2 1

PUBLISHER'S NOTE
While the author has made every effort to provide accurate telephone numbers
and Internet addresses at the time of publication, neither the publisher nor the
author assumes any responsibility for errors, or for changes that occur after publication. Further, publisher does not have any control over and does not assume
any responsibility for author or third-party Web sites or their content.

CONTENTS

♎ INTRODUCTION

Accessible Astrology

At a recent New York exhibit honoring the life of Princess Grace of Monaco (the former Hollywood star Grace Kelly) there was a surprise for astrology fans. A glass display case was filled with her astrological memorabilia: a jeweled Scorpio pendant, meticulous handwritten horoscopes of loved ones, and invitations to a gala Scorpio-theme birthday party. Even the catalogue of the exhibit prominently mentioned her sun sign. Like many of the rich and famous of her era, Princess Grace had access to astrologers, and she consulted them regularly.

At the time of Princess Grace's death in 1982, astrology was becoming widely available to the general public via books and horoscope magazines. Today, astrology is more accessible than ever to anyone who wishes to gain self-knowledge or to help make better life choices. As you approach the challenges and opportunities of 2009, let this guide help you discover and use all the tools astrology provides. You'll learn the important dates in your life this year, in addition to how the stars can help you improve relationships, find the right career, get organized, or support ecological programs. For those who are new to astrology or would like to know more about it, there are easy techniques to start putting astrology to work for you every day. You'll learn about your sun sign and how to decipher the mysterious symbols on a horoscope chart. Then you can use the convenient tables in this book to look up other planets in your horoscope, each of which sheds light on a different facet of your personal life.

Will the passion last, is Aries or Capricorn "the one," and where will you meet the perfect partner? Astrology is an age-old mating and dating coach. In our chapters, you'll

1

find answers to your burning questions about romance and tips about how to seduce every sign. We illustrate each sun-sign combination with famous pairs so you can visualize how some couples kept the flame of love burning and some fizzled out.

Whether it's money matters, fashion tips, or ways to sustain the planet, we'll provide guidance you can use every day. Can't decide whether to go to Italy or Mexico for this year's vacation? Try your sun sign's favored vacation spot. Most people have access to the Internet, where there's a mind-boggling variety of astrology sites. We've edited them down to the best sites where you can get free horoscopes, connect with other astrology fans, buy astrology software, and even find an accredited college that specializes in astrological studies.

There are so many ways to put astrology into your life. Before giving yourself or your home a makeover, consult your sun sign's special colors and styles to create a harmonious environment. Get in the best shape ever with a fitness program designed for your sign.

To make the most of each day, there are eighteen months of on-target daily horoscopes. So here's hoping you use your star power wisely and well to make 2009 a productive and happy year!

♎ CHAPTER 1

The Top Trends of 2009: A New Balancing Act

Astrologers judge the trends of a year by following the slow-moving planets, from Jupiter through Pluto. A change in sign indicates a new cycle, with new emphasis. The farthest planets (Uranus, Neptune, and Pluto) which stay in a sign for at least seven years, cause a very significant change in the atmosphere when they change signs. Shifts in Jupiter, which changes every year, and Saturn, every two years, are more obvious in current events and daily lives. Jupiter generally brings a fortunate, expansive emphasis to its new sign, while Saturn's two-year cycle is a reality check, bringing tests of maturity, discipline, and responsibility.

The Power of Little Pluto

Though astronomers have demoted tiny Pluto from being a full-fledged planet to a dwarf planet, astrologers have been tracking its influence since Pluto was discovered in 1930 and have witnessed that this minuscule celestial body has a powerful effect on both a personal and global level. So Pluto, which moved into the sign of Capricorn last year, will still be called a "planet" by astrologers and will be given just as much importance as before.

Down-to-Earth Capricorn Is Balanced with Forward-Looking Aquarius

Last year, the emphasis was on the earth signs of Capricorn and Virgo, which still continues for most of this year. Until 2024, Pluto will exert its influence in this practical, building, healing earth sign. Capricorn relates to structures, institutions, order, mountains and mountain countries, mineral rights, issues involving the elderly and growing older—all of which will be emphasized in the coming years. It is the sign of established order, corporations, big business—all of which will be accented. Possibly, it will fall to business structures to create a new sense of order in the world.

You should now feel the rumblings of change in the Capricorn area of your horoscope and in the world at large. The last time Pluto was in Capricorn was the years up to and during the Revolutionary War; therefore this should be an important time in the U.S. political scene, as well as a reflection of the aging and maturing of American society in general. Both the rise and the fall of the Ottoman Empire happened under Pluto in Capricorn.

The Aquarius Factor

This year, Jupiter moves from conservative Capricorn to more liberal, experimental, humanitarian Aquarius. During the year that Jupiter remains in a sign, the fields associated with that sign are the ones that currently arouse excitement and enthusiasm, usually providing excellent opportunities for expansion, fame, and fortune.

Jupiter in Aquarius promotes freedom-loving, liberal influences, which should balance the more conservative serious Capricorn-Virgo atmosphere. As it joins and expands the influence of Neptune, also in Aquarius, there should be many artistic and scientific breakthroughs. International politics also comes under this influence, as Neptune in Aquarius raises issues of global boundaries and political structures not being as solid as they seem. This could continue to produce rebellion and chaos in the environment. However, with the generally benevolent force of Jupiter backing up the creative side of Neptune, it is possible that highly original and effective solutions to global problems will be found, which could transcend the current social and cultural barriers.

Another place we notice the Jupiter influence is in fashion, which should veer into a more original and experimental mode, perhaps reminiscent of the 1960s, with brighter colors and more high-tech fabrics.

Those born under Aquarius should have many opportunities during the year. However, the key is to keep your feet on the ground. The flip side of Jupiter is that there are no limits. You can expand off the planet under a Jupiter transit, which is why the planet is often called the "Gateway to Heaven." If something is going to burst (such as an artery) or overextend or go over the top in some way, it could happen under a supposedly lucky Jupiter transit, so beware.

Those born under Leo may find their best opportunities working with partners this year, as Jupiter will be transiting their seventh house of relationships.

Saturn in Virgo: The Maturing of the Baby Boomers, Reforms in Care and Maintenance

Saturn, the planet of limitation, testing, and restriction, will be transiting Virgo for most of the year. This is a time when Virgo issues—health care and maintenance, education, and moral standards and controls—will come to the fore. For most of this year, we will be adjusting the structures of our lives, making changes so that we can function at an optimal efficient level. That means making game plans and to-do lists, clearing out clutter, and organizing and simplifying our lives. We'll be challenged with a reality check in areas where we have been too optimistic or expansive.

5

Saturn in Libra

Saturn moves into Libra on October 29. This is one of Saturn's best positions, where it can steady the scales of justice and promote balanced, responsible judgment. There should be much deliberation over duty, honor, and fairness, which will be ongoing for the next two years. Far-reaching new legislation and diplomatic moves are possible, perhaps resolving difficult international standoffs. Because this placement works well with the humanitarian Aquarius influence of Jupiter and Neptune, there should be new hope of resolving conflicts. Previously, Saturn was in Libra during the early 1920s, the early 1950s, and again in the early 1980s.

Continuing Trends

Uranus and Neptune continue to do a kind of astrological dance called a "mutual reception." This is a supportive relationship where Uranus is in Pisces, the sign ruled by Neptune, while Neptune is in Aquarius, the sign ruled by Uranus. When this dance is over in 2011, it is likely that we will be living under very different political and social circumstances.

Uranus in Pisces

Uranus, known as the Great Awakener, tends to cause both upheaval and innovation in the sign it transits. During previous episodes of Uranus in Pisces, great religions and spiritual movements have come into being, most recently Mormonism and Christian Fundamentalism. In its most positive mode, Pisces promotes imagination and creativity, the art of illusion in theater and film, and the inspiration of great artists.

A water sign, Pisces is naturally associated with all things liquid—such as oceans, oil, and alcohol—and with those creatures that live in the water—fish, the fishing industry, fish habitats, and fish farming. Currently there is a great debate going on about overfishing, contamination of fish, and fish farming. The underdogs, the enslaved, and the disenfranchised should also benefit from Uranus in Pisces. Since Uranus is a disruptive influence that aims to challenge the status quo, the forces of nature that manifest now will most likely be in the Pisces area—the oceans, seas, and rivers. We have so far seen unprecedented rainy seasons, floods, mud slides, and disastrous hurricanes. Note that 2005's devastating Hurricane Katrina hit an area known for both the oil and fishing industries.

Pisces is associated with the prenatal phase of life, which is related to regenerative medicine. The controversy over embryonic stem cell research will continue to be debated, but recent developments may make the arguments moot. Petroleum issues, both in the oil-producing countries and offshore oil drilling, will come to a head. Uranus in Pisces suggests that development of new hydroelectric sources may provide the power we need to continue our current power-thirsty lifestyle.

As in previous eras, there should continue to be a flourishing of the arts. We are seeing many new artistic forms developing now, such as computer-created actors and special effects. The sky's the limit on this influence.

Those who have problems with Uranus are those who resist change, so the key is to embrace the future.

Neptune in Aquarius

Neptune is a planet of imagination and creativity, but also of deception and illusion. Neptune is associated with hospitals, which have been the subject of much controversy. On the positive side, hospitals are acquiring cutting-edge technology. The atmosphere of many hospitals is already changing from the intimidating and sterile environment of the past to that of a health-promoting spa. Alternative therapies, such as massage, diet counseling, and aromatherapy, are becoming commonplace, which expresses this Neptune

7

trend. New procedures in plastic surgery, also a Neptune glamour field, and antiaging therapies are giving the illusion of youth.

However, issues involving the expense and quality of health care, medication, and the evolving relationship between doctors, drug companies, and HMOs reflect a darker side of this trend.

Eclipses Are Movers and Shakers

Six eclipses this year, more than usual, could shake up the financial markets and rock your world in January, July, and late December. The three eclipses in July are the ones to watch, especially the total solar eclipse at the time of the new moon on July 22, which is sandwiched between two lunar eclipses on July 7 and August 5. As several recent studies have shown the stock market to be linked to the lunar cycle, it might be wise to track investments more carefully during this time.

What About the New Planets?

Our solar system is getting crowded, as astronomers continue to discover new objects circling the sun. In addition to the familiar planets, there are dwarf planets, comets, cometoids, asteroids, and strange icy bodies in the Kuiper Belt beyond Neptune. A dwarf planet christened Eris, discovered in 2005, is now being observed and analyzed by astrologers. Eris was named after a goddess of discord and strife. In mythology, she was a troublemaker who made men think their opinions were right and others wrong. What an appropriate name for a planet discovered during a time of discord in the Middle East and elsewhere! Eris has a companion moon named Dysnomia for her daughter, described as a demon spirit of lawlessness. With mythological associations like these, we wonder what the effect of this mother-daughter duo will be. Once

Eris's orbit is established, astrologers will track the impact of this planet on our horoscopes. Eris takes about 560 years to orbit the sun, which means its emphasis in a given astrological sign will affect several generations.

♎ CHAPTER 2

How Astrology Works: The Basics

It's hard to believe, but once the inner workings of astrology were a mystery accessible only to a select few scholars. Now it's easy to pick up enough basic knowledge to go beyond the realm of your sun sign into the deeper areas of this fascinating subject, which combines science, art, spirituality, and psychology. In this chapter, we'll show you how astrology works. You'll be able to define a sign and figure out why astrologers say what they do about each sign. As you look at your astrological chart, you'll have a good idea of what's going on in each portion of the horoscope. Let's get started.

Know the Difference Between Signs and Constellations

Most readers know their signs, but many often confuse them with constellations. *Signs* are actually a type of celestial real estate, located on the *zodiac*, an imaginary 360-degree belt circling the earth. This belt is divided into twelve equal 30-degree portions, which are the *signs*. There's a lot of confusion about the difference between the *signs* and the *constellations* of the zodiac, patterns of stars which originally marked the twelve divisions, like signposts. Though a *sign* is named after the *constellation* that once marked the same area, the constellations are no longer in the same place relative to the earth that they were many centuries ago. Over hundreds of years, the earth's orbit has shifted, so that from our point of view here on earth, the constellations seem to have moved. However, the signs remain in place. (Most Western astrology uses the twelve-equal-part division of the zodiac, though there are some other methods of astrology that still use the constellations instead of the signs.)

Most people think of themselves in terms of their sun sign. A *sun sign* refers to the sign the sun is orbiting through at a given moment (from our point of view here on earth). For instance, if someone says, "I'm an Aries," the sun was passing through Aries when that person was born. However, there are nine other planets (plus asteroids, fixed stars, and sensitive points) that also form our total astrological personality, and some or many of these will be located in other signs. No one is completely "Aries," with all their astrological components in one sign! (Please note that, in astrology, the sun and moon are usually referred to as "planets," though of course they're not. Though there is some controversy over Pluto, it is still called a "planet" by astrologers.)

As we mentioned before, the sun signs are *places* on the zodiac. They do not *do* anything (the planets are the doers). However, they are associated with many things, depending on their location on the zodiac.

How Do We Define a Sign's Characteristics?

The definitions of the signs evolved systematically from four interrelated components: a sign's element, its quality, its polarity or sex, and its order in the progression of the zodiac. All these factors work together to tell us what the sign is like.

The system is magically mathematical: the number 12—as in the twelve signs of the zodiac—is divisible by 4, by 3, and by 2. There are four elements, three qualities, and two polarities, which follow one another in sequence around the zodiac.

The four elements (earth, air, fire, and water) are the building blocks of astrology. The use of an element to describe a sign probably dates from man's first attempts to categorize what he saw. Ancient sages believed that all things were composed of combinations of these basic elements—

11

earth, air, fire, and water. This included the human character, which was fiery/choleric, earthy/melancholy, airy/sanguine, or watery/phlegmatic. The elements also correspond to our emotional (water), physical (earth), mental (air), and spiritual (fire) natures. The energies of each of the elements were then observed to related to the time of year when the sun was passing though a certain segment of the zodiac.

Those born with the sun in fire signs—Aries, Leo, Sagittarius—embody the characteristics of that element. Optimism, warmth, hot tempers, enthusiasm, and "spirit" are typical of these signs. Taurus, Virgo, and Capricorn are "earthy"—more grounded, physical, materialistic, organized, and deliberate than fire sign people. Air sign people—Gemini, Libra, and Aquarius—are mentally oriented communicators. Water signs—Cancer, Scorpio, and Pisces—are emotional, sensitive, and creative.

Think of what each element does to the others: water puts out fire or evaporates under heat. Air fans the flames or blows them out. Earth smothers fire, drifts and erodes with too much wind, and becomes mud or fertile soil with water. Those are often perfect analogies for the relationships between people of different sun-sign elements. This astrochemistry was one of the first ways man described his relationships. Fortunately, no one is entirely "air" or "water." We all have a bit, or a lot, of each element in our horoscopes. It is this unique mix that defines each astrological personality.

Within each element, there are three qualities that describe types of behavior associated with the sign. Those of cardinal signs are activists, go-getters. These four signs—Aries, Cancer, Libra, and Capricorn—begin each season. Fixed signs, which happen in the middle of the season, are associated with builders and stabilizers. You'll find that Taurus, Leo, Scorpio, and Aquarius are usually gifted with concentration, stamina, and focus. Mutable signs—Gemini, Virgo, Sagittarius, and Pisces—fall at the end of each season and thus are considered catalysts for change. People born under mutable signs are flexible and adaptable.

The polarity of a sign is either its positive or negative "charge." It can be masculine, active, positive, and yang, like air or fire signs, or it can be feminine, reactive, negative, and yin, like the water and earth signs. The polarities alternate, moving energy around the zodiac like the poles of a battery.

Finally, we consider the sign's place in the order of the zodiac. This is vital to the balance of all the forces and the transmission of energy moving through the signs. You may have noticed that your sign is quite different from your neighboring sign on either side. Yet each seems to grow out of its predecessor like links in a chain and transmits a syntheses of energy gathered along the "chain" to the following sign, beginning with the fire-powered positive charge of Aries.

How the Signs Add Up

SIGN	ELEMENT	QUALITY	POLARITY	PLACE
Aries	fire	cardinal	masculine	first
Taurus	earth	fixed	feminine	second
Gemini	air	mutable	masculine	third
Cancer	water	cardinal	feminine	fourth
Leo	fire	fixed	masculine	fifth
Virgo	earth	mutable	feminine	sixth
Libra	air	cardinal	masculine	seventh
Scorpio	water	fixed	feminine	eighth
Sagittarius	fire	mutable	masculine	ninth
Capricorn	earth	cardinal	feminine	tenth
Aquarius	air	fixed	masculine	eleventh
Pisces	water	mutable	feminine	twelfth

Each Sign Has a Special Planet

Each sign has a "ruling" planet that is most compatible with its energies. Mars adds its fiery assertive characteristics to Aries. The sensual beauty and comfort-loving side of Venus rules Taurus, whereas the idealistic side of Venus rules Libra. Quick-moving Mercury rules two mutable signs, Gemini and Virgo. Its mental agility belongs to Gemini while its analytical side is best expressed in Virgo. The changeable emotional moon is associated with Cancer, while the outgoing Leo personality is ruled by the sun. Scorpio originally shared Mars, but when Pluto was discovered in this century, its powerful magnetic energies were deemed more suitable to the intense vibrations of the fixed water sign Scorpio. Though Pluto has, as of this writing, been downgraded, it is still considered by astrologers to be a powerful force in the horoscope. Disciplined Capricorn is ruled by Saturn, and expansive Sagittarius by Jupiter. Unpredictable Aquarius is ruled by Uranus and creative, imaginative Pisces by Neptune. In a horoscope, if a planet is placed in the sign it rules, it is sure to be especially powerful.

The Layout of a Horoscope Chart

A horoscope chart is a map of the heavens at a given moment in time. It looks like a wheel with twelve spokes. In between each of the "spokes" is a section called a *house*.

Each house deals with a different area of life and is influenced by a special sign and a planet. Astrologers look at the houses to tell in what area of life an event is happening or about to happen.

The house is governed by the sign passing over the spoke (or cusp of the house) at that particular moment. Though the first house is naturally associated with Aries and Mars, it would also have an additional Capricorn influence if that sign was passing over the house cusp at the time the chart was cast. The sequence of the houses starts with the first house located at the left center spoke (or the number 9 position, if you were reading a clock). The houses are then read *counterclockwise* around the chart, with the fourth house at the bottom of the chart, the tenth house at the top or twelve o'clock position.

Where do the planets belong? Around the horoscope, planets are placed within the houses according to their location at the time of the chart. That is why it is so important to have an accurate time; with no specific time, the planets have no specific location in the houses and one cannot determine which area of life they will apply to. Since the signs move across the houses as the earth turns, planets in a house will naturally intensify the importance of that house. The house that contains the sun is naturally one of the most prominent.

The First House: Self

The sign passing over the first house at the time of your birth is known as your ascendant, or rising sign. The first house is the house of "firsts"—the first impression you make, how you initiate matters, the image you choose to project. This is where you advertise yourself, where you project your personality. Planets that fall here will intensify the way you come across to others. It is the home of Aries and the planet Mars.

The Second House: The Material You

This house is where you experience the material world, what you value. Here are your attitudes about money, possessions, and finances, as well as your earning and spending capacity. On a deeper level, this house reveals your sense of self-worth, the inner values that draw wealth in various forms. It is the natural home of Taurus and the planet Venus.

The Third House: Your Thinking Process

This house describes how you communicate with others, how you reach out to others nearby and interact with the immediate environment. It shows how your thinking process works and the way you express your thoughts. Are you articulate or tongue-tied? Can you think on your feet? This house also shows your first relationships, your experiences with brothers and sisters, as well as how you deal with people close to you, such as your neighbors or pals. It's where you take short trips, write letters, or use the telephone. It shows how your mind works in terms of left-brain logical and analytical functions. It is the home of Gemini and the planet Mercury.

The Fourth House: Your Home Life

The fourth house shows the foundation of life, the psychological underpinnings. Located at the bottom of the chart, this house shows how you are nurtured and made to feel secure—your roots! It shows your early home environment and the circumstances at the end of your life (your final "home"), as well as the place you call home now. Astrologers look here for information about the parental nurturers in your life. It is the home of Cancer and the moon.

The Fifth House: Your Self-Expression

The Leo house is where the creative potential develops. Here you express yourself and procreate, in the sense that children are outgrowths of your creative ability. But this house most represents your inner childlike self, who delights in play. If your inner security has been established by the time you reach this house, you are now free to have fun, romance, and love affairs and to give of yourself. This is also the place astrologers look for playful love affairs, flirtations, and brief romantic encounters (rather than long-term commitments). It is the home of Leo and the sun.

The Sixth House: Care and Maintenance

The sixth house has been called the "care and maintenance" department. This house shows how you take care of your body and organize yourself to perform efficiently in the world. Here is where you get things done, where you look after others and fulfill service duties, such as taking care of pets. Here is what you do to survive on a day-to-day basis. The sixth house demands order in your life; otherwise there would be chaos. The house is your "job" (as opposed to your career, which is the domain of the tenth house), your diet, and your health and fitness regimens. It is the home of Virgo and the planet Mercury.

The Seventh House: Your Relationships

This house shows your attitude toward your partners and those with whom you enter commitments, contracts, or agreements. Here is the way your relate to others, as well as your close, intimate, one-on-one relationships (including open enemies—those you "face off" with). Open hostilities, lawsuits, divorces, and marriages happen here. If the first house represents the "I," the seventh or opposite house is the "not I"—the complementary partner you attract by the way you come across. If you are having trouble with partnerships, consider what you are attracting by the energies of your first and seventh house. It is the home of Libra and the planet Venus.

The Eighth House: Your Power House

The eighth house refers to how you merge with something or someone, and how you handle power and control. This is one of the most mysterious and powerful houses, where your energy transforms itself from "I" to "we." As you give up power and control by uniting with something or someone, two kinds of energies merge and become something greater, leading to a regeneration of the self on a higher level. Here are your attitudes toward sex, shared resources, and taxes (what you share with the government). Because this house involves what belongs to others, you face issues of control and power struggles, or undergo a deep psychological transformation as you bond with another. Here you transcend yourself through dreams, drugs, and occult or psychic experiences that reflect the collective unconscious. It is the home of Scorpio and the planet Pluto.

The Ninth House: Your Worldview

The ninth house shows your search for wisdom and higher knowledge: your belief system. As the third house represents the "lower mind," its opposite on the wheel, the ninth house, is the "higher mind," the abstract, intuitive, spiritual mind that asks "big" questions, like "Why we are here?" After the third house has explored what was close at hand, the ninth stretches out to broaden you mentally with higher education and travel. Here you stretch spiritually with religious activity. Since you are concerned with how everything is related, you tend to push boundaries and take risks. Here is where you express your ideas in a book or thesis, where you pontificate, philosophize, or preach. It is the home of Sagittarius and the planet Jupiter.

The Tenth House: Your Public Life

The tenth house is associated with your public life and high-profile activities. Located directly overhead at the "high noon" position on the horoscope wheel, this is the most "visible" house in the chart, the one where the world sees you. It deals with your career (but not your routine "job") and your reputation. Here is where you go public, take on responsibilities (as opposed to the fourth house, where you stay home). This will affect the career you choose and your "public relations." This house is also associated with your father figure or the main authority figure in your life. It is the home of Capricorn and the planet Saturn.

The Eleventh House: Your Social Concerns

The eleventh house is where you extend yourself to a group, a goal, or a belief system. This house is where you define what you really want: the kinds of friends you have, your political affiliations, and the kind of groups you identify with as an equal. Here is where you become concerned with "what other people think" or where you rebel against social conventions. It's where you become a socially conscious humanitarian or a partying social butterfly. It's where you look to others to stimulate you and discover your kinship to the rest of humanity. The sign on this house can help you understand what you gain and lose from friendships. It is the home of Aquarius and the planet Uranus.

The Twelfth House: Where You Become Selfless

Old-fashioned astrologers used to put a rather negative spin on this house, calling it the "house of self-undoing." When we "undo ourselves," we surrender control, boundaries, limits, and rules. The twelfth house is where the boundaries between yourself and others become blurred and you become selfless. But instead of being self-undoing, the twelfth house can be a place of great creativity and talent. It is the place where you can tap into the collective unconscious, where your imagination is limitless.

In your trip around the zodiac, you've gone from the "I" of self-assertion in the first house to the final house, which symbolizes the dissolution that happens before rebirth. The twelfth house is where accumulated experiences are processed in the unconscious. Spiritually oriented astrologers look to this house for evidence of past lives and karma. Places where we go for solitude or to do spiritual or reparatory work belong here, such as retreats, religious institutions, or hospitals. Here is also where we withdraw from society voluntarily or involuntarily, and where we are put in prison because of antisocial activity. Selfless giving through charitable acts is part of this house, as is helpless receiving or dependence on charity.

In your daily life, the twelfth house reveals your deepest intimacies, your best-kept secrets, especially those you hide from yourself and repress deep in the unconscious. It is where we surrender a sense of a separate self to a deep feeling of wholeness, such as selfless service in religion or any activity that involves merging with the greater whole. Many sports stars have important planets in the twelfth house, which enable them to play in the zone, finding an inner, almost mystical, strength that transcends their limits. The twelfth house is the home of Pisces and the planet Neptune.

Which Are the Most Powerful Houses?

Houses are stronger or weaker depending on how many planets are inhabiting them. If there are many planets in a given house, it follows that the activities of that house will be especially important in your life. If the planet that rules the house is also located there, this too adds power to the house. The most powerful houses are the first, fourth, seventh, and tenth. These are the houses on "the angles" of a horoscope.

CHAPTER 3

Access All Your Planets

Did you know that astrology offers you not one but ten opportunities to get to know yourself (and others) better? Of course, you know your sun sign, which gives you some very useful generic information. But there are nine other members of your planetary team, each of which has a specific role to play in your total astrological personality. It's the way all these planets express themselves through their sign and their relationship to one another that makes your horoscope unique. The complete horoscope chart then lights up with colorations from many different signs and planets.

If you know all the planets (including the sun and moon), you'll be more capable of predicting how the subject of the chart will act in a given situation. If you want to know what turns someone on, consult his Venus. How about mastering a fear? Look up Saturn. Does someone anger easily? Check their Mars.

The planets are the doers of the horoscope, each representing a basic force in life. The sign and house where the planet is located indicate how and where its force will operate. For a moment, think of the horoscope as real estate. Prime property is close to the rising sign or at the top of the chart. If two or more planets are grouped together in one sign, they usually operate like a team, playing off each other, rather than expressing their energy singularly. But a loner, a planet that stands far away from the others, is usually outstanding and often calls the shots.

The sign of a planet also has a powerful influence. In some signs, the planet's energies are very much at home and can easily express themselves. In others, the planet has to work harder and is slightly out of sorts. The sign that most corresponds to the planet's energies is said to be ruled by that planet and obviously is the best place for that planet to be. The next best place is a sign where it is exalted, or especially harmonious. On the other hand, there are places in the horoscope where a planet has to stretch itself to play its role, such as the sign opposite a planet's rulership, which embodies the opposite area of life, and the sign opposite its exaltation. However, a planet that must work harder can also be more complete, because it must grow to meet the challenges of living in a more difficult sign. Like world leaders who've had to struggle for greatness, this planet may actually develop strength and character.

Here's a list of the best places for each planet to be. Note that, as new planets were discovered in this century, they replaced the traditional rulers of signs which best complemented their energies.

ARIES—Mars
TAURUS—Venus, in its most sensual form
GEMINI—Mercury, in its communicative role
CANCER—the moon
LEO—the sun
VIRGO—also Mercury, this time in its more critical capacity
LIBRA—also Venus, in its more aesthetic, judgmental form
SCORPIO—Pluto, co-ruled by Mars
SAGITTARIUS—Jupiter
CAPRICORN—Saturn
AQUARIUS—Uranus, replacing Saturn, its original ruler
PISCES—Neptune, replacing Jupiter, its original ruler

Those who have many planets in exalted signs are lucky indeed, for here is where the planet can accomplish the most and be its most influential and creative.

SUN—exalted in Aries, where its energy creates action
MOON—exalted in Taurus, where instincts and reactions operate on a highly creative level
MERCURY—exalted in Aquarius, where it can reach analytical heights

22

VENUS—exalted in Pisces, a sign whose sensitivity encourages love and creativity

MARS—exalted in Capricorn, a sign that puts energy to work productively

JUPITER—exalted in Cancer, where it encourages nurturing and growth

SATURN—at home in Libra, where it steadies the scales of justice and promotes balanced, responsible judgment

URANUS—powerful in Scorpio, where it promotes transformation

NEPTUNE—especially favored in Cancer, where it gains the security to transcend to a higher state

PLUTO—exalted in Pisces, where it dissolves the old cycle, to make way for transition to the new

The Personal Planets: Mercury, Venus, and Mars

These planets work in your immediate personal life.

Mercury affects how you communicate and how your mental processes work. Are you a quick study who grasps information rapidly, or do you learn more slowly and thoroughly? How is your concentration? Can you express yourself easily? Are you a good writer? All these questions can be answered by your Mercury placement.

Venus shows what you react to. What turns you on? What appeals to you aesthetically? Are you charming to others? Are you attractive to look at? Your taste, your refinement, your sense of balance and proportion are all Venus-ruled.

Mars is your outgoing energy, your drive and ambition. Do you reach out for new adventures? Are you assertive? Are you motivated? Self-confident? Hot-tempered? How you channel your energy and drive is revealed by your Mars placement.

Mercury Shows How Your Mind Works

Since Mercury never travels far from the sun, read Mercury in your sun sign, and then the signs preceding and following it. Then decide which reflects the way you think.

Mercury in Aries

Your mind is very active and assertive. It approaches a plan aggressively. You never hesitate to say what you think, never shy away from a battle. In fact, you may relish a verbal confrontation. Tact is not your strong point, so you may have to learn not to trip over your tongue.

Mercury in Taurus

This is a much more cautious Mercury. Though you may be a slow learner, you have good concentration and mental stamina. You want to make your ideas really happen. You'll attack a problem methodically and consider every angle thoroughly, never jumping to conclusions. You'll stick with a subject until you master it.

Mercury in Gemini

You are a wonderful communicator with great facility for expressing yourself both verbally and in writing. You love gathering all kinds of information. You probably finish other people's sentences and express yourself with eloquent hand gestures. You can talk to anybody anytime and probably have phone and E-mail bills to prove it. You read anything from sci-fi to Shakespeare and might need an extra room just for your book collection. Though you learn fast, you may lack focus and discipline. Watch a tendency to jump from subject to subject.

Mercury in Cancer

You rely on intuition more than logic. Your mental processes are usually colored by your emotions, so you may seem shy or hesitant to voice your opinions. However, this placement gives you the advantage of great imagination and empathy in the way you communicate with others.

Mercury in Leo

You are enthusiastic and very dramatic in the way you express yourself. You like to hold the attention of groups and could be a great public speaker. Your mind thinks big, so you'd prefer to deal with the overall picture rather than with the details.

Mercury in Virgo

This is one of the best places for Mercury. It should give you critical ability, attention to details, and thorough analysis. Your mind focuses on the practical side of things. This type of thinking is very well suited to being a teacher or editor.

Mercury in Libra

You're either a born diplomat who smoothes over ruffled feathers or a talented debater. Many lawyers have this placement. However, since you're forever weighing the pros and cons of a situation, you may vacillate when making decisions.

Mercury in Scorpio

This is an investigative mind that stops at nothing to get the answers. You may have a sarcastic, stinging wit, a gift for the cutting remark. There's always a grain of truth to your verbal sallies, thanks to your penetrating insight.

Mercury in Sagittarius

You are a super salesman with a tendency to expound. Though you are very broad-minded, you can be dogmatic when it comes to telling others what's good for them. You won't hesitate to tell the truth as you see it, so watch a tendency toward tactlessness. On the plus side, you have a great sense of humor. This position of Mercury is often considered by astrologers to be at a disadvantage because Sagittarius opposes Gemini, the sign Mercury rules, and squares off with Virgo, another Mercury-ruled sign. What often happens is that Mercury in Sagittarius oversteps its bounds and loses sight of the facts in a situation. Do a reality check before making promises that you may not be able to deliver.

Mercury in Capricorn

This placement endows good mental discipline. You have a love of learning and a very orderly approach to your subjects. You will patiently plod through the facts and figures until you have mastered the tasks. You grasp structured situations easily, but may be short on creativity.

Mercury in Aquarius

An independent, original thinker, you'll have more cutting-edge ideas than the average person. You'll be quick to check out any unusual opportunities. Your opinions are so well-researched and grounded that once your mind is made up, it is difficult to change.

Mercury in Pisces

You have the psychic intuitive mind of a natural poet. Learn to make use of your creative imagination. You may think in terms of helping others, but check a tendency to be vague and forgetful of details.

Venus Is the Popularity Planet

Venus tells how you relate to others and to your environment. It shows where you receive pleasure and what you love to do. Find your Venus placement on the chart in this book by looking for the year of your birth in the left-hand column. Then follow the line of that year across the page until you reach the time period of your birthday. The sign heading that column will be your Venus. If you were born on a day when Venus was changing signs, check the signs preceding or following that day to determine if that feels more like your Venus nature.

Venus in Aries

You can't stand to be bored, confined, or ordered around. But a good challenge, maybe even a rousing row, turns you on. Confess—don't you pick a fight now and then just to get someone stirred up? You're attracted by the chase, not the catch, which could cause some problems in your love life, if the object of your affection becomes too attainable. You like to wear red and can spot a trend before anyone else.

Venus in Taurus

All your senses work in high gear. You love to be surrounded by glorious tastes, smells, textures, sounds, and visuals—austerity is not for you. Neither is being rushed. You like time to enjoy your pleasures. Soothing surroundings with plenty of creature comforts are your cup of tea. You like to feel secure in your nest, with no sudden jolts or surprises. You like familiar objects—in fact, you may hate to let anything or anyone go.

Venus in Gemini

You are a lively, sparkling personality who thrives in a situation that affords a constant variety and a frequent change of scenery. A varied social life is important to you, with plenty of mental stimulation and a chance to engage in some light flirtation. Commitment may be difficult, because playing the field is so much fun.

Venus in Cancer

An atmosphere where you feel protected, coddled, and mothered is best for you. You love to be surrounded by children in a cozy, homelike situation. You are attracted to those who are tender and nurturing, who make you feel secure and well provided for. You may be quite secretive about your emotional life or attracted to clandestine relationships.

Venus in Leo

First-class attention in large doses turns you on, and so does the glitter of real gold and the flash of mirrors. You like to feel like a star at all times, surrounded by your admiring audience. The side effect is that you may be attracted to flatterers and tinsel, while the real gold requires some digging.

Venus in Virgo

Everything neatly in its place? On the surface, you are attracted to an atmosphere where everything is in perfect order, but underneath are some basic, earthy urges. You are attracted to those who appeal to your need to teach, be of service, or play out a Pygmalion fantasy. You are at your best when you are busy doing something useful.

Venus in Libra

Elegance and harmony are your key words. You can't abide an atmosphere of contention. Your taste tends toward the classic, with light harmonies of color—nothing clashing, trendy, or outrageous. You love doing things with a partner and should be careful to pick one who is decisive, but patient enough to let you weigh the pros and cons. And steer clear of argumentative types.

Venus in Scorpio

Mysteries intrigue you—in fact, anything that is too open and aboveboard is a bit of a bore. You surely have a stack of whodunits by the bed, along with an erotic magazine or two. You like to solve puzzles. You may also be fascinated with the occult, crime, or scientific research. Intense, all-or-nothing situations add spice to your life, and you love to ferret out the secrets of others. But you could get burned by your flair for living dangerously. The color black, spicy food, dark wood furniture, and heady perfume put you in the right mood.

Venus in Sagittarius

If you are not actually a world traveler, your surroundings are sure to reflect your love of faraway places. You like a casual outdoor atmosphere and a dog or two to pet. There should be plenty of room for athletic equipment and suitcases. You're attracted to kindred souls who love to travel and who share your freedom-loving philosophy of life. Athletics and spiritual or New Age pursuits could be other interests.

Venus in Capricorn

No fly-by-night relationships for you! You want substance in life, and you are attracted to whatever will help you get where you are going. Status objects turn you on. And so do those who have a serious responsible, businesslike approach, or who remind you of a beloved parent. It is characteristic of this placement to be attracted to someone of a different generation. Antiques, traditional clothing, and dignified behavior are becoming to you.

Venus in Aquarius

This Venus wants to make friends, to be "cool." You like to be in a group, particularly one pushing a worthy cause. You feel quite at home surrounded by people, and could even court fame, yet all the while, you tend to remain detached from intense commitment. Original ideas and unpredictable people fascinate you. You prefer spontaneity and delightful surprises, rather than a well-planned schedule of events.

Venus in Pisces

This Venus loves to give of yourself, and you find plenty of takers. Stray animals and people appeal to your heart and your pocketbook, but be careful to look at their motives realistically once in a while. You are extremely vulnerable to sob stories of all kinds. Fantasy, the arts (especially film, dance, and theater), and psychic or spiritual activities also speak to you.

Mars: The Action Hero

Mars is the mover and shaker in your life. It shows how you pursue your goals, whether you have energy to burn or proceed in a slow, steady pace. It will also show how you get angry. Do you explode, or do a slow burn, or hold everything inside and then get revenge later?

To find your Mars, turn to the chart on pages 64–73. Then find your birth year in the left-hand column and trace the line across horizontally until you come to the column headed by the month of your birth. There you will find an abbreviation of your Mars sign. If the description of your Mars sign doesn't ring true, read the description of the signs preceding and following it. You might have been born on a day when Mars was changing signs, in which case your Mars might fall into the adjacent sign.

Mars in Aries

In the sign it rules, Mars shows its brilliant fiery nature. You have an explosive temper and can be quite impatient. On the other hand, you have tremendous courage, energy, and drive. You'll let nothing stand in your way as you race to be first! Obstacles are met head-on and broken through by force. However, problems that require patience and persistence to solve can have you exploding in rage. You're a great starter, but not necessarily around for the finish.

Mars in Taurus

Slow, steady, concentrated energy gives you the power to last until the finish line. You've great stamina, and you never give up. Your tactic is to wear away obstacles with your persistence. Often you come out a winner because you've had the patience to hang in there. When angered, you do a slow burn.

Mars in Gemini

You can't sit still for long. This Mars craves variety. You often have two or more things going on at once—it's all an amusing game to you. Your life can get very complicated, but that only adds spice and stimulation. What drives you into a nervous, hyper state? Boredom, sameness, routine, and confinement. You can do wonderful things with your hands, and you have a way with words.

Mars in Cancer

You rarely attack head-on. Instead, you'll keep things to yourself, make plans in secret, and always cover your actions. This might be interpreted by some as manipulative, but you are only being self-protective. You get furious when anyone knows too much about you. But you do like to know all about others. Your mothering and feeding instincts can be put to good use, if you work in the food, hotel, or child-care related businesses. You may have to overcome your fragile sense of security, which prompts you not to take risks and to get physically upset when criticized. Don't take things so personally!

Mars in Leo

You have a very dominant personality that takes center stage—modesty is not one of your traits, nor is taking a back seat. You prefer giving the orders and have been known to make a dramatic scene if they are not obeyed. Properly used, this Mars confers leadership ability, endurance, and courage.

Mars in Virgo

You are the faultfinder of the zodiac, who notices every detail. Mistakes of any kind make you very nervous. You may worry, even if everything is going smoothly. You may not express your anger directly, but you sure can nag. You have definite likes and dislikes, and you are sure you can do the job better than anyone else. You are certainly more industrious and detail-oriented than other signs. Your Mars energy is often most positively expressed in some kind of teaching role.

Mars in Libra

This Mars will have a passion for beauty, justice, and art. Generally, you will avoid confrontations at all costs. You prefer to spend your energy finding diplomatic solutions or weighing pros and cons. Your other techniques are passive aggression or exercising your well-known charm to get people to do what you want.

Mars in Scorpio

This is a powerful placement, so intense that it demands careful channeling into worthwhile activities. Otherwise, you could become obsessed with your sexuality or might use your need for power and control to manipulate others. You are strong-willed, shrewd, and very private about your affairs, and you'll usually have a secret agenda behind your actions. Your great stamina, focus, and discipline would be excellent assets for careers in the military or medical fields, especially research or surgery. When angry, you don't get mad—you get even!

Mars in Sagittarius

This expansive Mars often propels people into sales, travel, athletics or philosophy. Your energies function well when you are on the move. You have a hot temper and are inclined to say what you think before you consider the consequences. You shoot for high goals—and talk endlessly about them—but you may be weak on groundwork. This Mars needs a solid foundation. Watch a tendency to take unnecessary risks.

Mars in Capricorn

This is an ambitious Mars with an excellent sense of timing. You have an eye for those who can be of use to you, and you may dismiss people ruthlessly when you're angry. But you drive yourself hard and deliver full value. This is a good placement for an executive. You'll aim for status and a high material position in life, and keep climbing despite the odds. A great Mars to have!

Mars in Aquarius

This is the most rebellious Mars. You seem to have a drive to assert yourself against the status quo. You may enjoy provoking people, shocking them out of traditional views. Or this placement could express itself in an offbeat sex life. Somehow you often find yourself in unconventional situations. You enjoy being a leader of an active group, which pursues forward-looking studies, politics, or goals.

Mars in Pisces

This Mars is a good actor who knows just how to appeal to the sympathies of others. You create and project wonderful fantasies or use your sensitive antennae to crusade for those less fortunate. You get what you want through creating a veil of illusion and glamour. This is a good Mars for someone in the creative and imaginative fields—a dancer, a performer, a photographer, or an actor. Many famous film stars have this placement. Watch a tendency to manipulate by making others feel sorry for you.

Jupiter Is the Optimist

This big, bright, swirling mass of gases is associated with abundance, prosperity, and the kind of windfall you get without too much hard work. You're optimistic under Jupiter's influence, when anything seems possible. You'll travel, expand your mind with higher education, and publish to share your knowledge widely. On the other hand, Jupiter's influence is neither discriminating nor disciplined. It represents the principle of growth without judgment. Therefore, if not kept in check, it could result in extravagance, weight gain, laziness, and carelessness.

Be sure to look up your Jupiter in the tables in this book. When the current position of Jupiter is favorable, you may get that lucky break. This is a great time to try new things, take risks, travel, or get more education. Opportunities seem to open up easily, so take advantage of them.

Once a year, Jupiter changes signs. That means you are due for an expansive time every twelve years, when Jupiter travels through your sun sign. You'll also have periods every four years when Jupiter is in the same element as your sun sign.

Jupiter in Aries

You are the soul of enthusiasm and optimism. Your luckiest times are when you are getting started on an exciting project or selling an ideal that you really believe in. You may have to watch a tendency to be arrogant with those who do not share your enthusiasm. You follow your impulses, often ignoring budget or other commonsense limitations. To produce real, solid benefits, you'll need patience and the will to follow though wherever this Jupiter falls in your horoscope.

Jupiter in Taurus

You'll spend money on beautiful material things, especially those that come from nature—items made of rare woods, natural fabrics, or precious gems, for instance. You can't have too much comfort or too many sensual pleasures. Watch a tendency to overindulge in good food, or to over-pamper yourself with nothing but the best. Spartan living is not for you! You may be especially lucky in matters of real estate.

Jupiter in Gemini

You are the great talker of the zodiac, and you may be a great writer too. But restlessness could be your weak point. You jump around and talk too much; you could be a jack-of-all-trades. Keeping a secret is especially difficult, so you'll also have to watch a tendency to spill the beans. Since you love to be at the center of a beehive of activity, you'll have a vibrant social life. Your best opportunities will come through your talent for language; speaking, writing, communicating, and selling.

Jupiter in Cancer

You are luckiest in situations where you can find emotional closeness or deal with basic security needs, such as food, nurturing, or shelter. You may be a great collector, and you may simply love to accumulate things—you are the one who stashes things away for a rainy day. You probably have a very good memory and love children—in fact, you may have many children to care for. The food, hotel, child-care, and shipping businesses hold good opportunities for you.

Jupiter in Leo

You are a natural showman who loves to live in a larger-than-life way. Yours is a personality full of color that always finds its way into the limelight. You can't have too much attention. Showbiz is a natural place for you, and so is any area where you can play to a crowd. Exercising your flair for drama, your natural playfulness, and your romantic nature brings you good fortune. But watch a tendency to be overextravagant or to monopolize center stage.

Jupiter in Virgo

You actually love those minute details others find boring. To you, they make all the difference between the perfect and the ordinary. You are the fine craftsman who spots every flaw. You expand your awareness by finding the most efficient methods and by being of service to others. Many will be drawn to medical or teaching fields. You'll also have luck in publishing, crafts, nutrition, and service professions. Watch out for a tendency to overwork.

Jupiter in Libra

This is an other-directed Jupiter that develops best with a partner, for the stimulation of others helps you grow. You are also most comfortable in harmonious, beautiful situations, and you work well with artistic people. You have a great sense of fair play and an ability to evaluate the pros and cons of a situation. You usually prefer to play the role of diplomat rather than that of adversary.

Jupiter in Scorpio

You love the feeling of power and control, of taking things to their limit. You can't resist a mystery, and your shrewd, penetrating mind sees right through to the heart of most situations and people. You have luck in work that provides for solutions to matters of life and death. You may be drawn to undercover work, behind-the-scenes intrigue, psychotherapy, the occult, and sex-related ventures. Your challenge will be to develop a sense of moderation and tolerance for other beliefs. You may have luck in handling other people's money—insurance, taxes, and inheritance can bring you a windfall.

Jupiter in Sagittarius

Independent, outgoing, and idealistic, you'll shoot for the stars. This Jupiter compels you to travel far and wide, both physically and mentally, via higher education. You may have luck while traveling in an exotic place. You also have luck with outdoor ventures, exercise, and animals, particularly horses. Since you tend to be very open about your opinions, watch a tendency to be tactless and to exaggerate. Instead, use your wonderful sense of humor to make your point.

Jupiter in Capricorn

Jupiter is much more restrained in Capricorn, the sign of rules and authority. Here, Jupiter can make you overwork and heighten any ambition or sense of duty you may have. You'll expand in areas that advance your position, putting you higher up the social or corporate ladder. You are lucky working within the establishment in a very structured situation, where you can show off your ability to organize and reap rewards for your hard work.

Jupiter in Aquarius

This is another freedom-loving Jupiter, with great tolerance and originality. You are at your best when you are working for a humanitarian cause and in the company of many supporters. This is a good Jupiter for a political career. You'll relate to all kinds of people on all social levels. You have an abundance of original ideas, but you are best off away from routine and any situation that imposes rigid rules. You need mental stimulation!

Jupiter in Pisces

You are a giver whose feelings and pocketbook are easily touched by others, so choose your companions with care. You could be the original sucker for a hard-luck story. Better find a worthy hospital or charity to appreciate your selfless support. You have a great creative imagination and may attract good fortune in fields related to oil, perfume, pharmaceuticals, petroleum, dance, footwear, and alcohol. But beware not to overindulge in alcohol—focus on a creative outlet instead.

Saturn Puts on the Brakes

Jupiter speeds you up with lucky breaks, and then along comes Saturn to slow you down with the disciplinary brakes. It is the planet that can help you achieve lasting goals. Saturn has unfairly been called a malefic planet, one of the bad guys of the zodiac. On the contrary, Saturn is one of our best friends—the kind who tells you what you need to hear, even if it's not good news. Under a Saturn transit, we grow up, take responsibility for our lives, and emerge from whatever test this planet has in store as far wiser, more capable, and mature human beings. After all, it is when we are under pressure that we grow stronger.

When Saturn hits a critical point in your horoscope, you can count on an experience that will make you slow up, pull back, and reexamine your life. It is a call to eliminate what is not working and to shape up. By the end of its twenty-eight-year trip around the zodiac, Saturn will have tested you in all areas of your life. The major tests happen in seven-year cycles, when Saturn passes over the angles of your chart—your rising sign, the top of your chart or midheaven, your descendant, and the nadir or bottom of your chart. This is when the real life-changing experiences happen. But you are also in for a testing period whenever Saturn passes a planet in your chart or stresses that planet from a distance. Therefore, it is useful to check your planetary positions with the timetable of Saturn to prepare in advance, or at least to brace yourself.

When Saturn returns to its location at the time of your birth, at approximately age twenty-eight, you'll have your first Saturn return. At this time, a person usually takes stock or settles down to find his mission in life and assumes full adult duties and responsibilities.

Another way Saturn helps us is to reveal the karmic lessons from previous lives and give us the chance to overcome them. So look at Saturn's challenges as much-needed opportunities for self-improvement. Under a Jupiter influence, you'll have more fun, but Saturn gives you solid, long-lasting results.

Look up your natal Saturn in the tables in this book for clues on where you need work.

Saturn in Aries

Saturn here puts the brakes on Aries's natural drive and enthusiasm. There is often an angry side to this placement. You don't let anyone push you around and you know what's best for yourself. Following orders is not your strong point, nor is diplomacy. You tend to be quick to go on the offensive in relationships, attacking first, before anyone attacks you. Because no one quite lives up to your standards, you often wind up doing everything yourself. You'll have to learn to cooperate and tone down any self-centeredness. Pat Buchanan has this Saturn.

Saturn in Taurus

A big issue is getting control of the cash flow. There will be lean periods that can be frightening, but you have the patience and endurance to stick them out and the methodical drive to prosper in the end. Learn to take a philosophical attitude like Ben Franklin, who also had this placement, and who said, "A penny saved is a penny earned."

Saturn in Gemini

You are a serious student of life, who may have difficulty communicating or sharing your knowledge. You may be shy, speak slowly, or have fears about communicating, like Eleanor Roosevelt. You dwell in the realms of science, theory, or abstract analysis, even when you are dealing with the emotions, like Sigmund Freud, who also had this placement.

Saturn in Cancer

Your tests come with establishing a secure emotional base. In doing so, you may have to deal with some very basic fears centering on your early home environment. Most of your Saturn tests will have emotional roots in those early-childhood experiences. You may have difficulty remaining objective in terms of what you try to achieve, so it will be especially important for you to deal with negative feelings such as guilt, paranoia, jealousy, resentment, and suspicion. Galileo and Michelangelo also navigated these murky waters.

Saturn in Leo

This is an authoritarian Saturn—a strict, demanding parent who may deny the pleasure principle in your zeal to see that rules are followed. Though you may feel guilty about taking the spotlight, you are very ambitious and loyal. You have to watch a tendency toward rigidity, also toward overwork and holding back affection. Joseph Kennedy and Billy Graham share this placement.

Saturn in Virgo

This is a cautious, exacting Saturn, intensely hard on yourself. Most of all, you give yourself the roughest time with your constant worries about every little detail, often making yourself sick. You may have difficulties setting priorities and getting the job done. Your tests will come in learning tolerance and understanding of others. Charles de Gaulle, Mae West, and Nathaniel Hawthorne had this meticulous Saturn.

Saturn in Libra

Saturn is exalted here, which makes this planet an ally. You may choose very serious, older partners in life, perhaps stemming from a fear of dependency. You need to learn to stand solidly on your own before you commit to another. Since you are extremely cautious, you deliberate every involvement—with good reason. It is best that you find an occupation that makes good use of your sense of duty and honor. Steer clear of fly-by-night situations. Both Khrushchev and Mao Tse-tung had this placement.

Saturn in Scorpio

You have great staying power. This Saturn tests you in situations involving the control of others. You may feel drawn to some kind of intrigue or undercover work, like J. Edgar Hoover. Or there may be an air of mystery surrounding your life and death, like Marilyn Monroe and Robert Kennedy, who both had this placement. There are lessons to be learned from your sexual involvements. Often sex is used for manipulation or is somehow out of the ordinary. The Roman emperor Caligula and the transsexual Christine Jorgensen are extreme cases.

Saturn in Sagittarius

Your challenges and lessons will come from tests of your spiritual and philosophical values, as happened to Martin Luther King Jr. and Gandhi. You are high-minded and sincere with this reflective, moral placement. Uncompromising in your ethical standards, you could become a benevolent despot.

Saturn in Capricorn

With the help of Saturn at maximum strength, your judgment will improve with age. And, like Spencer Tracy's screen image, you'll be the gray-haired hero with a strong sense of responsibility. You advance in life slowly but steadily, always with a strong hand at the helm and an eye for the advantageous situation. Like Pat Robertson, you're likely to stand for conservative values. Negatively, you may be a loner, prone to periods of melancholy.

Saturn in Aquarius

Your tests come from relationships with groups. Do you care too much about what others think? Do you feel like an outsider, like Greta Garbo? You may fear being different from others and therefore slight your own unique, forward-looking gifts. Or like Lord Byron and Howard Hughes, you may take the opposite tack and rebel in the extreme. You can apply discipline to accomplish great humanitarian goals, as Albert Schweitzer did.

Saturn in Pisces

Your fear of the unknown and the irrational may lead you to the safety and protection of an institution. You may go on the run like Jesse James to avoid looking too deeply inside. Or you might go in the opposite, more positive direction and develop a disciplined psychoanalytic approach, which puts you more in control of your feelings. Some of you will take refuge in work with hospitals, charities, or religious institutions. Queen Victoria, who had this placement, symbolized an era when institutions of all kinds were sustained. Discipline applied to artistic work, especially poetry and dance, or spiritual work, such as yoga or meditation, might be helpful.

How Uranus, Neptune, and Pluto Influence Your Generation

These three planets remain in signs such a long time that a whole generation bears the imprint of the sign. Mass movements, great sweeping changes, fads that characterize a generation, and even the issues of the conflicts and wars of the time are influenced by these outer three planets. When one of these distant planets changes signs, there is a definite shift in the atmosphere, the feeling of the end of an era.

Since these planets are so far away from the sun—too distant to be seen by the naked eye—they pick up signals from the universe at large. These planetary receivers literally link the sun with distant energies, and then perform a similar function in your horoscope by linking your central character with intuitive, spiritual, transformative forces from the cosmos. Each planet has a special domain and will reflect this in the area of your chart where it falls.

Uranus Is the Surprise Ingredient

Uranus is the surprise ingredient that sets you and your generation apart. There is nothing ordinary about this quirky green planet that seems to be traveling on its side, surrounded by a swarm of moons. Is it any wonder that astrologers assigned it to Aquarius, the most eccentric and gregarious sign? Uranus seems to wend its way around the sun, marching to its own tune.

Significantly, Uranus follows Saturn, the planet of limitations and structures. Often we get caught up in the structures we have created to give ourselves a sense of security. However, if we lose contact with our spiritual roots in the process, Uranus is likely to jolt us out of our comfortable rut and wake us up.

Uranus energy is electrical, happening in sudden flashes. It is not influenced by karma or past events, nor does it regard tradition, sex, or sentiment. Uranus's key words are surprise and awakening. Suddenly, there's that flash of inspiration, that bright idea, or that totally new approach that revolutionizes whatever scheme you were undertaking. A Uranus event takes you by surprise, for better or for worse. The Uranus place in your life is where you awaken and become your own person, leaving the structures of Saturn behind. And it is probably the most unconventional place in your chart.

Look up the sign of Uranus at the time of your birth and see where you follow your own tune.

Uranus in Aries

Birth Dates:
  March 31, 1927–November 4, 1927
  January 13, 1928–June 6, 1934

October 10, 1934–March 28, 1935

Your generation is original, creative, and pioneering. It developed the computer, the airplane, and the cyclotron. You let nothing hold you back from exploring the unknown, and you have a powerful mixture of fire and electricity behind you. Women of your generation were among the first to be liberated. You were the unforgettable style setters. You have a surprise in store for everyone. As with Yoko Ono, Grace Kelly, and Jacqueline Onassis, your life may be jolted by sudden and violent changes.

Uranus in Taurus

Birth dates:
  June 6, 1934–October 10, 1934
  March 28, 1935–August 7, 1941
  October 5, 1941–May 15, 1942

The great territorial shakeups of World War II began during your generation. You're independent; you're probably self-employed or you would like to be. You have original ideas about making money, and you brace yourself for sudden changes of fortune. This Uranus can cause shakeups, particularly in finances, but it can also make you a born entrepreneur, like Martha Stewart.

Uranus in Gemini

Birth dates:
  August 7, 1941–October 5, 1941
  May 15, 1942–August 30, 1948
  November 12, 1948–June 10, 1949

You were the first children to be influenced by television, and in your adult years, your generation stocks up on answering machines, cell phones, computers, and fax machines—any new way you can communicate. You have an inquiring mind, but your interests may be rather short-lived. This Uranus can be easily fragmented if there is no structure and focus.

Uranus in Cancer

Birth date:

    August 30–November 12, 1948

    June 10, 1949–August 24, 1955

    January 28, 1956–June 10, 1956

This generation came at a time when divorce was becoming commonplace, so your home image is unconventional. You may have an unusual relationship with your parents, or come from a broken home or an unconventional one. You'll have unorthodox ideas about parenting, intimacy, food, and shelter. You may also be interested in dreams, psychic phenomena, and memory work.

Uranus in Leo

Birth date:

    August 24, 1955–January 28, 1956

    June 10, 1956–November 1, 1961

    January 10, 1962–August 10, 1962

This generation understood how to use electronic media. Many of your group are now leaders in the high-tech industries, and you also understand how to use the new media to promote yourself. Like Isadora Duncan, you may have a very eccentric kind of charisma and a life that is sparked by unusual love affairs. Your children may have traits that are out of the ordinary. Where this planet falls in your chart, you'll have a love of freedom, be a bit of an egomaniac, and show the full force of your personality in a unique way, like tennis great Martina Navratilova.

Uranus in Virgo

Birth dates:

    November 1, 1961–January 10, 1962

    August 10, 1962–September 28, 1968

    May 20, 1969–June 24, 1969

You'll have highly individual work methods, and many will be finding newer, more practical ways to use computers. Like Einstein, who had this placement, you'll break the rules brilliantly. Your generation came at a time of student rebellions, the civil rights movement, and the general acceptance of health foods. Chances are, you're concerned about pollution and cleaning up the environment. You may also be involved with nontraditional healing methods.

Uranus in Libra

Birth dates:
    September 28, 1968–May 20, 1969
    June 24, 1969–November 21, 1974
    May 1, 1975–September 8, 1975
Your generation will be always changing partners. Born during the era of women's liberation, you may have come from a broken home and may have no clear image of what a marriage entails. There will be many sudden splits and experiments before you settle down. Your generation will be much involved in legal and political reforms and in changing artistic and fashion looks.

Uranus in Scorpio

Birth dates:
    November 21, 1974–May 1, 1975
    September 8, 1975–February 17, 1981
    March 20, 1981–November 16, 1981
Interest in transformation, meditation, and life after death signaled the beginning of New Age consciousness. Your generation recognizes no boundaries, no limits, and no external controls. You'll have new attitudes toward death and dying, psychic phenomena, and the occult. Like Mae West and Casanova, you'll shock 'em sexually.

Uranus in Sagittarius

Birth date:
    February 17, 1981–March 20, 1981
    November 16, 1981–February 15, 1988
    May 27, 1988–December 2, 1988
Could this generation be the first to travel in outer space? The new generation with this placement included Charles Lindbergh and a time when the first zeppelins and

the Wright Brothers were conquering the skies. Uranus here forecasts great discoveries, mind expansion, and long-distance travel. Like Galileo and Martin Luther, those born in these years will generate new theories about the cosmos and man's relation to it.

Uranus in Capricorn

Birth Dates:
    December 20, 1904–January 30, 1912
    September 4, 1912–November 12, 1912
    February 15, 1988–May 27, 1988
    December 2, 1988–April 1, 1995
    June 9, 1995–January 12, 1996
This generation, now reaching adulthood, will challenge traditions. In these years, we got organized with the help of technology put to practical use. The Internet was born after the great economic boom of the 1990s. Great leaders who were movers and shakers of history, like Julius Caesar and Henry VIII, were born under this placement.

Uranus in Aquarius

Birth Dates:
    January 30, 1912–September 4, 1912
    November 12, 1912–April 1, 1919
    August 16, 1919–January 22, 1920
    April 1, 1995–June 9, 1995
    January 12, 1996–March 10, 2003
    September 15, 2003–December 30, 2003
Uranus in Aquarius is the strongest placement for this planet. Recently, we've had the opportunity to witness the full force of its power of innovation, as well as its sudden wake-up calls and insistence on humanitarian values. This was a time of high-tech development, when home computers became as ubiquitous as television. It was a time of globalization, surprise attacks (9/11), and underdeveloped countries demanding attention. The last generation with this placement produced great innovative minds, such as Leonard Bernstein and Orson Welles. The next will be-

come another radical breakthrough generation, much concerned with global issues that involve all humanity.

Uranus in Pisces

Birth Dates:
  April 1, 1919–August 16, 1919
  January 22, 1920–March 31, 1927
  November 4, 1927–January 12, 1928
  March 10, 2003–September 15, 2003
  December 30, 2003–May 28, 2010
Uranus is now in Pisces, ushering in a new generation. In the past century, Uranus in Pisces focused attention on the rise of electronic entertainment—radio and the cinema—and the secretiveness of Prohibition. This produced a generation of idealists exemplified by Judy Garland's theme, "Somewhere over the Rainbow." Uranus in Pisces also hints at stealth activities, at hospital and prison reform, at high-tech drugs and medical experiments, at shake-ups in and new locations for Pisces-ruled off-shore petroleum drilling. Issues regarding the water and oil supply, water-related storm damage (Hurricaine Katrina), sudden hurricanes, droughts, and floods demand our attention.

Neptune Is the Magic Solvent

Neptune is often maligned as the planet of illusions that dissolves reality, enabling you to escape the material world. Under Neptune's influence, you see what you want to see. But Neptune also encourages you to create. It embodies glamour, subtlety, mystery, and mysticism, and governs anything that takes you beyond the mundane world, including out-of-body experiences.

Neptune breaks through and transcends your ordinary perceptions to take you to another level, where you experience either confusion or ecstasy. Its force can pull you off course only if you allow this to happen. Those who use Neptune wisely can translate their daydreams into poetry, theater, design, or inspired moves in the business world, avoiding the tricky con artist side of this planet.

Find your Neptune listed below:

Neptune in Cancer

Birth Dates:
    July 19, 1901–December 25, 1901
    May 21, 1902–September 23, 1914
    December 14, 1914–July 19, 1915
    March 19, 1916–May 2, 1916
Dreams of the homeland, idealistic patriotism, and glamorization of the nurturing assets of women characterized this time. You who were born here have unusual psychic ability and deep insights into basic needs of others.

Neptune in Leo

Birth Dates:
    September 23, 1914–December 14, 1914
    July 19, 1915–March 19, 1916
    May 2, 1916–September 21, 1928
    February 19, 1929–July 24, 1929
Neptune in Leo brought us the glamour and high living of the 1920s and the big spenders of that time. Neptune temptations of gambling, seduction, theater, and lavish entertaining distracted from the realities of the age. Those born in that generation also made great advances in the arts.

Neptune in Virgo

Birth Dates:
    September 21, 1928–February 19, 1929
    July 24, 1929–October 3, 1942
    April 17, 1943–August 2, 1943
Neptune in Virgo encompassed the 1930s, the Great Depression, and the beginning of World War II, when a new order was born. This was a time of facing what didn't work. Many were unemployed and found solace at the movies, watching the great Virgo star Greta Garbo or the escapist

dance films of Busby Berkley. New public services were born. Those with Neptune in Virgo later spread the gospel of health and fitness. This generation's devotion to spending hours at the office inspired the word workaholic.

Neptune in Libra

Birth dates:
  October 3, 1942–April 17, 1943
  August 2, 1943–December 24, 1955
  March 12, 1956–October 19, 1956
  June 15, 1957–August 6, 1957
This was the time of World War II, and the immediate postwar period, when the world regained balance and returned to relative stability. Neptune in Libra was the romantic generation who would later be concerned with relating. As this generation matured, there was a new trend toward marriage and commitment. Racial and sexual equality become important issues, as they redesigned traditional roles to suit modern times.

Neptune in Scorpio

Birth dates:
  December 24, 1955–March 12, 1956
  October 19, 1956–June 15, 1957
  August 6, 1957–January 4, 1970
  May 3, 1970–November 6, 1970
Neptune in Scorpio brought in a generation that would become interested in transformative power. Born in an era that glamorized sex, drugs, rock and roll, and Eastern religion, they matured in a more sobering time of AIDS, cocaine abuse, and New Age spirituality. As they evolve, they will become active in healing the planet from the results of the abuse of power.

Neptune in Sagittarius

Birth dates:
  January 4, 1970–May 3, 1970
  November 6, 1970–January 19, 1984

June 23, 1984–November 21, 1984

Neptune in Sagittarius was the time when space travel became a reality. The Neptune influence glamorized new approaches to mysticism, religion, and mind expansion. This generation will take a new approach to spiritual life, with emphasis on visions, mysticism, and clairvoyance.

Neptune in Capricorn

Birth dates:
  January 19, 1984–June 23, 1984
  November 21, 1984–January 29, 1998

Neptune in Capricorn brought a time when delusions about material power were glamorized in the mideighties and nineties. There was a boom in the stock market, and the Internet era spawned young tycoons who later lost all their wealth. It was also a time when the psychic and occult worlds spawned a new category of business enterprise, and sold services on television.

Neptune in Aquarius

Birth dates:
  January 29, 1998–April 4, 2011

This should continue to be a time of breakthroughs. Here the creative influence of Neptune reaches a universal audience. This is a time of dissolving barriers and globalization—when we truly become one world. During this transit of high-tech Aquarius, new kinds of entertainment media reach across cultural differences. However, the transit of Neptune has also raised boundary issues between cultures, especially in Middle Eastern countries with Neptune-ruled oil fields. As Neptune raises issues of social and political structures not being as solid as they seem, this could continue to produce rebellion and chaos in the environment. However, by using imagination (Neptune) in partnership with a global view (Aquarius), we could reach creative solutions.

Those born with this placement should be true citizens of the world, with a remarkable creative ability to transcend social and cultural barriers.

Pluto Can Transform You

Though Pluto is a tiny, mysterious body in space, its influence is great. When Pluto zaps a strategic point in your horoscope, your life changes dramatically.

Little Pluto is the power behind the scenes; it affects you at deep levels of consciousness, causing events to come to the surface that will transform you and your generation. Nothing escapes, or is sacred, with this probing planet. Its purpose is to wipe out the past so something new can happen.

The Pluto place in your horoscope is where you have invisible power (Mars governs the visible power), where you can transform, heal, and affect the unconscious needs of the masses. Pluto tells lots about how your generation projects power and what makes it seem cool to others. And when Pluto changes signs, there is a whole new concept of what's cool. Pluto's strange elliptical orbit occasionally runs inside the orbit of neighboring Neptune. Because of its eccentric path, the length of time Pluto stays in any given sign can vary from thirteen to thirty-two years. It covered only seven signs in the last century.

Pluto in Gemini

Late 1800s–May 26, 1914

This was a time of mass suggestion and breakthroughs in communications, when many brilliant writers, such as Ernest Hemingway and F. Scott Fitzgerald, were born. Henry Miller, D. H. Lawrence, and James Joyce scandalized society by using explicit sexual images and language in their literature. "Muckraking" journalists exposed corruption. Pluto-ruled Scorpio president Theodore Roosevelt said, "Speak softly, but carry a big stick." This generation had an intense need to communicate and made major breakthroughs in knowledge. A compulsive restlessness and a thirst for a variety of experiences characterize many of this generation.

Pluto in Cancer

Birth Dates:

May 26, 1914–June 14, 1939

Dictators and mass media arose to wield emotional power over the masses. Women's rights were a popular issue. Deep sentimental feelings, acquisitiveness, and possessiveness characterized these times and people. Most of the great stars of the Hollywood era who embodied the American image were born during this period: Grace Kelly, Esther Williams, Frank Sinatra, and Lana Turner, to name a few.

Pluto in Leo

Birth Dates:

June 14, 1939–August 19, 1957

The performing arts played on the emotions of the masses. Mick Jagger, John Lennon, and rock and roll were born at this time. So were baby boomers like Bill and Hillary Clinton. Those born here tend to be self-centered, powerful, and boisterous. This generation does its own thing, for better or for worse. They are quick to embrace self-transformation in the form of antiaging and plastic surgery techniques, to stay forever young and stay relevant in society.

Pluto in Virgo

Birth Dates:

August 19, 1957–October 5, 1971

April 17, 1972–July 30, 1972

This is the yuppie generation that sparked a mass movement toward fitness, health, and career. It is a much more sober, serious, and driven generation than the fun-loving Pluto in Leo. During this time, machines were invented to process detail work efficiently. Inventions took a practical turn with answering machines, fax machines, car phones, and home-office equipment—all making the workplace far more efficient.

Pluto in Libra

Birth Dates:
  October 5, 1971–April 17, 1972
  July 30, 1972–November 5, 1983
  May 18, 1984–August 27, 1984

A mellower generation, people born at this time are concerned with partnerships, working together, and finding diplomatic solutions to problems. Marriage is important to this generation, and they will define it by combining traditional values with equal partnership. This was a time of women's liberation, gay rights, the ERA, and legal battles over abortion—all of which transformed our ideas about relationships.

Pluto in Scorpio

Birth Dates:
  November 5, 1983–May 18, 1984
  August 27, 1984–January 17, 1995

Pluto was in its ruling sign for a comparatively short period of time. However, this was a time of record achievements, destructive sexually transmitted diseases, nuclear power controversies, and explosive political issues. Pluto destroys in order to create new understanding—the phoenix rising from the ashes—which should be some consolation for those of you who felt Pluto's force before 1995. Sexual shockers were par for the course during these intense years, when black clothing, transvestites, body piercing, tattoos, and sexually explicit advertising pushed the boundaries of good taste.

Pluto in Sagittarius

Birth Dates:
  January 17, 1995–April 20, 1995
  November 10, 1995–January 27, 2008
  June 13, 2008–November 26, 2008

During the most recent Pluto transit, we were pushed to expand our horizons and find deeper spiritual meaning in life.

Pluto's opposition with Saturn in 2001 brought an enormous conflict between traditional societies and the forces of change. It signaled a time when religious convictions exerted power in our political life as well.

Since Sagittarius is associated with travel, Pluto, the planet of extremes, made space travel a reality for wealthy adventurers, who paid for the privilege of travel on space shuttles. Globalization transformed business and traditional societies as outsourcing became the norm.

New dimensions in electronic publishing, concern with animal rights and the environment, and an increasing emphasis on extreme forms of religion were other signs of Pluto in Sagittarius. Charismatic religious leaders asserted themselves and questions of the boundaries between church and state arose. There were also sexual scandals associated with the church, which transformed the religious power structure.

Pluto in Capricorn

Birth Dates:
  January 25, 2008–June 13, 2008
  November 26, 2008–January 20, 2024

As Pluto in Jupiter-ruled Sagittarius signaled a time of expansion and globalization, Pluto's entry into Saturn-ruled Capricorn last year signaled a time of adjustment, of facing reality and limitations, then finding pragmatic solutions. It will be a time when a new structure is imposed, when we become concerned with what actually works.

As Capricorn is associated with corporations and also with responsibility and duty, look for dramatic changes in business practices, hopefully with more attention paid to ethical and social responsibility as well as the bottom line. Big business will have enormous power during this transit, perhaps handling what governments have been unable to accomplish. There will be an emphasis on trimming down, perhaps a new belt-tightening regime. And, since Capricorn is the sign of Father Time, there will be a new emphasis on the aging of the population. The generation born now is sure to be a more practical and realistic one than that of their older Pluto in Sagittarius siblings.

VENUS SIGNS 1901–2009

	Aries	Taurus	Gemini	Cancer	Leo	Virgo
1901	3/29–4/22	4/22–5/17	5/17–6/10	6/10–7/5	7/5–7/29	7/29–8/23
1902	5/7–6/3	6/3–6/30	6/30–7/25	7/25–8/19	8/19–9/13	9/13–10/7
1903	2/28–3/24	3/24–4/18	4/18–5/13	5/13–6/9	6/9–7/7	7/7–8/17
						9/6–11/8
1904	3/13–5/7	5/7–6/1	6/1–6/25	6/25–7/19	7/19–8/13	8/13–9/6
1905	2/3–3/6	3/6–4/9	7/8–8/6	8/6–9/1	9/1–9/27	9/27–10/21
	4/9–5/28	5/28–7/8				
1906	3/1–4/7	4/7–5/2	5/2–5/26	5/26–6/20	6/20–7/16	7/16–8/11
1907	4/27–5/22	5/22–6/16	6/16–7/11	7/11–8/4	8/4–8/29	8/29–9/22
1908	2/14–3/10	3/10–4/5	4/5–5/5	5/5–9/8	9/8–10/8	10/8–11/3
1909	3/29–4/22	4/22–5/16	5/16–6/10	6/10–7/4	7/4–7/29	7/29–8/23
1910	5/7–6/3	6/4–6/29	6/30–7/24	7/25–8/18	8/19–9/12	9/13–10/6
1911	2/28–3/23	3/24–4/17	4/18–5/12	5/13–6/8	6/9–7/7	7/8–11/18
1912	4/13–5/6	5/7–5/31	6/1–6/24	6/24–7/18	7/19–8/12	8/13–9/5
1913	2/3–3/6	3/7–5/1	7/8–8/5	8/6–8/31	9/1–9/26	9/27–10/20
	5/2–5/30	5/31–7/7				
1914	3/14–4/6	4/7–5/1	5/2–5/25	5/26–6/19	6/20–7/15	7/16–8/10
1915	4/27–5/21	5/22–6/15	6/16–7/10	7/11–8/3	8/4–8/28	8/29–9/21
1916	2/14–3/9	3/10–4/5	4/6–5/5	5/6–9/8	9/9–10/7	10/8–11/2
1917	3/29–4/21	4/22–5/15	5/16–6/9	6/10–7/3	7/4–7/28	7/29–8/21
1918	5/7–6/2	6/3–6/28	6/29–7/24	7/25–8/18	8/19–9/11	9/12–10/5
1919	2/27–3/22	3/23–4/16	4/17–5/12	5/13–6/7	6/8–7/7	7/8–11/8
1920	4/12–5/6	5/7–5/30	5/31–6/23	6/24–7/18	7/19–8/11	8/12–9/4
1921	2/3–3/6	3/7–4/25	7/8–8/5	8/6–8/31	9/1–9/25	9/26–10/20
	4/26–6/1	6/2–7/7				
1922	3/13–4/6	4/7–4/30	5/1–5/25	5/26–6/19	6/20–7/14	7/15–8/9
1923	4/27–5/21	5/22–6/14	6/15–7/9	7/10–8/3	8/4–8/27	8/28–9/20
1924	2/13–3/8	3/9–4/4	4/5–5/5	5/6–9/8	9/9–10/7	10/8–11/12
1925	3/28–4/20	4/21–5/15	5/16–6/8	6/9–7/3	7/4–7/27	7/28–8/21

Libra	Scorpio	Sagittarius	Capricorn	Aquarius	Pisces
8/23–9/17	9/17–10/12	10/12–1/16	1/16–2/9 11/7–12/5	2/9–3/5 12/5–1/11	3/5–3/29
10/7–10/31	10/31–11/24	11/24–12/18	12/18–1/11	2/6–4/4	1/11–2/6 4/4–5/7
8/17–9/6 11/8–12/9	12/9–1/5			1/11–2/4	2/4–2/28
9/6–9/30	9/30–10/25	1/5–1/30 10/25–11/18	1/30–2/24 11/18–12/13	2/24–3/19 12/13–1/7	3/19–4/13
10/21–11/14	11/14–12/8	12/8–1/1/06			1/7–2/3
8/11–9/7	9/7–10/9 12/15–12/25	10/9–12/15 12/25–2/6	1/1–1/25	1/25–2/18	2/18–3/14
9/22–10/16	10/16–11/9	11/9–12/3	2/6–3/6 12/3–12/27	3/6–4/2 12/27–1/20	4/2–4/27
11/3–11/28	11/28–12/22	12/22–1/15			1/20–2/4
8/23–9/17	9/17–10/12	10/12–11/17	1/15–2/9 11/17–12/5	2/9–3/5 12/5–1/15	3/5–3/29
10/7–10/30	10/31–11/23	11/24–12/17	12/18–12/31	1/1–1/15 1/29–4/4	1/16–1/28 4/5–5/6
11/19–12/8	12/9–12/31		1/1–1/10	1/11–2/2	2/3–2/27
9/6–9/30	1/1–1/4 10/1–10/24	1/5–1/29 10/25–11/17	1/30–2/23 11/18–12/12	2/24–3/18 12/13–12/31	3/19–4/12
10/21–11/13	11/14–12/7	12/8–12/31		1/1–1/6	1/7–2/2
8/11–9/6	9/7–10/9 12/6–12/30	10/10–12/5 12/31	1/1–1/24	1/25–2/17	2/18–3/13
9/22–10/15	10/16–11/8	1/1–2/6 11/9–12/2	2/7–3/6 12/3–12/26	3/7–4/1 12/27–12/31	4/2–4/26
11/3–11/27	11/28–12/21	12/22–12/31		1/1–1/19	1/20–2/13
8/22–9/16	9/17–10/11	1/1–1/14 10/12–11/6	1/15–2/7 11/7–12/5	2/8–3/4 12/6–12/31	3/5–3/28
10/6–10/29	10/30–11/22	11/23–12/16	12/17–12/31	1/1–4/5	4/6–5/6
11/9–12/8	12/9–12/31		1/1–1/9	1/10–2/2	2/3–2/26
9/5–9/30	1/1–1/3 9/31–10/23	1/4–1/28 10/24–11/17	1/29–2/22 11/18–12/11	2/23–3/18 12/12–12/31	3/19–4/11
10/21–11/13	11/14–12/7	12/8–12/31		1/1–1/6	1/7–2/2
8/10–9/6	9/7–10/10 11/29–12/31	10/11–11/28	1/1–1/24	1/25–2/16	2/17–3/12
9/21–10/14	1/1 10/15–11/7	1/2–2/6 11/8–12/1	2/7–3/5 12/2–12/25	3/6–3/31 12/26–12/31	4/1–4/26
11/13–11/26	11/27–12/21	12/22–12/31		1/1–1/19	1/20–2/12
8/22–9/15	9/16–10/11	1/1–1/14 10/12–11/6	1/15–2/7 11/7–12/5	2/8–3/3 12/6–12/31	3/4–3/27

VENUS SIGNS 1901–2009

	Aries	Taurus	Gemini	Cancer	Leo	Virgo
1926	5/7–6/2	6/3–6/28	6/29–7/23	7/24–8/17	8/18–9/11	9/12–10/5
1927	2/27–3/22	3/23–4/16	4/17–5/11	5/12–6/7	6/8–7/7	7/8–11/9
1928	4/12–5/5	5/6–5/29	5/30–6/23	6/24–7/17	7/18–8/11	8/12–9/4
1929	2/3–3/7	3/8–4/19	7/8–8/4	8/5–8/30	8/31–9/25	9/26–10/19
	4/20–6/2	6/3–7/7				
1930	3/13–4/5	4/6–4/30	5/1–5/24	5/25–6/18	6/19–7/14	7/15–8/9
1931	4/26–5/20	5/21–6/13	6/14–7/8	7/9–8/2	8/3–8/26	8/27–9/19
1932	2/12–3/8	3/9–4/3	4/4–5/5	5/6–7/12	9/9–10/6	10/7–11/1
			7/13–7/27	7/28–9/8		
1933	3/27–4/19	4/20–5/28	5/29–6/8	6/9–7/2	7/3–7/26	7/27–8/20
1934	5/6–6/1	6/2–6/27	6/28–7/22	7/23–8/16	8/17–9/10	9/11–10/4
1935	2/26–3/21	3/22–4/15	4/16–5/10	5/11–6/6	6/7–7/6	7/7–11/8
1936	4/11–5/4	5/5–5/28	5/29–6/22	6/23–7/16	7/17–8/10	8/11–9/4
1937	2/2–3/8	3/9–4/13	7/7–8/3	8/4–8/29	8/30–9/24	9/25–10/18
	4/14–6/3	6/4–7/6				
1938	3/12–4/4	4/5–4/28	4/29–5/23	5/24–6/18	6/19–7/13	7/14–8/8
1939	4/25–5/19	5/20–6/13	6/14–7/8	7/9–8/1	8/2–8/25	8/26–9/19
1940	2/12–3/7	3/8–4/3	4/4–5/5	5/6–7/4	9/9–10/5	10/6–10/31
			7/5–7/31	8/1–9/8		
1941	3/27–4/19	4/20–5/13	5/14–6/6	6/7–7/1	7/2–7/26	7/27–8/20
1942	5/6–6/1	6/2–6/26	6/27–7/22	7/23–8/16	8/17–9/9	9/10–10/3
1943	2/25–3/20	3/21–4/14	4/15–5/10	5/11–6/6	6/7–7/6	7/7–11/8
1944	4/10–5/3	5/4–5/28	5/29–6/21	6/22–7/16	7/17–8/9	8/10–9/2
1945	2/2–3/10	3/11–4/6	7/7–8/3	8/4–8/29	8/30–9/23	9/24–10/18
	4/7–6/3	6/4–7/6				
1946	3/11–4/4	4/5–4/28	4/29–5/23	5/24–6/17	6/18–7/12	7/13–8/8
1947	4/25–5/19	5/20–6/12	6/13–7/7	7/8–8/1	8/2–8/25	8/26–9/18
1948	2/11–3/7	3/8–4/3	4/4–5/6	5/7–6/28	9/8–10/5	10/6–10/31
			6/29–8/2	8/3–9/7		
1949	3/26–4/19	4/20–5/13	5/14–6/6	6/7–6/30	7/1–7/25	7/26–8/19
1950	5/5–5/31	6/1–6/26	6/27–7/21	7/22–8/15	8/16–9/9	9/10–10/3
1951	2/25–3/21	3/22–4/15	4/16–5/10	5/11–6/6	6/7–7/7	7/8–11/9

Libra	Scorpio	Sagittarius	Capricorn	Aquarius	Pisces
10/6–10/29	10/30–11/22	11/23–12/16	12/17–12/31	1/1–4/5	4/6–5/6
11/10–12/8	12/9–12/31	1/1–1/7	1/8	1/9–2/1	2/2–2/26
9/5–9/28	1/1–1/3	1/4–1/28	1/29–2/22	2/23–3/17	3/18–4/11
	9/29–10/23	10/24–11/16	11/17–12/11	12/12–12/31	
10/20–11/12	11/13–12/6	12/7–12/30	12/31	1/1–1/5	1/6–2/2
8/10–9/6	9/7–10/11	10/12–11/21	1/1–1/23	1/24–2/16	2/17–3/12
	11/22–12/31				
9/20–10/13	1/1–1/3	1/4–2/6	2/7–3/4	3/5–3/31	4/1–4/25
	10/14–11/6	11/7–11/30	12/1–12/24	12/25–12/31	
11/2–11/25	11/26–12/20	12/21–12/31		1/1–1/18	1/19–2/11
8/21–9/14	9/15–10/10	1/1–1/13	1/14–2/6	2/7–3/2	3/3–3/26
		10/11–11/5	11/6–12/4	12/5–12/31	
10/5–10/28	10/29–11/21	11/22–12/15	12/16–12/31	1/1–4/5	4/6–5/5
11/9–12/7	12/8–12/31		1/1–1/7	1/8–1/31	2/1–2/25
9/5–9/27	1/1–1/2	1/3–1/27	1/28–2/21	2/22–3/16	3/17–4/10
	9/28–10/22	10/23–11/15	11/16–12/10	12/11–12/31	
10/19–11/11	11/12–12/5	12/6–12/29	12/30–12/31	1/1–1/5	1/6–2/1
8/9–9/6	9/7–10/13	10/14–11/14	1/1–1/22	1/23–2/15	2/16–3/11
	11/15–12/31				
9/20–10/13	1/1–1/3	1/4–2/5	2/6–3/4	3/5–3/30	3/31–4/24
	10/14–11/6	11/7–11/30	12/1–12/24	12/25–12/31	
11/1–11/25	11/26–12/19	12/20–12/31		1/1–1/18	1/19–2/11
8/21–9/14	9/15–10/9	1/1–1/12	1/13–2/5	2/6–3/1	3/2–3/26
		10/10–11/5	11/6–12/4	12/5–12/31	
10/4–10/27	10/28–11/20	11/21–12/14	12/15–12/31	1/1–4/5	4/6–5/5
11/9–12/7	12/8–12/31		1/1–1/7	1/8–1/31	2/1–2/24
9/3–9/27	1/1–1/2	1/3–1/27	1/28–2/20	2/21–3/16	3/17–4/9
	9/28–10/21	10/22–11/15	11/16–12/10	12/11–12/31	
10/19–11/11	11/12–12/5	12/6–12/29	12/30–12/31	1/1–1/4	1/5–2/1
8/9–9/6	9/7–10/15	10/16–11/7	1/1–1/21	1/22–2/14	2/15–3/10
	11/8–12/31				
9/19–10/12	1/1–1/4	1/5–2/5	2/6–3/4	3/5–3/29	3/30–4/24
	10/13–11/5	11/6–11/29	11/30–12/23	12/24–12/31	
11/1–11/25	11/26–12/19	12/20–12/31		1/1–1/17	1/18–2/10
8/20–9/14	9/15–10/9	1/1–1/12	1/13–2/5	2/6–3/1	3/2–3/25
		10/10–11/5	11/6–12/5	12/6–12/31	
10/4–10/27	10/28–11/20	11/21–12/13	12/14–12/31	1/1–4/5	4/6–5/4
11/10–12/7	12/8–12/31		1/1–1/7	1/8–1/31	2/1–2/24

VENUS SIGNS 1901–2009

	Aries	Taurus	Gemini	Cancer	Leo	Virgo
1952	4/10–5/4	5/5–5/28	5/29–6/21	6/22–7/16	7/17–8/9	8/10–9/3
1953	2/2–3/3	3/4–3/31	7/8–8/3	8/4–8/29	8/30–9/24	9/25–10/18
	4/1–6/5	6/6–7/7				
1954	3/12–4/4	4/5–4/28	4/29–5/23	5/24–6/17	6/18–7/13	7/14–8/8
1955	4/25–5/19	5/20–6/13	6/14–7/7	7/8–8/1	8/2–8/25	8/26–9/18
1956	2/12–3/7	3/8–4/4	4/5–5/7	5/8–6/23	9/9–10/5	10/6–10/31
			6/24–8/4	8/5–9/8		
1957	3/26–4/19	4/20–5/13	5/14–6/6	6/7–7/1	7/2–7/26	7/27–8/19
1958	5/6–5/31	6/1–6/26	6/27–7/22	7/23–8/15	8/16–9/9	9/10–10/3
1959	2/25–3/20	3/21–4/14	4/15–5/10	5/11–6/6	6/7–7/8	7/9–9/20
					9/21–9/24	9/25–11/9
1960	4/10–5/3	5/4–5/28	5/29–6/21	6/22–7/15	7/16–8/9	8/10–9/2
1961	2/3–6/5	6/6–7/7	7/8–8/3	8/4–8/29	8/30–9/23	9/24–10/17
1962	3/11–4/3	4/4–4/28	4/29–5/22	5/23–6/17	6/18–7/12	7/13–8/8
1963	4/24–5/18	5/19–6/12	6/13–7/7	7/8–7/31	8/1–8/25	8/26–9/18
1964	2/11–3/7	3/8–4/4	4/5–5/9	5/10–6/17	9/9–10/5	10/6–10/31
			6/18–8/5	8/6–9/8		
1965	3/26–4/18	4/19–5/12	5/13–6/6	6/7–6/30	7/1–7/25	7/26–8/19
1966	5/6–5/31	6/1–6/26	6/27–7/21	7/22–8/15	8/16–9/8	9/9–10/2
1967	2/24–3/20	3/21–4/14	4/15–5/10	5/11–6/6	6/7–7/8	7/9–9/9
					9/10–10/1	10/2–11/9
1968	4/9–5/3	5/4–5/27	5/28–6/20	6/21–7/15	7/16–8/8	8/9–9/2
1969	2/3–6/6	6/7–7/6	7/7–8/3	8/4–8/28	8/29–9/22	9/23–10/17
1970	3/11–4/3	4/4–4/27	4/28–5/22	5/23–6/16	6/17–7/12	7/13–8/8
1971	4/24–5/18	5/19–6/12	6/13–7/6	7/7–7/31	8/1–8/24	8/25–9/17
1972	2/11–3/7	3/8–4/3	4/4–5/10	5/11–6/11		
			6/12–8/6	8/7–9/8	9/9–10/5	10/6–10/30
1973	3/25–4/18	4/18–5/12	5/13–6/5	6/6–6/29	7/1–7/25	7/26–8/19
1974	5/5–5/31	6/1–6/25	6/26–7/21	7/22–8/14	8/15–9/8	9/9–10/2
1975	2/24–3/20	3/21–4/13	4/14–5/9	5/10–6/6	6/7–7/9	7/10–9/2
					9/3–10/4	10/5–11/9
1976	4/8–5/2	5/2–5/27	5/27–6/20	6/20–7/14	7/14–8/8	8/8–9/1
1977	2/2–6/6	6/6–7/6	7/6–8/2	8/2–8/28	8/28–9/22	9/22–10/17
1978	3/9–4/2	4/2–4/27	4/27–5/22	5/22–6/16	6/16–7/12	7/12–8/6
1979	4/23–5/18	5/18–6/11	6/11–7/6	7/6–7/30	7/30–8/24	8/24–9/17

Libra	Scorpio	Sagittarius	Capricorn	Aquarius	Pisces
9/4–9/27	1/1–1/2	1/3–1/27	1/28–2/20	2/21–3/16	3/17–4/9
	9/28–10/21	10/22–11/15	11/16–12/10	12/11–12/31	
10/19–11/11	11/12–12/5	12/6–12/29	12/30–12/31	1/1–1/5	1/6–2/1
8/9–9/6	9/7–10/22	10/23–10/27	1/1–1/22	1/23–2/15	2/16–3/11
	10/28–12/31				
9/19–10/13	1/1–1/6	1/7–2/5	2/6–3/4	3/5–3/30	3/31–4/24
	10/14–11/5	11/6–11/30	12/1–12/24	12/25–12/31	
11/1–11/25	11/26–12/19	12/20–12/31		1/1–1/17	1/18–2/11
8/20–9/14	9/15–10/9	1/1–1/12	1/13–2/5	2/6–3/1	3/2–3/25
		10/10–11/5	11/6–12/6	12/7–12/31	
10/4–10/27	10/28–11/20	11/21–12/14	12/15–12/31	1/1–4/6	4/7–5/5
11/10–12/7	12/8–12/31		1/1–1/7	1/8–1/31	2/1–2/24
9/3–9/26	1/1–1/2	1/3–1/27	1/28–2/20	2/21–3/15	3/16–4/9
	9/27–10/21	10/22–11/15	11/16–12/10	12/11–12/31	
10/18–11/11	11/12–12/4	12/5–12/28	12/29–12/31	1/1–1/5	1/6–2/2
8/9–9/6	9/7–12/31		1/1–1/21	1/22–2/14	2/15–3/10
9/19–10/12	1/1–1/6	1/7–2/5	2/6–3/4	3/5–3/29	3/30–4/23
	10/13–11/5	11/6–11/29	11/30–12/23	12/24–12/31	
11/1–11/24	11/25–12/19	12/20–12/31		1/1–1/16	1/17–2/10
8/20–9/13	9/14–10/9	1/1–1/12	1/13–2/5	2/6–3/1	3/2–3/25
		10/10–11/5	11/6–12/7	12/8–12/31	
10/3–10/26	10/27–11/19	11/20–12/13	2/7–2/25	1/1–2/6	4/7–5/5
			12/14–12/31	2/26–4/6	
11/10–12/7	12/8–12/31		1/1–1/6	1/7–1/30	1/31–2/23
9/3–9/26	1/1	1/2–1/26	1/27–2/20	2/21–3/15	3/16–4/8
	9/27–10/21	10/22–11/14	11/15–12/9	12/10–12/31	
10/18–11/10	11/11–12/4	12/5–12/28	12/29–12/31	1/1–1/4	1/5–2/2
8/9–9/7	9/8–12/31		1/1–1/21	1/22–2/14	2/15–3/10
9/18–10/11	1/1–1/7	1/8–2/5	2/6–3/4	3/5–3/29	3/30–4/23
	10/12–11/5	11/6–11/29	11/30–12/23	12/24–12/31	
10/31–11/24	11/25–12/18	12/19–12/31		1/1–1/16	1/17–2/10
8/20–9/13	9/14–10/8	1/1–1/12	1/13–2/4	2/5–2/28	3/1–3/24
		10/9–11/5	11/6–12/7	12/8–12/31	
10/3–10/26	10/27–11/19	11/20–12/13	12/14–12/31	3/1–4/6	4/7–5/4
			1/30–2/28	1/1–1/29	
11/10–12/7	12/8–12/31		1/1–1/6	1/7–1/30	1/31–2/23
9/1–9/26	9/26–10/20	1/1–1/26	1/26–2/19	2/19–3/15	3/15–4/8
10/17–11/10	11/10–12/4	12/4–12/27	12/27–1/20/78		1/4–2/2
8/6–9/7	9/7–1/7			1/20–2/13	2/13–3/9
9/17–10/11	10/11–11/4	1/7–2/5	2/5–3/3	3/3–3/29	3/29–4/23
		11/4–11/28	11/28–12/22	12/22–1/16/80	

VENUS SIGNS 1901–2009

	Aries	Taurus	Gemini	Cancer	Leo	Virgo
1980	2/9–3/6	3/6–4/3	4/3–5/12 6/5–8/6	5/12–6/5 8/6–9/7	9/7–10/4	10/4–10/30
1981	3/24–4/17	4/17–5/11	5/11–6/5	6/5–6/29	6/29–7/24	7/24–8/18
1982	5/4–5/30	5/30–6/25	6/25–7/20	7/20–8/14	8/14–9/7	9/7–10/2
1983	2/22–3/19	3/19–4/13	4/13–5/9	5/9–6/6	6/6–7/10 8/27–10/5	7/10–8/27 10/5–11/9
1984	4/7–5/2	5/2–5/26	5/26–6/20	6/20–7/14	7/14–8/7	8/7–9/1
1985	2/2–6/6	6/7–7/6	7/6–8/2	8/2–8/28	8/28–9/22	9/22–10/16
1986	3/9–4/2	4/2–4/26	4/26–5/21	5/21–6/15	6/15–7/11	7/11–8/7
1987	4/22–5/17	5/17–6/11	6/11–7/5	7/5–7/30	7/30–8/23	8/23–9/16
1988	2/9–3/6	3/6–4/3	4/3–5/17 5/27–8/6	5/17–5/27 8/28–9/22	9/7–10/4 9/22–10/16	10/4–10/29
1989	3/23–4/16	4/16–5/11	5/11–6/4	6/4–6/29	6/29–7/24	7/24–8/18
1990	5/4–5/30	5/30–6/25	6/25–7/20	7/20–8/13	8/13–9/7	9/7–10/1
1991	2/22–3/18	3/18–4/13	4/13–5/9	5/9–6/6	6/6–7/11 8/21–10/6	7/11–8/21 10/6–11/9
1992	4/7–5/1	5/1–5/26	5/26–6/19	6/19–7/13	7/13–8/7	8/7–8/31
1993	2/2–6/6	6/6–7/6	7/6–8/1	8/1–8/27	8/27–9/21	9/21–10/16
1994	3/8–4/1	4/1–4/26	4/26–5/21	5/21–6/15	6/15–7/11	7/11–8/7
1995	4/22–5/16	5/16–6/10	6/10–7/5	7/5–7/29	7/29–8/23	8/23–9/16
1996	2/9–3/6	3/6–4/3	4/3–8/7	8/7–9/7	9/7–10/4	10/4–10/29
1997	3/23–4/16	4/16–5/10	5/10–6/4	6/4–6/28	6/28–7/23	7/23–8/17
1998	5/3–5/29	5/29–6/24	6/24–7/19	7/19–8/13	8/13–9/6	9/6–9/30
1999	2/21–3/18	3/18–4/12	4/12–5/8	5/8–6/5	6/5–7/12 8/15–10/7	7/12–8/15 10/7–11/9
2000	4/6–5/1	5/1–5/25	5/25–6/13	6/13–7/13	7/13–8/6	8/6–8/31
2001	2/2–6/6	6/6–7/5	7/5–8/1	8/1–8/26	8/26–9/20	9/20–10/15
2002	3/7–4/1	4/1–4/25	4/25–5/20	5/20–6/14	6/14–7/10	7/10–8/7
2003	4/21–5/16	5/16–6/9	6/9–7/4	7/4–7/29	7/29–8/22	8/22–9/15
2004	2/8–3/5	3/5–4/3	4/3–8/7	8/7–9/6	9/6–10/3	10/3–10/28
2005	3/22–4/15	4/15–5/10	5/10–6/3	6/3–6/28	6/28–7/23	7/23–8/17
2006	5/3–5/29	5/29–6/24	6/24–7/19	7/19–8/12	8/12–9/6	9/6–9/30
2007	2/21–3/16	3/17–4/10	4/11–5/7	5/8–6/4	6/5–7/13 8/8–10/6	7/14–8/7 10/7–11/7
2008	4/6–4/30	5/1–5/24	5/25–6/17	6/18–7/11	7/12–8/4	8/5–8/29
2009	2/2–4/11 4/24–6/6	6/6–7/5	7/5–7/31	731/–8/26	8/26–9/20	9/20–10/14

Libra	Scorpio	Sagittarius	Capricorn	Aquarius	Pisces
10/30–11/24	11/24–12/18	12/18–1/11/81			1/16–2/9
8/18–9/12	9/12–10/9	10/9–11/5	1/11–2/4 11/5–12/8	2/4–2/28 12/8–1/23/82	2/28–3/24
10/2–10/26	10/26–11/18	11/18–12/12	1/23–3/2 12/12–1/5/83	3/2–4/6	4/6–5/4
11/9–12/6	12/6–1/1/84			1/5–1/29	1/29–2/22
9/1–9/25	9/25–10/20	1/1–1/25 10/20–11/13	1/25–2/19 11/13–12/9	2/19–3/14 12/10–1/4	3/14–4/7
10/16–11/9 8/7–9/7	11/9–12/3 9/7–1/7	12/3–12/27	12/28–1/19	 1/20–2/13	1/4–2/2 2/13–3/9
9/16–10/10	10/10–11/3	1/7–2/5 11/3–11/28	2/5–3/3 11/28–12/22	3/3–3/28 12/22–1/15	3/28–4/22
10/29–11/23	11/23–12/17	12/17–1/10			1/15–2/9
8/18–9/12	9/12–10/8	10/8–11/5	1/10–2/3 11/5–12/10	2/3–2/27 12/10–1/16/90	2/27–3/23
10/1–10/25	10/25–11/18	11/18–12/12	1/16–3/3 12/12–1/5	3/3–4/6	4/6–5/4
11/9–12/6	12/6–12/31	12/31–1/25/92		1/5–1/29	1/29–2/22
8/31–9/25	9/25–10/19	10/19–11/13	1/25–2/18 11/13–12/8	2/18–3/13 12/8–1/3/93	3/13–4/7
10/16–11/9 8/7–9/7	11/9–12/2 9/7–1/7	12/2–12/26	12/26–1/19	 1/19–2/12	1/3–2/2 2/12–3/8
9/16–10/10	10/10–11/13	1/7–2/4 11/3–11/27	2/4–3/2 11/27–12/21	3/2–3/28 12/21–1/15	3/28–4/22
10/29–11/23	11/23–12/17	12/17–1/10/97			1/15–2/9
8/17–9/12	9/12–10/8	10/8–11/5	1/10–2/3 11/5–12/12	2/3–2/27 12/12–1/9	2/27–3/23
9/30–10/24	10/24–11/17	11/17–12/11	1/9–3/4	3/4–4/6	4/6–5/3
11/9–12/5	12/5–12/31	12/31–1/24		1/4–1/28	1/28–2/21
8/31–9/24	9/24–10/19	10/19–11/13	1/24–2/18 11/13–12/8	2/18–3/12 12/8	3/13–4/6
10/15–11/8	11/8–12/2	12/2–12/26	12/26/01– 1/18/02	12/8/00–1/3/01	1/3–2/2
8/7–9/7	9/7–1/7/03		12/26/01–1/18	1/18–2/11	2/11–3/7
9/15–10/9	10/9–11/2	1/7–2/4 11/2–11/26	2/4–3/2 11/26–12/21	3/2–3/27 12/21–1/14/04	3/27–4/21
10/28–11/22	11/22–12/16	12/16–1/9/05		1/1–1/14	1/14–2/8
8/17–9/11	9/11–10/8	10/8–11/15	1/9–2/2 11/5–12/15	2/2–2/26 12/15–1/1/06	2/26–3/22
9/30–10/24	10/24–11/17	11/17–12/11	1/1–3/5	3/5–4/6	4/6–5/3
11/8–12/4	12/5–12/29	12/30–1/24/08		1/3–1/26	1/27–2/20
8/6–9/7	9/7–1/7			1/20–2/13	2/13–3/9
8/30–9/22	9/23–10/17	10/18–11/11	1/24–2/16 11/12–12/6	2/17–3/11 12/7–1/2/09	3/12–4/5
10/14–11/7	11/7–12/1	12/1–12/25	12/25–1/19/10	12/7/08– 1/31/09	1/3–2/2 4/11–4/24

How to Use the Mars, Jupiter, and Saturn Tables

Find the year of your birth on the left side of each column. The dates when the planet entered each sign are listed on the right side of each column. (Signs are abbreviated to three letters.) Your birthday should fall on or between each date listed, and your planetary placement should correspond to the earlier sign of that period.

All planet changes are calculated for the Greenwich Mean Time zone.

MARS SIGNS 1901–2009

Year	Mon	Day	Sign	Year	Mon	Day	Sign
1901	MAR	1	Leo		OCT	1	Vir
	MAY	11	Vir		NOV	20	Lib
	JUL	13	Lib	1905	JAN	13	Scp
	AUG	31	Scp		AUG	21	Sag
	OCT	14	Sag		OCT	8	Cap
	NOV	24	Cap		NOV	18	Aqu
1902	JAN	1	Aqu		DEC	27	Pic
	FEB	8	Pic	1906	FEB	4	Ari
	MAR	19	Ari		MAR	17	Tau
	APR	27	Tau		APR	28	Gem
	JUN	7	Gem		JUN	11	Can
	JUL	20	Can		JUL	27	Leo
	SEP	4	Leo		SEP	12	Vir
	OCT	23	Vir		OCT	30	Lib
	DEC	20	Lib		DEC	17	Scp
1903	APR	19	Vir	1907	FEB	5	Sag
	MAY	30	Lib		APR	1	Cap
	AUG	6	Scp		OCT	13	Aqu
	SEP	22	Sag		NOV	29	Pic
	NOV	3	Cap	1908	JAN	11	Ari
	DEC	12	Aqu		FEB	23	Tau
1904	JAN	19	Pic		APR	7	Gem
	FEB	27	Ari		MAY	22	Can
	APR	6	Tau		JUL	8	Leo
	MAY	18	Gem		AUG	24	Vir
	JUN	30	Can		OCT	10	Lib
	AUG	15	Leo		NOV	25	Scp

1909	JAN	10	Sag		MAR	9	Pic
	FEB	24	Cap		APR	16	Ari
	APR	9	Aqu		MAY	26	Tau
	MAY	25	Pic		JUL	6	Gem
	JUL	21	Ari		AUG	19	Can
	SEP	26	Pic		OCT	7	Leo
	NOV	20	Ari	1916	MAY	28	Vir
1910	JAN	23	Tau		JUL	23	Lib
	MAR	14	Gem		SEP	8	Scp
	MAY	1	Can		OCT	22	Sag
	JUN	19	Leo		DEC	1	Cap
	AUG	6	Vir	1917	JAN	9	Aqu
	SEP	22	Lib		FEB	16	Pic
	NOV	6	Scp		MAR	26	Ari
	DEC	20	Sag		MAY	4	Tau
1911	JAN	31	Cap		JUN	14	Gem
	MAR	14	Aqu		JUL	28	Can
	APR	23	Pic		SEP	12	Leo
	JUN	2	Ari		NOV	2	Vir
	JUL	15	Tau	1918	JAN	11	Lib
	SEP	5	Gem		FEB	25	Vir
	NOV	30	Tau		JUN	23	Lib
1912	JAN	30	Gem		AUG	17	Scp
	APR	5	Can		OCT	1	Sag
	MAY	28	Leo		NOV	11	Cap
	JUL	17	Vir		DEC	20	Aqu
	SEP	2	Lib	1919	JAN	27	Pic
	OCT	18	Scp		MAR	6	Ari
	NOV	30	Sag		APR	15	Tau
1913	JAN	10	Cap		MAY	26	Gem
	FEB	19	Aqu		JUL	8	Can
	MAR	30	Pic		AUG	23	Leo
	MAY	8	Ari		OCT	10	Vir
	JUN	17	Tau		NOV	30	Lib
	JUL	29	Gem	1920	JAN	31	Scp
	SEP	15	Can		APR	23	Lib
1914	MAY	1	Leo		JUL	10	Scp
	JUN	26	Vir		SEP	4	Sag
	AUG	14	Lib		OCT	18	Cap
	SEP	29	Scp		NOV	27	Aqu
	NOV	11	Sag	1921	JAN	5	Pic
	DEC	22	Cap		FEB	13	Ari
1915	JAN	30	Aqu		MAR	25	Tau

	MAY	6	Gem		OCT	26	Scp
	JUN	18	Can		DEC	8	Sag
	AUG	3	Leo	1928	JAN	19	Cap
	SEP	19	Vir		FEB	28	Aqu
	NOV	6	Lib		APR	7	Pic
	DEC	26	Scp		MAY	16	Ari
1922	FEB	18	Sag		JUN	26	Tau
	SEP	13	Cap		AUG	9	Gem
	OCT	30	Aqu		OCT	3	Can
	DEC	11	Pic		DEC	20	Gem
1923	JAN	21	Ari	1929	MAR	10	Can
	MAR	4	Tau		MAY	13	Leo
	APR	16	Gem		JUL	4	Vir
	MAY	30	Can		AUG	21	Lib
	JUL	16	Leo		OCT	6	Scp
	SEP	1	Vir		NOV	18	Sag
	OCT	18	Lib		DEC	29	Cap
	DEC	4	Scp	1930	FEB	6	Aqu
1924	JAN	19	Sag		MAR	17	Pic
	MAR	6	Cap		APR	24	Ari
	APR	24	Aqu		JUN	3	Tau
	JUN	24	Pic		JUL	14	Gem
	AUG	24	Aqu		AUG	28	Can
	OCT	19	Pic		OCT	20	Leo
	DEC	19	Ari	1931	FEB	16	Can
1925	FEB	5	Tau		MAR	30	Leo
	MAR	24	Gem		JUN	10	Vir
	MAY	9	Can		AUG	1	Lib
	JUN	26	Leo		SEP	17	Scp
	AUG	12	Vir		OCT	30	Sag
	SEP	28	Lib		DEC	10	Cap
	NOV	13	Scp	1932	JAN	18	Aqu
	DEC	28	Sag		FEB	25	Pic
1926	FEB	9	Cap		APR	3	Ari
	MAR	23	Aqu		MAY	12	Tau
	MAY	3	Pic		JUN	22	Gem
	JUN	15	Ari		AUG	4	Can
	AUG	1	Tau		SEP	20	Leo
1927	FEB	22	Gem		NOV	13	Vir
	APR	17	Can	1933	JUL	6	Lib
	JUN	6	Leo		AUG	26	Scp
	JUL	25	Vir		OCT	9	Sag
	SEP	10	Lib		NOV	19	Cap

	DEC	28	Aqu		FEB	17	Tau
1934	FEB	4	Pic		APR	1	Gem
	MAR	14	Ari		MAY	17	Can
	APR	22	Tau		JUL	3	Leo
	JUN	2	Gem		AUG	19	Vir
	JUL	15	Can		OCT	5	Lib
	AUG	30	Leo		NOV	20	Scp
	OCT	18	Vir	1941	JAN	4	Sag
	DEC	11	Lib		FEB	17	Cap
1935	JUL	29	Scp		APR	2	Aqu
	SEP	16	Sag		MAY	16	Pic
	OCT	28	Cap		JUL	2	Ari
	DEC	7	Aqu	1942	JAN	11	Tau
1936	JAN	14	Pic		MAR	7	Gem
	FEB	22	Ari		APR	26	Can
	APR	1	Tau		JUN	14	Leo
	MAY	13	Gem		AUG	1	Vir
	JUN	25	Can		SEP	17	Lib
	AUG	10	Leo		NOV	1	Scp
	SEP	26	Vir		DEC	15	Sag
	NOV	14	Lib	1943	JAN	26	Cap
1937	JAN	5	Scp		MAR	8	Aqu
	MAR	13	Sag		APR	17	Pic
	MAY	14	Scp		MAY	27	Ari
	AUG	8	Sag		JUL	7	Tau
	SEP	30	Cap		AUG	23	Gem
	NOV	11	Aqu	1944	MAR	28	Can
	DEC	21	Pic		MAY	22	Leo
1938	JAN	30	Ari		JUL	12	Vir
	MAR	12	Tau		AUG	29	Lib
	APR	23	Gem		OCT	13	Scp
	JUN	7	Can		NOV	25	Sag
	JUL	22	Leo	1945	JAN	5	Cap
	SEP	7	Vir		FEB	14	Aqu
	OCT	25	Lib		MAR	25	Pic
	DEC	11	Scp		MAY	2	Ari
1939	JAN	29	Sag		JUN	11	Tau
	MAR	21	Cap		JUL	23	Gem
	MAY	25	Aqu		SEP	7	Can
	JUL	21	Cap		NOV	11	Leo
	SEP	24	Aqu		DEC	26	Can
	NOV	19	Pic	1946	APR	22	Leo
1940	JAN	4	Ari		JUN	20	Vir

	AUG	9	Lib		OCT	12	Cap
	SEP	24	Scp		NOV	21	Aqu
	NOV	6	Sag		DEC	30	Pic
	DEC	17	Cap	1953	FEB	8	Ari
1947	JAN	25	Aqu		MAR	20	Tau
	MAR	4	Pic		MAY	1	Gem
	APR	11	Ari		JUN	14	Can
	MAY	21	Tau		JUL	29	Leo
	JUL	1	Gem		SEP	14	Vir
	AUG	13	Can		NOV	1	Lib
	OCT	1	Leo		DEC	20	Scp
	DEC	1	Vir	1954	FEB	9	Sag
1948	FEB	12	Leo		APR	12	Cap
	MAY	18	Vir		JUL	3	Sag
	JUL	17	Lib		AUG	24	Cap
	SEP	3	Scp		OCT	21	Aqu
	OCT	17	Sag		DEC	4	Pic
	NOV	26	Cap	1955	JAN	15	Ari
1949	JAN	4	Aqu		FEB	26	Tau
	FEB	11	Pic		APR	10	Gem
	MAR	21	Ari		MAY	26	Can
	APR	30	Tau		JUL	11	Leo
	JUN	10	Gem		AUG	27	Vir
	JUL	23	Can		OCT	13	Lib
	SEP	7	Leo		NOV	29	Scp
	OCT	27	Vir	1956	JAN	14	Sag
	DEC	26	Lib		FEB	28	Cap
1950	MAR	28	Vir		APR	14	Aqu
	JUN	11	Lib		JUN	3	Pic
	AUG	10	Scp		DEC	6	Ari
	SEP	25	Sag	1957	JAN	28	Tau
	NOV	6	Cap		MAR	17	Gem
	DEC	15	Aqu		MAY	4	Can
1951	JAN	22	Pic		JUN	21	Leo
	MAR	1	Ari		AUG	8	Vir
	APR	10	Tau		SEP	24	Lib
	MAY	21	Gem		NOV	8	Scp
	JUL	3	Can		DEC	23	Sag
	AUG	18	Leo	1958	FEB	3	Cap
	OCT	5	Vir		MAR	17	Aqu
	NOV	24	Lib		APR	27	Pic
1952	JAN	20	Scp		JUN	7	Ari
	AUG	27	Sag		JUL	21	Tau

	SEP	21	Gem		NOV	6	Vir
	OCT	29	Tau	1965	JUN	29	Lib
1959	FEB	10	Gem		AUG	20	Scp
	APR	10	Can		OCT	4	Sag
	JUN	1	Leo		NOV	14	Cap
	JUL	20	Vir		DEC	23	Aqu
	SEP	5	Lib	1966	JAN	30	Pic
	OCT	21	Scp		MAR	9	Ari
	DEC	3	Sag		APR	17	Tau
1960	JAN	14	Cap		MAY	28	Gem
	FEB	23	Aqu		JUL	11	Can
	APR	2	Pic		AUG	25	Leo
	MAY	11	Ari		OCT	12	Vir
	JUN	20	Tau		DEC	4	Lib
	AUG	2	Gem	1967	FEB	12	Scp
	SEP	21	Can		MAR	31	Lib
1961	FEB	5	Gem		JUL	19	Scp
	FEB	7	Can		SEP	10	Sag
	MAY	6	Leo		OCT	23	Cap
	JUN	28	Vir		DEC	1	Aqu
	AUG	17	Lib	1968	JAN	9	Pic
	OCT	1	Scp		FEB	17	Ari
	NOV	13	Sag		MAR	27	Tau
	DEC	24	Cap		MAY	8	Gem
1962	FEB	1	Aqu		JUN	21	Can
	MAR	12	Pic		AUG	5	Leo
	APR	19	Ari		SEP	21	Vir
	MAY	28	Tau		NOV	9	Lib
	JUL	9	Gem		DEC	29	Scp
	AUG	22	Can	1969	FEB	25	Sag
	OCT	11	Leo		SEP	21	Cap
1963	JUN	3	Vir		NOV	4	Aqu
	JUL	27	Lib		DEC	15	Pic
	SEP	12	Scp	1970	JAN	24	Ari
	OCT	25	Sag		MAR	7	Tau
	DEC	5	Cap		APR	18	Gem
1964	JAN	13	Aqu		JUN	2	Can
	FEB	20	Pic		JUL	18	Leo
	MAR	29	Ari		SEP	3	Vir
	MAY	7	Tau		OCT	20	Lib
	JUN	17	Gem		DEC	6	Scp
	JUL	30	Can	1971	JAN	23	Sag
	SEP	15	Leo		MAR	12	Cap

	MAY	3	Aqu		JUN	6	Tau
	NOV	6	Pic		JUL	17	Gem
	DEC	26	Ari		SEP	1	Can
1972	FEB	10	Tau		OCT	26	Leo
	MAR	27	Gem	1978	JAN	26	Can
	MAY	12	Can		APR	10	Leo
	JUN	28	Leo		JUN	14	Vir
	AUG	15	Vir		AUG	4	Lib
	SEP	30	Lib		SEP	19	Scp
	NOV	15	Scp		NOV	2	Sag
	DEC	30	Sag		DEC	12	Cap
1973	FEB	12	Cap	1979	JAN	20	Aqu
	MAR	26	Aqu		FEB	27	Pic
	MAY	8	Pic		APR	7	Ari
	JUN	20	Ari		MAY	16	Tau
	AUG	12	Tau		JUN	26	Gem
	OCT	29	Ari		AUG	8	Can
	DEC	24	Tau		SEP	24	Leo
1974	FEB	27	Gem		NOV	19	Vir
	APR	20	Can	1980	MAR	11	Leo
	JUN	9	Leo		MAY	4	Vir
	JUL	27	Vir		JUL	10	Lib
	SEP	12	Lib		AUG	29	Scp
	OCT	28	Scp		OCT	12	Sag
	DEC	10	Sag		NOV	22	Cap
1975	JAN	21	Cap		DEC	30	Aqu
	MAR	3	Aqu	1981	FEB	6	Pic
	APR	11	Pic		MAR	17	Ari
	MAY	21	Ari		APR	25	Tau
	JUL	1	Tau		JUN	5	Gem
	AUG	14	Gem		JUL	18	Can
	OCT	17	Can		SEP	2	Leo
	NOV	25	Gem		OCT	21	Vir
1976	MAR	18	Can		DEC	16	Lib
	MAY	16	Leo	1982	AUG	3	Scp
	JUL	6	Vir		SEP	20	Sag
	AUG	24	Lib		OCT	31	Cap
	OCT	8	Scp		DEC	10	Aqu
	NOV	20	Sag	1983	JAN	17	Pic
1977	JAN	1	Cap		FEB	25	Ari
	FEB	9	Aqu		APR	5	Tau
	MAR	20	Pic		MAY	16	Gem
	APR	27	Ari		JUN	29	Can

	AUG	13	Leo	1990	JAN	29	Cap
	SEP	30	Vir		MAR	11	Aqu
	NOV	18	Lib		APR	20	Pic
1984	JAN	11	Scp		MAY	31	Ari
	AUG	17	Sag		JUL	12	Tau
	OCT	5	Cap		AUG	31	Gem
	NOV	15	Aqu		DEC	14	Tau
	DEC	25	Pic	1991	JAN	21	Gem
1985	FEB	2	Ari		APR	3	Can
	MAR	15	Tau		MAY	26	Leo
	APR	26	Gem		JUL	15	Vir
	JUN	9	Can		SEP	1	Lib
	JUL	25	Leo		OCT	16	Scp
	SEP	10	Vir		NOV	29	Sag
	OCT	27	Lib	1992	JAN	9	Cap
	DEC	14	Scp		FEB	18	Aqu
1986	FEB	2	Sag		MAR	28	Pic
	MAR	28	Cap		MAY	5	Ari
	OCT	9	Aqu		JUN	14	Tau
	NOV	26	Pic		JUL	26	Gem
1987	JAN	8	Ari		SEP	12	Can
	FEB	20	Tau	1993	APR	27	Leo
	APR	5	Gem		JUN	23	Vir
	MAY	21	Can		AUG	12	Lib
	JUL	6	Leo		SEP	27	Scp
	AUG	22	Vir		NOV	9	Sag
	OCT	8	Lib		DEC	20	Cap
	NOV	24	Scp	1994	JAN	28	Aqu
1988	JAN	8	Sag		MAR	7	Pic
	FEB	22	Cap		APR	14	Ari
	APR	6	Aqu		MAY	23	Tau
	MAY	22	Pic		JUL	3	Gem
	JUL	13	Ari		AUG	16	Can
	OCT	23	Pic		OCT	4	Leo
	NOV	1	Ari		DEC	12	Vir
1989	JAN	19	Tau	1995	JAN	22	Leo
	MAR	11	Gem		MAY	25	Vir
	APR	29	Can		JUL	21	Lib
	JUN	16	Leo		SEP	7	Scp
	AUG	3	Vir		OCT	20	Sag
	SEP	19	Lib		NOV	30	Cap
	NOV	4	Scp	1996	JAN	8	Aqu
	DEC	18	Sag		FEB	15	Pic

	MAR	24	Ari		MAR	1	Tau
	MAY	2	Tau		APR	13	Gem
	JUN	12	Gem		MAY	28	Can
	JUL	25	Can		JUL	13	Leo
	SEP	9	Leo		AUG	29	Vir
	OCT	30	Vir		OCT	15	Lib
1997	JAN	3	Lib		DEC	1	Scp
	MAR	8	Vir	2003	JAN	17	Sag
	JUN	19	Lib		MAR	4	Cap
	AUG	14	Scp		APR	21	Aqu
	SEP	28	Sag		JUN	17	Pic
	NOV	9	Cap		DEC	16	Ari
	DEC	18	Aqu	2004	FEB	3	Tau
1998	JAN	25	Pic		MAR	21	Gem
	MAR	4	Ari		MAY	7	Can
	APR	13	Tau		JUN	23	Leo
	MAY	24	Gem		AUG	10	Vir
	JUL	6	Can		SEP	26	Lib
	AUG	20	Leo		NOV	11	Sep
	OCT	7	Vir		DEC	25	Sag
	NOV	27	Lib	2005	FEB	6	Cap
1999	JAN	26	Scp		MAR	20	Aqu
	MAY	5	Lib		MAY	1	Pic
	JUL	5	Scp		JUN	12	Ari
	SEP	2	Sag		JUL	28	Tau
	OCT	17	Cap	2006	FEB	17	Gem
	NOV	26	Aqu		APR	14	Can
2000	JAN	4	Pic		JUN	3	Leo
	FEB	12	Ari		JUL	22	Vir
	MAR	23	Tau		SEP	8	Lib
	MAY	3	Gem		OCT	23	Scp
	JUN	16	Can		DEC	6	Sag
	AUG	1	Leo	2007	JAN	16	Cap
	SEP	17	Vir		FEB	25	Aqu
	NOV	4	Lib		APR	6	Pic
	DEC	23	Scp		MAY	15	Ari
2001	FEB	14	Sag		JUNE	24	Tau
	SEP	8	Cap		AUG	7	Gem
	OCT	27	Aqu		SEP	28	Can
	DEC	8	Pic		DEC	31	Gem*
2002	JAN	18	Ari				

*Repeat means planet is retrograde.

2008	MAR	4	Can
	MAY	9	Leo
	JUL	1	Vir
	AUG	19	Lib
	OCT	3	Scp
	NOV	16	Sag
	DEC	27	Cap

2009	FEB	4	Aqu
	MAR	14	Pic
	APR	22	Ari
	MAY	31	Tau
	JUL	11	Gem
	AUG	25	Can
	OCT	16	Leo

JUPITER SIGNS 1901–2009

1901	JAN	19	Cap
1902	FEB	6	Aqu
1903	FEB	20	Pic
1904	MAR	1	Ari
	AUG	8	Tau
	AUG	31	Ari
1905	MAR	7	Tau
	JUL	21	Gem
	DEC	4	Tau
1906	MAR	9	Gem
	JUL	30	Can
1907	AUG	18	Leo
1908	SEP	12	Vir
1909	OCT	11	Lib
1910	NOV	11	Scp
1911	DEC	10	Sag
1913	JAN	2	Cap
1914	JAN	21	Aqu
1915	FEB	4	Pic
1916	FEB	12	Ari
	JUN	26	Tau
	OCT	26	Ari
1917	FEB	12	Tau
	JUN	29	Gem
1918	JUL	13	Can
1919	AUG	2	Leo
1920	AUG	27	Vir
1921	SEP	25	Lib
1922	OCT	26	Scp
1923	NOV	24	Sag

1924	DEC	18	Cap
1926	JAN	6	Aqu
1927	JAN	18	Pic
	JUN	6	Ari
	SEP	11	Pic
1928	JAN	23	Ari
	JUN	4	Tau
1929	JUN	12	Gem
1930	JUN	26	Can
1931	JUL	17	Leo
1932	AUG	11	Vir
1933	SEP	10	Lib
1934	OCT	11	Scp
1935	NOV	9	Sag
1936	DEC	2	Cap
1937	DEC	20	Aqu
1938	MAY	14	Pic
	JUL	30	Aqu
	DEC	29	Pic
1939	MAY	11	Ari
	OCT	30	Pic
	DEC	20	Ari
1940	MAY	16	Tau
1941	MAY	26	Gem
1942	JUN	10	Can
1943	JUN	30	Leo
1944	JUL	26	Vir
1945	AUG	25	Lib
1946	SEP	25	Scp
1947	OCT	24	Sag

Year	Month	Day	Sign		Year	Month	Day	Sign
1948	NOV	15	Cap			OCT	19	Vir
1949	APR	12	Aqu		1968	FEB	27	Leo
	JUN	27	Cap			JUN	15	Vir
	NOV	30	Aqu			NOV	15	Lib
1950	APR	15	Pic		1969	MAR	30	Vir
	SEP	15	Aqu			JUL	15	Lib
	DEC	1	Pic			DEC	16	Scp
1951	APR	21	Ari		1970	APR	30	Lib
1952	APR	28	Tau			AUG	15	Scp
1953	MAY	9	Gem		1971	JAN	14	Sag
1954	MAY	24	Can			JUN	5	Scp
1955	JUN	13	Leo			SEP	11	Sag
	NOV	17	Vir		1972	FEB	6	Cap
1956	JAN	18	Leo			JUL	24	Sag
	JUL	7	Vir			SEP	25	Cap
	DEC	13	Lib		1973	FEB	23	Aqu
1957	FEB	19	Vir		1974	MAR	8	Pic
	AUG	7	Lib		1975	MAR	18	Ari
1958	JAN	13	Scp		1976	MAR	26	Tau
	MAR	20	Lib			AUG	23	Gem
	SEP	7	Scp			OCT	16	Tau
1959	FEB	10	Sag		1977	APR	3	Gem
	APR	24	Scp			AUG	20	Can
	OCT	5	Sag			DEC	30	Gem
1960	MAR	1	Cap		1978	APR	12	Can
	JUN	10	Sag			SEP	5	Leo
	OCT	26	Cap		1979	FEB	28	Can
1961	MAR	15	Aqu			APR	20	Leo
	AUG	12	Cap			SEP	29	Vir
	NOV	4	Aqu		1980	OCT	27	Lib
1962	MAR	25	Pic		1981	NOV	27	Scp
1963	APR	4	Ari		1982	DEC	26	Sag
1964	APR	12	Tau		1984	JAN	19	Cap
1965	APR	22	Gem		1985	FEB	6	Aqu
	SEP	21	Can		1986	FEB	20	Pic
	NOV	17	Gem		1987	MAR	2	Ari
1966	MAY	5	Can		1988	MAR	8	Tau
	SEP	27	Leo			JUL	22	Gem
1967	JAN	16	Can			NOV	30	Tau
	MAY	23	Leo		1989	MAR	11	Gem
						JUL	30	Can

1990	AUG	18	Leo
1991	SEP	12	Vir
1992	OCT	10	Lib
1993	NOV	10	Scp
1994	DEC	9	Sag
1996	JAN	3	Cap
1997	JAN	21	Aqu
1998	FEB	4	Pic
1999	FEB	13	Ari
	JUN	28	Tau
	OCT	23	Ari
2000	FEB	14	Tau
	JUN	30	Gem
2001	JUL	14	Can
2002	AUG	1	Leo
2003	AUG	27	Vir
2004	SEP	24	Lib
2005	OCT	26	Scp
2006	NOV	24	Sag
2007	DEC	17	Cap
2009	JAN	5	Aqu

SATURN SIGNS 1903–2009

1903	JAN	19	Aqu
1905	APR	13	Pic
	AUG	17	Aqu
1906	JAN	8	Pic
1908	MAR	19	Ari
1910	MAY	17	Tau
	DEC	14	Ari
1911	JAN	20	Tau
1912	JUL	7	Gem
	NOV	30	Tau
1913	MAR	26	Gem
1914	AUG	24	Can
	DEC	7	Gem
1915	MAY	11	Can
1916	OCT	17	Leo
	DEC	7	Can
1917	JUN	24	Leo
1919	AUG	12	Vir
1921	OCT	7	Lib
1923	DEC	20	Scp
1924	APR	6	Lib
	SEP	13	Scp
1926	DEC	2	Sag
1929	MAR	15	Cap
	MAY	5	Sag
	NOV	30	Cap
1932	FEB	24	Aqu
	AUG	13	Cap
	NOV	20	Aqu
1935	FEB	14	Pic
1937	APR	25	Ari
	OCT	18	Pic
1938	JAN	14	Ari
1939	JUL	6	Tau
	SEP	22	Ari
1940	MAR	20	Tau
1942	MAY	8	Gem
1944	JUN	20	Can
1946	AUG	2	Leo
1948	SEP	19	Vir
1949	APR	3	Leo
	MAY	29	Vir
1950	NOV	20	Lib
1951	MAR	7	Vir
	AUG	13	Lib
1953	OCT	22	Scp
1956	JAN	12	Sag
	MAY	14	Scp
	OCT	10	Sag
1959	JAN	5	Cap
1962	JAN	3	Aqu
1964	MAR	24	Pic
	SEP	16	Aqu
	DEC	16	Pic

1967	MAR	3	Ari	1988	FEB	13	Cap
1969	APR	29	Tau		JUN	10	Sag
1971	JUN	18	Gem		NOV	12	Cap
1972	JAN	10	Tau	1991	FEB	6	Aqu
	FEB	21	Gem	1993	MAY	21	Pic
1973	AUG	1	Can		JUN	30	Aqu
1974	JAN	7	Gem	1994	JAN	28	Pic
	APR	18	Can	1996	APR	7	Ari
1975	SEP	17	Leo	1998	JUN	9	Tau
1976	JAN	14	Can		OCT	25	Ari
	JUN	5	Leo	1999	MAR	1	Tau
1977	NOV	17	Vir	2000	AUG	10	Gem
1978	JAN	5	Leo		OCT	16	Tau
	JUL	26	Vir	2001	APR	21	Gem
1980	SEP	21	Lib	2003	JUN	3	Can
1982	NOV	29	Scp	2005	JUL	16	Leo
1983	MAY	6	Lib	2007	SEP	2	Vir
	AUG	24	Scp	2009	OCT	29	Lib
1985	NOV	17	Sag				

CHAPTER 4

Moods and the Moon

How many love songs have been written about the moon?
We'll bet the moon easily wins over the sun for mentions
in romantic song and poetry, for dreamy representations in
painting and photography. The most fascinating aspect of
the moon is its connection with our emotions, its ability to
evoke strong feelings by the mere sight of its glowing light
in the night sky. With the moon, we're moody, romantic,
caring, or concerned with our inner self. On the other hand,
we associate the sun with radiance, confidence, or an outgoing emotional atmosphere.

Astrologers often refer to the sun and moon as the lights.
This is an appropriate description, since the sun and moon
are not really planets, but a star and a satellite. But it is
also true that these two bodies shed the most light on a
horoscope reading.

The sign the moon was transiting at the time of your
birth reveals secrets like what you really care about and
what makes you feel comfortable and secure. It represents
the receptive, reflective, female, and nurturing self. It also
reflects who nurtured you, the mother or mother figure in
your chart. In a man's chart, the moon position describes
his receptive, emotional, and yin side, as well as the woman
in his life who will have the deepest effect, usually his
mother. (Venus reveals the kind of woman who will attract
him physically.)

The moon is more at home in some signs than in others.
It rules maternal Cancer and is exalted in Taurus—both
comforting, home-loving signs where the natural emotional
energies of the moon are easily and productively expressed.
But when the moon is in the opposite signs—Capricorn and
Scorpio—it leaves the comfortable nest and deals with emo-

tional issues of power and achievement in the outside world. If you were born with the moon in one of these signs, you may find your emotional role in life more challenging.

To determine your moon sign, it is worthwhile to have an accurate horoscope cast, either by an astrologer, a computer program, or one of the online astrology sites that offer free charts. Since detailed moon tables are too extensive for this book, check through the following listing to find the moon sign that feels most familiar.

Moon in Aries

This placement makes you both independent and ardent. You are an idealist, and you tend to fall in and out of love easily. You love a challenge but could cool once your quarry is captured. Your emotional reactions are fast and fiery, quickly expressed and quickly forgotten. You may not think before expressing your feelings. It's not easy to hide how you feel. Channeling all your emotional energy could be one of your big challenges.

Moon in Taurus

You are a sentimental soul who is very fond of the good life and gravitates toward solid, secure relationships. You like displays of affection and creature comforts—all the tangible trappings of a cozy, safe, calm atmosphere. You are sensual and steady emotionally, but very stubborn, possessive, and determined. You can't be pushed and tend to dislike changes. You should make an effort to broaden your horizons and to take a risk sometimes. You may become very attached to your home turf, your garden, and your possessions. You may also be a collector of objects that are meaningful to you.

Moon in Gemini

You crave mental stimulation and variety in life, which you usually get via a varied social life, the excitement of flirtation, or multiple professional involvements. You may marry more than once and have a rather chaotic emotional life due to your difficulty with commitment and settling down, as well as your need to be constantly on the go. (Be sure to find a partner who is as outgoing as you are.) You will have to learn at some point to focus your energies because you tend to be somewhat fragmented—to do two things at once, to have two homes, or even to have two lovers. If you can find a creative way to express your many-faceted nature, you'll be ahead of the game.

Moon in Cancer

This is the most powerful lunar position, which is sure to make a deep imprint on your character. Your needs are very much associated with your reaction to the needs of others. You are very sensitive, caring, and self-protective, though some of you may mask this with a hard shell, like the moon-sensitive crab. This placement also gives an excellent memory, keen intuition, and an uncanny ability to perceive the needs of others. All of the lunar phases will affect you, especially full moons and eclipses, so you would do well to mark them on your calendar. Because you're happiest at home, you may work at home or turn your office into a second home, where you can nurture and comfort people. (You may tend to mother the world.) With natural psychic, intuitive ability, you might be drawn to occult work in some way. Or you may get professionally involved with providing food and shelter to others.

Moon in Leo

This warm, passionate moon takes everything to heart. You are attracted to all that is noble, generous, and aristocratic in life (and you may be a bit of a snob). You have an innate ability to take command emotionally, but you do need strong support, loyalty, and loud applause from those you love. You are possessive of your loved ones and your turf and will roar if anyone threatens to take over territory.

Moon in Virgo

You are rather cool until you decide if others measure up. But once someone or something meets your high standards, you hold up your end of the arrangement perfectly. You may, in fact, drive yourself too hard to attain some notion of perfection. Try to be a bit easier on yourself and others. Don't always act the censor! You love to be the teacher; you are drawn to situations where you can change others for the better, but sometimes you must learn to accept others for what they are—enjoy what you have!

Moon in Libra

Like other air-sign moons, you think before you feel. Therefore, you may not immediately recognize the emotional needs of others. However, you are relationship-oriented and may find it difficult to be alone or to do things alone. After you have learned emotional balance by leaning on yourself first, you can have excellent partnerships. It is best for you to avoid extremes, which set your scales swinging and can make your love life precarious. You thrive in a rather conservative, traditional, romantic relationship, where you receive attention and flattery—but not possessiveness—from your partner. You'll be your most charming in an elegant, harmonious atmosphere.

Moon in Scorpio

This is a moon that enjoys and responds to intense, passionate feelings. You may go to extremes and have a very dramatic emotional life, full of ardor, suspicion, jealousy, and obsession. It would be much healthier to channel your need for power and control into meaningful work. This is a good position for anyone in the fields of medicine, police work, research, the occult, psychoanalysis, or intuitive work, because life-and-death situations don't faze you. However, you do take personal disappointments very hard.

Moon in Sagittarius

You take life's ups and downs with good humor and the proverbial grain of salt. You'll love 'em and leave 'em or take off on a great adventure at a moment's notice. "Born free" could be your slogan. Attracted by the exotic, you have mental and physical wanderlust. You may be too much in search of new mental and spiritual stimulation to ever settle down.

Moon in Capricorn

Are you ever accused of being too cool and calculating? You have an earthy side, but you take prestige and position very seriously. Your strong drive to succeed extends to your romantic life, where you will be devoted to improving your lifestyle and rising to the top. A structured situation where you can advance methodically makes you feel wonderfully secure. You may be attracted to someone older or very much younger or from a different social world. It may be difficult to look at the lighter side of emotional relationships. Though this moon is placed in the sign of its detriment, the good news is that you tend to be very dutiful and responsible to those you care for.

Moon in Aquarius

You are a people collector with many friends of all backgrounds. You are happiest surrounded by people, and you may feel uneasy when left alone. Though you usually stay friends with lovers, intense emotions and demanding one-on-one relationships turn you off. You don't like anything to be too rigid or scheduled. Though tolerant and understanding, you can be emotionally unpredictable; you may opt for an unconventional love life. With plenty of space, you will be able to sustain relationships with liberal, freedom-loving types.

Moon in Pisces

You are very responsive and empathetic to others, especially if they have problems or are the underdog. (Be on guard against attracting too many people with sob stories.) You'll be happiest if you can express your creative imagination in the arts or in the spiritual or healing professions. Because you may tend to escape in fantasies or overreact to the moods of others, you need an emotional anchor to help you keep a firm foothold in reality. Steer clear of too much escapism (especially in alcohol) or reclusiveness. Places near water soothe your moods. Working in a field that gives you emotional variety will also help you be productive.

♎ CHAPTER 5

Timing Tips from the Stars

One of the differences between people who achieve their goals and those who never seem to hit the mark is that the achievers usually have more control over the way they use their time. Astrology offers many ways to take control of your time, which could give you the competitive edge. It can show you when to be proactive and make your moves or when to kick back and relax. There are times when your careful plans could be derailed, when sudden changes from out of the blue could upset your schedule or delay your projects. On the other hand, there are days when everything is more likely to go smoothly and effortlessly, people will respond to you favorably, and perhaps you have some extra sex appeal.

For instance, when mischievous Mercury creates havoc with communications, it's time to back up your vital computer files, read between the lines of contracts, and be very patient with coworkers. When Venus passes through your sign, you're more alluring, so it's time to try out a new outfit or hairstyle, and then ask someone you'd like to know better to dinner. Venus timing can also help you charm clients with a stunning sales pitch or make an offer they won't refuse.

In this chapter you will find the tricks of astrological time management. You can find your red-letter days as well as which times to avoid. You will also learn how to make the magic of the moon work for you. Use the information in this chapter and the planet tables in this book and also the moon sign listings in your daily forecasts.

Here are the happenings to note on your agenda:

• Dates of your sun sign (high-energy period)

- The month previous to your sun sign (low-energy time)
- Dates of planets in your sign this year
- Full and new moons (Pay special attention when these fall in your sun sign!)
- Eclipses
- Moon in your sun sign every month, as well as moon in the opposite sign (listed in daily forecast)
- Mercury retrogrades
- Other retrograde periods

Your Most Proactive Time

Every birthday starts off a new cycle of solar energy for you. You should feel a new surge of vitality as the powerful sun enters your sign. This is the time when predominant energies are most favorable to you. So go for it! Start new projects, and make your big moves (especially when the new moon is in your sign, doubling your charisma). You'll get the recognition you deserve now, when everyone is attuned to your sun sign. Look in the tables in this book to see if other planets will also be passing through your sun sign at this time. Venus (love, beauty), Mars (energy, drive), and Mercury (communication, mental sharpness) reinforce the sun and give an extra boost to your life in the areas they affect. Venus will rev up your social and love life, making you seem especially attractive. Mars amplifies your energy and drive. Mercury fuels your brainpower and helps you communicate. Jupiter signals an especially lucky period of expansion.

There are two downtimes related to the sun. During the month before your birthday period, when you are winding up your annual cycle, you could be feeling especially vulnerable and depleted. So at that time get extra rest, watch your diet, and take it easy. Don't overstress yourself. Use this time to gear up for a big push when the sun enters your sign.

Another downtime is when the sun is in the sign opposite your sun sign (six months from your birthday). This is a reactive time, when the prevailing energies are very different from yours. You may feel at odds with the world. You'll have to work harder for recognition because people are not on your wavelength. However, this could be a good time to work on a team, in cooperation with others, or behind the scenes.

Be a Moon Watcher

The moon is a powerful tool to divine the mood of the moment. You can work with the moon in two ways. Plan by the sign the moon is in; plan by the phase of the moon. The sign will tell you the kind of activities that suit the moon's mood. The phase will tell you the best time to start or finish a certain activity.

Working with the phases of the moon is as easy as looking up at the night sky. During the new moon, when both the sun and moon are in the same sign, begin new ventures—especially activities that are favored by that sign. Then you'll utilize the powerful energies pulling you in the same direction. You'll be focused outward, toward action, and in a doing mode. Postpone breaking off, terminating, deliberating, or reflecting—activities that require introspection and passive work. These are better suited to a later moon phase.

Get your project under way during the first quarter. Then go public at the full moon, a time of high intensity, when feelings come out into the open. This is your time to shine—to express yourself. Be aware, however, that because pressures are being released, other people will also be letting off steam. Since confrontations are possible, take advantage of this time either to air grievances or to avoid arguments.

About three days after the full moon comes the disseminating phase, a time when the energy of the cycle begins to wind down. From the last quarter of the moon to the next new moon, it's a time to cut off unproductive relationships, do serious thinking, and focus on inward-directed activities.

You'll feel some new and full moons more strongly than others, especially those new moons that fall in your sun sign and full moons in your opposite sign. Because that full moon happens at your low-energy time of year, it is likely to be an especially stressful time in a relationship, when any hidden problems or unexpressed emotions could surface.

Full and New Moons in 2009

All dates are calculated for eastern standard time and eastern daylight time.

Full Moon—January 10 in Cancer
New Moon—Janaury 26 in Aquarius (solar eclipse)

Full Moon—February 9 in Leo (lunar eclipse)
New Moon—February 24 in Pisces

Full Moon—March 10 in Virgo
New Moon—March 26 in Aries

Full Moon—April 9 in Libra
New Moon—April 24 in Taurus

Full Moon—May 9 in Scorpio
New Moon—May 24 in Gemini

Full Moon—June 7 in Sagittarius
New Moon—June 22 in Cancer

Full Moon—July 7 in Capricorn (lunar eclipse)
New Moon—July 21 in Cancer (second new moon in Cancer, solar eclipse)

Full Moon—August 5 in Aquarius (lunar eclipse)
New Moon—August 20 in Leo

Full Moon—September 4 in Pisces
New Moon—September 18 in Virgo

Full Moon—October 4 in Aries
New Moon—October 18 in Libra

Full Moon—November 2 in Taurus
New Moon—November 16 in Scorpio

Full Moon—December 2 in Gemini
New Moon—December 16 in Sagittarius
Full Moon—December 31 in Cancer (lunar eclipse)

Timing by the Moon's Sign

To forecast the daily emotional "weather," to determine your monthly high and low days, or to synchronize your activities with the cycles of the moon, take note of the moon's sign under your daily forecast at the end of the book. Here are some of the activities favored and the moods you are likely to encounter under each moon sign.

Moon in Aries: Get Moving

The new moon in Aries is an ideal time to start new projects. Everyone is pushy, raring to go, rather impatient, and short-tempered. Leave details and follow-up for later. Competitive sports or martial arts are great ways to let off steam. Quiet types could use some assertiveness, but it's a great day for dynamos. Be careful not to step on too many toes.

Moon in Taurus: Lay the Foundations for Success

Do solid, methodical tasks like follow-through or backup work. Make investments, buy real estate, do appraisals, or do some hard bargaining. Attend to your property. Get out in the country or spend some time in your garden. Enjoy creature comforts, music, a good dinner, or sensual love-making. Forget starting a diet—this is a day when you'll feel self-indulgent.

Moon in Gemini: Communicate

Talk means action today. Telephone, write letters, and fax!
Make new contacts; stay in touch with steady customers.
You can juggle lots of tasks today. It's a great time for
mental activity of any kind. Don't try to pin people down—
they too are feeling restless. Keep it light. Flirtations and
socializing are good. Watch gossip—and don't give away
secrets.

Moon in Cancer: Pay Attention to Loved Ones

This is a moody, sensitive, emotional time. People respond
to personal attention and mothering. Stay at home, have a
family dinner, or call your mother. Nostalgia, memories,
and psychic powers are heightened. You'll want to hang on
to people and things (don't clean out your closets now).
You could have shrewd insights into what others really
need and want. Pay attention to dreams, intuition, and
gut reactions.

Moon in Leo: Be Confident

Everybody is in a much more confident, warm, generous
mood. It's a good day to ask for a raise, show what you
can do, or dress like a star. People will respond to flattery
and enjoy a bit of drama and theater. You may be extravagant, treat yourself royally, and show off a bit—but don't
break the bank! Be careful not to promise more than you
can deliver.

Moon in Virgo: Be Practical

Do practical, down-to-earth chores. Review your budget,
make repairs, or be an efficiency expert. Not a day to ask
for a raise. Tend to personal care and maintenance. Have
a health checkup, go on a diet, or buy vitamins or health
food. Make your home spotless. Take care of details and
piled-up chores. Reorganize your work and life so they run

more smoothly and efficiently. Save money. Be prepared for others to be in critical, faultfinding moods.

Moon in Libra: Be Diplomatic

Attend to legal matters. Negotiate contracts. Arbitrate. Do things with your favorite partner. Socialize. Be romantic. Buy a special gift or a beautiful object. Decorate yourself or your surroundings. Buy new clothes. Throw a party. Have an elegant, romantic evening. Smooth over any ruffled feathers. Avoid confrontations. Stick to civilized discussions.

Moon in Scorpio: Solve Problems

This is a day to do things with passion. You'll have excellent concentration and focus. Try not to get too intense emotionally. Avoid sharp exchanges with loved ones. Others may tend to go to extremes, get jealous, or overreact. Great for troubleshooting, problem solving, research, scientific work—and making love. Pay attention to those psychic vibes.

Moon in Sagittarius: Sell and Motivate

A great time for travel, philosophical discussions, or setting long-range career goals. Work out, do sports, or buy athletic equipment. Others will be feeling upbeat, exuberant, and adventurous. Taking risks is favored. You may feel like gambling, betting on the horses, visiting a local casino, or buying a lottery ticket. Teaching, writing, and spiritual activities also get the green light. Relax outdoors. Take care of animals.

Moon in Capricorn: Get Organized

You can accomplish a lot now, so get on the ball! Attend to business. Issues concerning your basic responsibilities, duties, family, and elderly parents could crop up. You'll be expected to deliver on promises. Weed out the deadwood from your life. Get a dental checkup. Not a good day for gambling or taking risks.

Moon in Aquarius: Join the Group

A great day for doing things with groups—clubs, meetings, outings, politics, or parties. Campaign for your candidate. Work for a worthy cause. Deal with larger issues that affect humanity—the environment and metaphysical questions. Buy a computer or electronic gadget. Watch TV. Wear something outrageous. Try something you've never done before. Present an original idea. Don't stick to a rigid schedule; go with the flow. Take a class in meditation, mind control, or yoga.

Moon in Pisces: Be Creative

This can be a very creative day, so let your imagination work overtime. Film, theater, music, and ballet could inspire you. Spend some time resting and reflecting, reading, or writing poetry. Daydreams can also be profitable. Help those less fortunate. Lend a listening ear to someone who may be feeling blue. Don't overindulge in self-pity or escapism. People are especially vulnerable to substance abuse. Turn your thoughts to romance and someone special.

Eclipses Clear the Air

This is a year with six eclipses, an unusually high number. Eclipses can bring on milestones in your life, if they aspect a key point in your horoscope. In general, they shake up the status quo, bringing hidden areas out into the open. During this time, problems you've been avoiding or have brushed aside can surface to demand your attention. A good coping strategy is to accept whatever comes up as a challenge that could make a positive difference in your life. And don't forget the power of your sense of humor. If you can laugh at something, you'll never be afraid of it.

When the natural rhythms of the sun and moon are disturbed, it's best to postpone important activities. Be sure to mark eclipse days on your calendar, especially if the eclipse falls in your birth sign. This year, those born under Cancer, Leo, Aquarius, and Capricorn should take special note of the feelings that arise. If your moon is in one of these signs, you may be especially affected. With lunar eclipses, some possibilities could be a break from attachments, or the healing of an illness or substance abuse that was triggered by the subconscious. The temporary event could be a healing time, when you gain perspective. During solar eclipses, when you might be in a highly subjective state, pay attention to the hidden subconscious patterns that surface, the emotional truth that is revealed at this time.

The effect of the eclipse can reverberate for some time, often months after the event. But it is especially important to stay cool and make no major moves during the period known as the shadow of the eclipse, which begins about a week before and lasts until at least three days after the eclipse. After three days, the daily rhythms should return to normal, and you can proceed with business as usual.

This Year's Eclipse Dates

January 26: Solar Eclipse in Aquarius
February 9: Lunar Eclipse in Leo
July 7: Lunar Eclipse in Capricorn
July 22: Solar Eclipse in Cancer
August 5: Lunar eclipse in Aquarius
December 31: Lunar Eclipse in Cancer

Retrogrades: When the Planets Seem to Backstep

All the planets, except for the sun and moon, have times when they appear to move backward—or retrograde—as it seems from our point of view on Earth. At these times, planets do not work as they normally do. So it's best to "take a break" from that planet's energies in our life and to do some work on an inner level.

Mercury Retrograde: The Key Is in "Re"

Mercury goes into retrograde most often, and its effects can be especially irritating. When it reaches a short distance ahead of the sun several times a year, it seems to move backward from our point of view. Astrologers often compare retrograde motion to the optical illusion that occurs when we ride on a train that passes another train traveling at a different speed—the second train appears to be moving in reverse.

What this means to you is that the Mercury-ruled areas of your life—analytical thought processes, communications, scheduling—are subject to all kinds of confusion. Be prepared. Communications equipment can break down. Schedules may be changed on short notice. People are late for appointments or don't show up at all. Traffic is terrible. Major purchases malfunction, don't work out, or get delivered in the wrong color. Letters don't arrive or are delivered to the wrong address. Employees will make errors that have to be corrected later. Contracts don't work out or must be renegotiated.

Since most of us can't put our lives on "hold" during Mercury retrogrades, we should learn to tame the trickster and make it work for us. The key is in the prefix re-. This is the time to go back over things in your life, reflect on what you've done during the previous months. Now you can get deeper insights, and spot errors you've missed. So take time to review and reevaluate what has happened. Rest and reward yourself—it's a good time to take a vacation, especially if you revisit a favorite place. Reorganize your work and finish up projects that are backed up. Clean out your desk and closets. Throw away what you can't recycle. If you must sign contracts or agreements, do so with a contingency clause that lets you reevaluate the terms later.

Postpone major purchases or commitments for the time being. Don't get married (unless you're remarrying the same person). Try not to rely on other people keeping appointments, contracts, or agreements to the letter; have several alternatives. Double-check and read between the lines. Don't buy anything connected with communications or transportation (if you must, be sure to cover yourself).

Mercury retrograding through your sun sign will intensify its effect on your life.

If Mercury was retrograde when you were born, you may be one of the lucky people who don't suffer the frustrations of this period. If so, your mind probably works in a very intuitive, insightful way.

The sign in which Mercury is retrograding can give you an idea of what's in store—as well as the sun signs that will be especially challenged.

Mercury Retrogrades in 2009

Mercury has three major retrograde periods this year, then turns retrograde in late December, in time for New Year's Eve, when there is also a lunar eclipse and retrograding Mars. This means it will be especially important to watch all activities which involve mental processes and communication.

January 11 to February 1 from Aquarius to Capricorn
May 6 to May 30 in Taurus to Gemini
September 6 to September 29 from Libra to Virgo
December 26 in Capricorn until January 15, 2010

Venus Retrograde: Relationships Are Affected

Retrograding Venus can cause your relationships to take a backward step, or you may feel that a key relationship is on hold. Singles may be especially lonely, yet find it difficult to connect with someone special. If you wish to make amends in an already troubled relationship, make peaceful overtures at this time. You may feel more extravagant or overindulge in shopping or sweet treats. Shopping till you drop and buying what you cannot afford are bad at this time. It's *not* a good time to redecorate— you'll hate the color of the walls later. Postpone getting a new hairstyle. It only lasts for a relatively short time this year; however, Aries should take special note.

Venus Retrogrades in 2009

Venus retrogrades from March 6 to April 17, from Pisces to Aries.

Use the Power of Mars

Mars shows how and when to get where you want to go. Timing your moves with Mars on your side can give you a big push. On the other hand, pushing Mars the wrong way can guarantee that you'll run into frustrations around every corner. Your best times to forge ahead are during the weeks when Mars is traveling through your sun sign or your Mars sign (look these up in the planet tables in this book). Also consider times when Mars is in a compatible sign (fire signs with air signs, or earth signs with water signs). You'll be sure to have planetary power on your side.

Holiday Happenings

It should be a lively holiday season this year. Mars will start a lengthy retrograde in extravagant Leo beginning December 20, in the midst of the holiday season, followed by Mercury turning retrograde on December 26 and a lunar eclipse in Cancer on December 31. Your patience may be tested more than usual during this year's festivities, so plan ahead and perhaps do your shopping early. Be flexible with travel plans, if you are vacationing, especially if you are a Leo or Cancer. Be especially cautious during the New Year's lunar eclipse. Resolve to practice anger management and self-control, even when those around you are on a short fuse. The Mars retrograde in Leo will last until March of 2010, during which there are sure to be repercussions on the international level.

Mars Retrogrades in 2009

Mars turns retrograde in Leo on December 20 until March 10, 2010.

When Other Planets Retrograde

The slower-moving planets stay retrograde for many months at a time (Jupiter, Saturn, Neptune, Uranus, and Pluto).

When Saturn is retrograde, it's an uphill battle with self-discipline. You may not be in the mood for work. You may feel more like hanging out at the beach than getting things done.

Neptune retrograde promotes a dreamy escapism from reality, when you may feel you're in a fog (Pisces will feel this, especially).

Uranus retrograde may mean setbacks in areas where there have been sudden changes, when you may be forced to regroup or reevaluate the situation.

Pluto retrograde is a time to work on establishing proportion and balance in areas where there have been recent dramatic transformations.

When the planets move forward again, there's a shift in the atmosphere. Activities connected with each planet start moving ahead; plans that were stalled get rolling. Make a special note of those days on your calendar and proceed accordingly.

Other Retrogrades in 2009

The five slower-moving planets all go retrograde in 2009.

Jupiter retrogrades from June 15 to October 12 in Aquarius.

Saturn is retrograde as the year begins and turns direct on May 16 in Virgo.

Uranus retrogrades from July 1 to December 1 in Pisces.

Neptune retrogrades from May 28 to November 4 in Aquarius.

Pluto turns retrograde April 4 to September 11 in Capricorn.

♎ CHAPTER 6

Your Sign's Bottom Line in 2009: Is Success in Your Stars?

Though no sign wins the financial lottery—all have their share of billionaires and paupers—the signs of success are those who make the most of their particular financial talents. But every year, Jupiter, the planet of luck, gives an extra boost to a different sign. This year, it's the air signs (Gemini, Libra, and especially Aquarius) who should profit most from the lucky rays of Jupiter in Aquarius. Of all the signs, Aquarius is best suited for analyzing and coping with the unpredictable nature of the stock market and able to detach emotionally from investments. Most of us could benefit from using some Aquarius-inspired intuition, socially conscious investment philosophy, and experimental nature, especially in the area of our horoscope where Jupiter will be giving us growth opportunities.

Aries

You've got a taste for fast money, quick turnover, and edgy investments, with no patience for gradual, long-term gains. You're an impulse buyer with the nerve for risky tactics that could backfire. On the other hand, you're a pioneer who can see into the future, who dares to take a gamble on a new idea or product that could change the world . . . like Sam Walton of the Wal-Mart stores, who changed the way we shop. You need a backup plan in case one of your big ideas burns out. To protect your money, get a backup plan you can follow without thinking about it. Have a percentage of your income automatically put into a savings or retirement account. Then give yourself some extra funds to play with. Your weak point is your impatience; so you're not one to wait out a slow market or watch savings slowly accumulate. You're inspired by Aquarius this year, so it's time to support your long-range goals and ideals, by exploring socially conscious investments, especially in the clean-energy field.

Taurus

You're a saver who loves to see your cash, as well as your possessions, accumulate. You have no qualms about steadily increasing your fortune. You're a savvy trader and a shrewd investor, in there for long-term gains. You have low toleration for risk; you hate to lose anything. But you do enjoy luxuries, and may need to reward yourself frequently. You might pass up an opportunity because it seems too risky, but you should take a chance once in a while. Lucky Jupiter accents your career this year, which means new opportunities. So don't hesitate to explore job offers. You're especially lucky in real estate or any occupation that requires appraising and trading, as well as earth-centered businesses like farming and conservation.

Gemini

With Gemini, the cash can flow in and then out just as quickly. You naturally multi-task, and you are sure to have several projects going at once, as well as several credit cards, which can easily get out of hand. Saving is not one of your strong points—too boring. You fall in and out of love with different ideas; you have probably tried a round of savings techniques. Diversification is your best strategy. Have several different kinds of investments—at least one should be a long-term plan. Set savings goals and then regularly deposit small amounts into your accounts. Follow the lead of Gemini financial adviser Suze Orman and get a good relationship going with your money! With lucky Jupiter accenting travel this year, investigate foreign investment opportunities and jobs connected with travel and tourism.

Cancer

You can be a natural moneymaker with your peerless intuition. You can spot a winner that everyone else misses. Consider Cancer success stories like those of cosmetics queen Estee Lauder and Roxanne Quimby, of Burt's Bees, who turned her friend's stash of beeswax into a thriving cosmetics business. Who knew? So trust your intuition. You are a saver who always has a backup plan, just in case. Remember to treat and nurture yourself as well as others. Investments in the food industry, restaurants, hotels, shipping, and water-related industries are Cancer territory.

Leo

You love the first-class lifestyle, but may not always have the resources to support it. Finding a way to fund your extravagant tastes is the Leo challenge. Some courses in money management or an expert financial coach could set you on the right track. However, you're also a terrific salesperson, and you're fabulous in high-profile jobs that pay a lot. You're the community tastemaker; you satisfy your appetite for "the best" by working for a quality company that sells luxury goods, splendid real estate, dream vacations, and first-class travel—that way you'll have access to the lifestyle without having to pay for it. With Jupiter in Aquarius accenting partnerships, you might want to team up for investing purposes this year.

Virgo

Your sign is a stickler for details, which includes your money management. You like to follow your spending and saving closely; you enjoy planning, budgeting, and price comparison. Your sign usually has no problem sticking to a savings or investment plan. You have a critical eye for quality, and you like to bargain and to shop to get the best value. In fact, Warren Buffet, a Virgo billionaire, is known for value investing. You buy cheap and sell at a profit. Investing in health care, organic products, and food could be profitable for you, especially this year, when Jupiter accents the care and maintenance part of your life.

Libra

Oh, do you ever love to shop! And you often have an irresistible urge to acquire an exquisite object or a designer dress you can't really afford or to splurge on the perfect antique armoire. You don't like to settle for second-rate or bargain buys. Learning to prioritize your spending is especially difficult for your sign, so try to find a good money manager to do it for you. Following a strictly balanced budget is your key to financial success. With Libra's keen eye for quality and good taste, you are a savvy picker at auctions and antiques fairs, so you might be able to turn around your purchase for a profit. Jupiter in Aquarius will bless creativity and self-expression.

Scorpio

Scorpios prefer to stay in control of their finances at all times. You're sure to have a financial-tracking program on your computer. You're not an impulse buyer, unless you see something that immediately turns you on. Rely on your instincts! Scorpio is the sign of credit cards, taxes, and loans, so you are able to use these tools cleverly. Investing for Scorpio is rarely casual. You'll do extensive research and track your investments by reading the financial pages, annual reports, and profit-loss statements.

Sagittarius

Sagittarius is a natural gambler, with a high tolerance for risk. It's important for you to learn when to hold 'em, and when to fold 'em, as the song goes, by setting limits on your risk taking and covering your assets. You enjoy the thrill of playing the stock market, where you could win big and lose big. Money itself is rarely the object for Sagittarius—it's the game that counts. Since your sign rarely saves for a rainy day, your best strategy might be a savings plan that transfers a certain amount into a savings account. Regular bill-paying plans are another strategy to keep you on track. You could benefit from an inspirational money manager who gets you fired up about an investment plan. Go where the action is and circulate. Your ruling planet, Jupiter, blesses social contacts this year. Why not join an investment club?

Capricorn

You're one of the strongest money managers in the zodiac, which should serve you well this year when Jupiter, the planet of luck and expansion, is blessing your house of finance. You're a born bargain hunter and clever negotiator—a saver rather than a spender. You are the sign of self-discipline, which works well when it comes to sticking with a budget and living frugally while waiting for resources to accumulate. You are likely to plan carefully for your elder years, profiting from long-term investments. You have a keen sense of value, and you will pick up a bargain and then turn it around at a nice profit.

Aquarius

Luck is with you this year, with Jupiter blessing your sign. There should be many chances to speculate on forward-looking ventures. The Aquarius trait of unpredictability extends to your financial life, where you surprise us all with your ability to turn something totally unique into a money spinner. Consider your wealthy sign mate Oprah Winfrey, who has been able to intuit what the public will buy at a given moment. Some of your ideas might sound far-out, but they turn out to be right on the money. Investing in high-tech companies that are on the cutting edge of their field is good for Aquarius. You'll probably intuit which ones will stay the course. You'll feel good about investing in companies that improve the environment, such as new types of fuel, or ones that are related to your favorite cause.

Pisces

The typical Pisces is probably the sign least interested in money management. However, there are many billionaires born under your sign, such as Michael Dell, David Geffen, and Steve Jobs. Generally they have made money from innovative ideas and left the details to others. That might work for you. Find a Scorpio, Capricorn, or Virgo to help you set a profitable course and systematically save (which is not in your nature). Sign up for automatic bill paying so you won't have to think about it. If you keep in mind how much less stressful life will be and how much more you can do when you're not worried about paying bills, you might be motivated enough to stick to a sensible budget. Investment-wise, consider anything to do with water—off-shore drilling, water conservation and purifying, shipping, and seafood. Petroleum is also ruled by your sign, as are institutions related to hospitals.

♎ CHAPTER 7

Sun-Sign Seduction Secrets

Haven't found the one yet? Maybe you haven't been using astrology. If you want to charm a Capricorn, hook a Pisces, or corral a Taurus, here are sun-sign seduction tips guaranteed to keep your lover begging for more.

Aries: Play Hard to Get

This highly physical sign is walking dynamite with a brief attention span. Don't be too easy to get, ladies. A little challenge, a lively debate, and a merry chase only heat them up. They want to see what you're made of. Once you've lured them into your lair, be a challenge and a bit of a daredevil. Pull out your X-rated tricks. Don't give your all—let them know there's more where that came from. Make it exciting; show you're up for adventure. Wear bright red somewhere interesting. Since Aries rules the head and face, be sure to focus on these areas in your lovemaking. Use your lips, tongue, breath, and even your eyelashes to the max. Practice scalp massages and deep kissing techniques. Aries won't wait, so when you make your move, be sure you're ready to follow through. No head games or teasing!

To keep you happy, you've got to voice your *own* needs, because this lover will be focused on *his*. Teach him how to please, or this could be a one-sided adventure.

Taurus: Appeal to All Their Senses

Taurus wins as the most sensual sign, with the most sexual stamina. This man is earthy and lusty in bed; he can go on all night. This is not a sign to tease. Like a bull, he'll see red, not bed. So make him comfortable, and then bombard all his senses. Good food gets Taurus in the mood. So do the right music, fragrance, revealing clothes, and luxurious bedlinens. Give him a massage with delicious-smelling and -tasting oils; focus on the neck area.

Don't forget to turn off the phone! Taurus hates interruptions. Since they can be very vocal lovers, choose a setting where you won't be disturbed. And don't ever rush; enjoy a long, slow, delicious encounter.

Gemini: Be a Playmate

Playful Gemini loves games, so make your seduction fun. Be their lost twin soul or confidante. Good communication is essential, so share deep secrets and live out fantasies. This sign adores variety. Nothing bores Gemini more than making love the same way all the time, or bringing on the heavy emotions. So trot out all the roles you've been longing to play. Here's the perfect partner. But remember to keep it light and fun. Gemini's turn-on zone is the hands, and this sign gives the best massages. Gadgets that can be activated with a touch amuse Gemini. This sign is great at doing two things at once, like making love while watching an erotic film. Turn the cell phone off unless you want company. On the other hand, Gemini is your sign for superhot phone sex.

Gemini loves a change of scene. So experiment on the floor, in the shower, or on the kitchen table. Borrow a friend's apartment or rent a hotel room for variety.

Cancer: Use the Moon

The key to Cancer is to get this moon child in the mood. Consult the moon—a full moon is best. Wining, dining, old-fashioned courtship, and breakfast in bed are turn-ons. Whatever makes your Cancer feel secure will promote shedding inhibitions in the sack. (Don't try any of your

Aries daredevil techniques here!) Cancer prefers familiar, comfortable, homey surroundings. Cancer's turn-on zone is the breasts. Cancer women often have naturally inflated chests. Cancer men may fantasize about a well-endowed playmate. If your breasts are enhanced, show them off. Cancer will want to know all your deepest secrets, so invent a few good ones. But lots of luck delving into *their* innermost thoughts!

Take your Cancer near water. The sight and sound of the sea can be their aphrodisiac. A moonlit beach, a deserted swimming pool, a Jacuzzi, or a bubble bath are good seduction spots. Listen to the rain patter on the roof in a mountain cabin.

Leo: Offer the Royal Treatment

Leo must be the best and hear it from you often. In return, they'll perform for you, telling you just what you want to hear (true or not). They like a lover with style and endurance, and to be swept off their feet and into bed. Leos like to go first-class all the way, so build them up with lots of attention, wining and dining, and special gifts.

Never mention other lovers or make them feel second-best. A sure signal for Leo to look elsewhere is a competitive spouse. Leos take great pride in their bodies, so you should pour on the admiration. A few well-placed mirrors could inspire them. So would a striptease with beautiful lingerie, expensive fragrance on the sheets, and, if female, an occasional luxury hotel room, with champagne and caviar delivered by room service. Leo's erogenous zone is the lower back, so a massage with expensive oils would make your lion purr with pleasure.

Virgo: Let Them Be the Teacher

Virgo's standards are so sky-high that you may feel intimidated at first. The key to pleasing fussy Virgo lovers is to look for the hot fantasy beneath their cool surface. They're really looking for someone to make over. So let Virgo play teacher, and you play the willing student; the doctor-patient routine works as well. Be Eliza Doolittle to his Henry Higgins.

Let Virgo help you improve your life, quit smoking, learn French, and diet. Read an erotic book together, and then practice the techniques. Or study esoteric, erotic exercises from the Far East.

The Virgo erogenous zone is the tummy area, which should be your base of operations. Virgo likes things pristine and clean. Fall onto crisp, immaculate white sheets. Wear a sheer virginal white nightie. Smell shower-fresh with no heavy perfume. Be sure your surroundings pass the hospital test. A shower together afterward (with great-smelling soap) could get the ball rolling again.

Libra: Look Your Best

Libra must be turned on aesthetically. Make sure you look as beautiful as possible, and wear something stylishly seductive but never vulgar. Have a mental affair first, as you flirt and flatter this sign. Then proceed to the physical. Approach Libra like a dance partner, ready to waltz or tango.

Libra must be in the mood for love; otherwise, forget it. Any kind of ugliness is a turnoff. Provide an elegant and harmonious atmosphere, with no loud noise, clashing colors, or uncomfortable beds. Libra is not an especially spontaneous lover, so it is best to spend time warming them up. Libra's back is his erogenous zone, your cue to provide back rubs with scented potions. Once in bed, you can be a bit aggressive sexually. Libra loves strong, decisive moves. Set the scene, know what you want, and let Libra be happy to provide it.

Scorpio: Be an All-or-Nothing Lover

Scorpio is legendary in bed, often called the sex sign of the zodiac. But seducing them is often a power game. Scorpio likes to be in control, even the quiet, unassuming ones. Scorpio loves a mystery, so don't tell all. Keep them guessing about you, offering tantalizing hints along the way. The hint of danger often turns Scorpio on, so you'll find members of this sign experimenting with the exotic and highly erotic forms of sex. Sadomasochism, bondage, or anything that tests the limits of power could be a turn-on for Scorpio.

Invest in some sexy black leather and some powerful music. Clothes that lace, buckle, or zip tempt Scorpio to untie you. Present yourself as a mysterious package just waiting to be unwrapped.

Once in bed, there are no holds barred with Scorpio. They'll find your most pleasurable pressure points, and touch you as you've never been touched before. They are quickly aroused (the genital area belongs to this sign) and are willing to try anything. But they can be possessive. Don't expect your Scorpio to share you with anyone. It's all or nothing for them.

Sagittarius: Be a Happy Wanderer

Sagittarius men are the Don Juans of the zodiac—love-'em-and-leave-'em types who are difficult to pin down. Your seduction strategy is to join them in their many pursuits, and then hook them with love on the road. Sagittarius enjoys sex in venues that suggest movement; planes, SUVs, or boats. But a favorite turn-on place is outdoors, in nature. A deserted hiking path, a field of tall grass, or a remote woodland glade—all give the centaur sexy ideas. Athletic Sagittarius might go for some personal training in an empty gym. Join your Sagittarius for amorous aerobics, meditate together, and explore the tantric forms of sex. Lovemaking after hiking and skiing would be healthy fun.

Sagittarius enjoys lovers from exotic ethnic backgrounds, or lovers met in spiritual pursuits or on college campuses. Sagittarius are great cheerleaders and motivators, and will enjoy feeling that they have inspired you to be all that you can be.

There may be a canine or feline companion sharing your

Sagittarius lover's bed with you, so check your allergies. And bring Fido or Felix a toy to keep them occupied.

Capricorn: Take Their Mind off Business

The great news about Capricorn lovers is that they improve with age. They are probably the sexiest seniors. So stick around, if you have a young one. They're lusty in bed (it's not the sign of the goat for nothing), and can be quite raunchy and turned on by X-rated words and deeds. If this is not your thing, let them know. The Capricorn erogenous zone is the knees. Some discreet fondling in public places could be your opener. Capricorn tends to think of sex as part of a game plan for the future. They are well-organized, and might regard lovemaking as relaxation after a long day's work. This sign often combines business with pleasure. So look for a Capricorn where there's a convention, trade show, or work-related conference.

Getting Capricorn's mind off his agenda and onto yours could take some doing. Separate him from his buddies by whispering sexy secrets in his ear. Then convince him you're an asset to his image and a boon to his health. Though he may seem uptight at first, you'll soon discover he's a love animal who makes a wonderful and permanent pet.

Aquarius: Give Them Enough Space

This sign really does not want an all-consuming passion or an all-or-nothing relationship. Aquarius needs space. But once they feel free to experiment with a spontaneous and exciting partner, Aquarius can give you a far-out sexual adventure.

Passion begins in the mind, so a good mental buildup is key. Aquarius is an inventive sign who believes love is a playground without rules. Plan surprise, unpredictable encounters in unusual places. Find ways to make love transcendental, an extraordinary and unique experience. Be ready to try anything Aquarius suggests, if only once. Calves and ankles are the special Aquarius erogenous zone, so perfect your legwork.

Be careful not to be too possessive. Your Aquarius needs lots of space and tolerance for friends (including old lovers) and their many outside interests.

Pisces: Live Their Fantasies

Pisces is the sign of fantasy and imagination. This sign has great theatrical talent. Pisces looks for lovers who will take care of them. Pisces will return the favor! Here is someone who can psych out your deepest desires without mentioning them. Pisces falls for sob stories and is always ready to empathize. It wouldn't hurt to have a small problem for Pisces to help you overcome. It might help if you cry on his shoulder, for this sign needs to be needed. Use your imagination when setting the scene for love. A dramatic setting brings out Pisces theatrical talents. Or creatively use the element of water. Rain on the roof, waterfalls, showers, beach houses, water beds, and Jacuzzis could turn up the heat. Experiment with pulsating jets of water. Take midnight skinny-dips in deserted pools.

The Pisces erogenous zone is the feet. This is your cue to give a sensuous foot massage using scented lotions. Let him paint your toes. Beautiful toenails in sexy sandals are a special turn-on.

Your Hottest Love Match

Here's a tip for finding your hottest love match. If your lover's Mars sign makes favorable aspects to your Venus, is in the same element (earth, air, fire, water), or is in the same sign, your lover will do what you want done! Mars influences how we act when we make love, while Venus shows what we like done to us. Sometimes fighting and making up is the sexiest fun of all. If you're the type who needs a spark to keep lust alive (you know who you are!), then look for Mars and Venus in different signs of the same quality (fixed or cardinal or mutable). For instance, a fixed sign (Taurus, Leo, Scorpio, Aquarius) paired with another fixed sign can have a sexy tug-of-war before you finally surrender. Two cardinal signs (Aries, Cancer, Libra, Capricorn) set off passionate fireworks when they clash. Mutable signs (Gemini, Virgo, Sagittarius, Pisces) play a fascinating game of cat and mouse, never quite catching each other.

Your Most Seductive Time

The best time for love is when Venus is in your sign, making you the most desirable sign in the zodiac. This only lasts about three weeks (unless Venus is retrograde) so don't waste time! And find out the time this year when Venus is in your sign by consulting the Venus chart at the end of chapter three.

What's the Sexiest Sign?

It depends on what sign you are. Astrology has traditionally given this honor to Scorpio, the sign associated with the sex organs. However, we are all a combination of different signs (and turn-ons). Gemini's communicating ability and manual dexterity could deliver the magic touch. Cancer's tenderness and understanding could bring out your passion more than regal Leo.

Which Is the Most Faithful Sign?

The earth signs of Capricorn, Taurus, and Virgo are usually the most faithful. They tend to be more home- and family-oriented, and they are usually choosy about their mates. It's impractical, inconvenient, and probably expensive to play around, or so they think.

Who'll Play Around?

The mutable signs of Gemini, Pisces, and Sagittarius win the playboy or playgirl sweepstakes. These signs tend to be changeable, fickle, and easily bored. But they're so much fun!

♎ CHAPTER 8

Children of 2009, Born in Changing Times

Parents of several children may see a marked difference between children born in 2009 and their older siblings, because the cosmic atmosphere is changing, which should imprint the personalities of this year's children. Astrologers look to the slow-moving outer planets—Uranus, Neptune, and Pluto—to describe a generation.

This year, Uranus and Neptune are still passing through Pisces and Aquarius, both visionary and spiritual signs. However, there is also much more earth-sign emphasis than in previous years due to the earthly pull of Pluto in Capricorn, plus the closer planets. Saturn also in an earth sign, will counterbalance this spirituality with extreme practicality and pragmatism. This generation will be focused on getting the job done, on fixing up the planet, and on making things work.

Astrology can be an especially helpful tool when used to design an environment that enhances and encourages each child's positive qualities. Some parents start before conception, planning the birth of their child as far as possible to harmonize with the signs of other family members. However, each baby has its own schedule, so if yours arrives a week early or late, or elects a different sign than you'd planned, recognize that the new sign may be more in line with the mission your child is here to accomplish. In other words, if you were hoping for a Libra child and he arrives during Virgo, that Virgo energy may be just what is needed to stimulate or complement your family. Remember that there are many astrological elements besides the sun sign that indicate strong family ties. Usually each child will share

111

a particular planetary placement, an emphasis on a particular sign or house, or a certain chart configuration with his parents and other family members. Often there is a significant planetary angle that will define the parent-child relationship, such as family sun signs that form a T-square or a triangle.

One important thing you can do is to be sure the exact moment of birth is recorded. This will be essential in calculating an accurate astrological chart. The following descriptions can be applied to the sun or moon sign (if known) of a child—the sun sign will describe basic personality and the moon sign indicates the child's emotional needs.

The Aries Child

Baby Aries is quite a handful. This energetic child will walk—and run—as soon as possible, and perform daring feats of exploration. Caregivers should be vigilant. Little Aries seems to know no fear (and is especially vulnerable to head injuries). Many Aries children, in their rush to get on with life, seem hyperactive, and they are easily frustrated when they can't get their own way. Violent temper tantrums and dramatic physical displays are par for the course with this child, requiring a time-out mat or naughty chair.

The very young Aries should be monitored carefully, since he is prone to take risks and may injure himself. Aries love to take things apart and may break toys easily, but with encouragement, the child will develop formidable coordination. Aries's bossy tendencies should be molded into leadership qualities, rather than bullying, which should be easy to do with this year's babies. Encourage these children to take out aggressions and frustrations in active, competitive sports, where they usually excel. When young Aries learns to focus energies long enough to master a subject and learns consideration for others, the indomitable Aries spirit will rise to the head of the class.

Aries born in 2009 will be a more subdued version of this sign, but still loaded with energy. The Capricorn effect should make little Aries easier to discipline and more focused on achievement. A natural leader!

The Taurus Child

This is a cuddly, affectionate child who eagerly explores the world of the senses, especially the senses of taste and touch. The Taurus child can be a big eater and will put on weight easily if not encouraged to exercise. Since this child likes comfort and gravitates to beauty, try coaxing little Taurus to exercise to music, or take him or her out of doors, with hikes or long walks. Though Taurus may be a slow learner, this sign has an excellent retentive memory and generally masters a subject thoroughly. Taurus is interested in results and will see each project patiently through to completion, continuing long after others have given up. This year's earth sign planets will give him a wonderful sense of support and accomplishment.

Choose Taurus toys carefully to help develop innate talents. Construction toys, such as blocks or erector sets, appeal to their love of building. Paints or crayons develop their sense of color. Many Taurus have musical talent and love to sing, which is apparent at a young age.

This year's Taurus will want a pet or two, and a few plants of his own. Give little Taurus a small garden, and watch the natural green thumb develop. This child has a strong sense of acquisition and an early grasp of material value. After filling a piggy bank, Taurus graduates to a savings account, before other children have started to learn the value of money.

This year's Taurus gets a bonanza of good luck and support from Jupiter, Pluto, and Saturn, all in compatible earth signs. These should give little Taurus an especially easygoing disposition and provide many opportunities to live up to his sign's potential.

The Gemini Child

Little Gemini will talk as soon as possible, filling the air with questions and chatter. This is a friendly child who enjoys social contact, seems to require company, and adapts quickly to different surroundings. Geminis have quick minds that easily grasp the use of words, books, and telephones, and will probably learn to talk and read at an earlier age than most. Though they are fast learners, Gemini may have a short attention span, darting from subject to subject. Projects and games that help focus the mind could be used to help them concentrate. Musical instruments, typewriters, and computers help older Gemini children combine mental with manual dexterity. Geminis should be encouraged to finish what they start before they go on to another project. Otherwise, they can become jack-of-all-trade types who have trouble completing anything they do. Their disposition is usually cheerful and witty, making these children popular with their peers and delightful company at home.

This year's Gemini baby should go to the head of the class. Uranus in Pisces could inspire Gemini to make an unusual career choice, perhaps in a financial field. When he grows up, this year's Gemini may change jobs several times before he finds a position that satisfies his need for stimulation and variety.

The Cancer Child

This emotional, sensitive child is especially influenced by patterns set in early life. Young Cancers cling to their first memories as well as their childhood possessions. They thrive in calm emotional waters, with a loving, protective mother, and usually remain close to her (even if their relationship with her was difficult) throughout their lives. Divorce and death—anything that disturbs the safe family unit—are devastating to Cancers, who may need extra support and reassurance during a family crisis.

They sometimes need a firm hand to push the positive, creative side of their personality and discourage them from getting swept away by emotional moods or resorting to emotional manipulation to get their way. If this child is praised and encouraged to find creative expression, Cancers will be able to express their positive side consistently, on a firm, secure foundation.

This year's Cancer baby should be a social, cooperative child, oriented toward others, thanks to Jupiter and Pluto blessing relationships.

The Leo Child

Leo children love the limelight and will plot to get the lion's share of attention. These children assert themselves with flair and drama, and can behave like tiny tyrants to get their way. But in general, they have a sunny, positive disposition and are rarely subject to blue moods.

At school, they're the types voted most popular, head cheerleader, or homecoming queen. Leo is sure to be noticed for personality, if not for stunning looks or academic work; the homely Leo will be a class clown, and the unhappy Leo can be the class bully.

Above all, a Leo child cannot tolerate being ignored for long. Drama or performing-arts classes, sports, and school politics are healthy ways for Leo to be a star. But Leos must learn to take lesser roles occasionally, or they will have some painful putdowns in store. Usually, their popularity is well earned; they are hard workers who try to measure up to their own high standards—and usually succeed.

This year's Leo should be a less flamboyant, more down-to-earth version of his sign, as the earthy planets exert their influence. This should add more financial and practical talents to the expressive Leo personality.

The Virgo Child

The young Virgo can be a quiet, rather serious child, with a quick, intelligent mind. Early on, little Virgo shows far more attention to detail and concern with small things than other children. Little Virgo has a built-in sense of order and a fascination with how things work. It is important for these children to have a place of their own, which they can order as they wish and where they can read or busy themselves with crafts and hobbies. This child's personality can be very sensitive. Little Virgo may get hyper and overreact to seemingly small irritations, which can take the form of stomach upsets or delicate digestive systems. But this child will flourish where there is mental stimulation and a sense of order. Virgos thrive in school, especially in writing or language skills, and they seem truly happy when buried in books. Chances are, young Virgo will learn to read ahead of classmates. Hobbies that involve detail work or that develop fine craftsmanship are especially suited to young Virgos.

Baby Virgo of 2009 is likely to be an especially high achiever with Saturn, also in Virgo, adding focus and discipline, while Jupiter transiting the house of self-expression endows extra creativity.

The Libra Child

The Libra child learns early about the power of charm and appearance. This is often a very physically appealing child with an enchanting dimpled smile, who is naturally sociable and enjoys the company of both children and adults. It is a rare Libra child who is a discipline problem, but when their behavior is unacceptable, they respond better to calm discussion than displays of emotion, especially if the discussion revolves around fairness. Because young Libras without a strong direction tend to drift with the mood of the group, these children should be encouraged to develop their unique talents and powers of discrimination, so they can later stand on their own.

In school, this child is usually popular and will often have to choose between social invitations and studies. In the teen years, social pressures mount as the young Libra begins to look for a partner. This is the sign of best friends, so Libra's choice of companions can have a strong effect on his future direction. Beautiful Libra girls may be tempted to go steady or have an unwise early marriage. Chances are, both sexes will fall in and out of love several times in their search for the ideal partner.

Little Libra of 2009 is an especially social, talkative child, who gets along well with siblings as Jupiter in Capricorn enhances family life. This child is endowed with much imagination and creativity, as well as communication skills.

The Scorpio Child

The Scorpio child may seem quiet and shy, but will surprise others with intense feelings and formidable willpower. Scorpio children are single-minded when they want something and intensely passionate about whatever they do. One of a caregiver's tasks is to teach this child to balance activities and emotions, yet at the same time to make the most of his great concentration and intense commitment.

Since young Scorpios do not show their depth of feelings easily, parents will have to learn to read almost imperceptible signs that troubles are brewing beneath the surface. Both Scorpio boys and girls enjoy games of power and control on or off the playground. Scorpio girls may take an early interest in the opposite sex, masquerading as tomboys, while Scorpio boys may be intensely competitive and loners. When her powerful energies are directed into work, sports, or challenging studies, Scorpio is a superachiever, focused on a goal. With trusted friends, young Scorpio is devoted and caring—the proverbial friend through thick and thin, loyal for life.

Scorpio 2009 has a strong financial emphasis, which could make these children big money earners in adulthood. Uranus in Pisces in their house of creativity should put them on the cutting edge of whichever field they choose.

The Sagittarius Child

This restless, athletic child will be out of the playpen and off on explorative adventures as soon as possible. Little Sagittarius is remarkably well-coordinated, attempting daredevil feats on any wheeled vehicle from scooters to skateboards. These natural athletes need little encouragement to channel their energies into sports. Their cheerful friendly dispositions earn them popularity in school, and once they have found a subject where their talent and imagination can soar, they will do well academically. They love animals, especially horses, and will be sure to have a pet or two, if not a home zoo. When they are old enough to take care of themselves, they'll clamor to be off on adventures of their own, away from home, if possible.

This is a child who loves to travel, who will not get homesick at summer camp, and who may sign up to be a foreign-exchange student or spend summers abroad. Outdoor adventure appeals to little Sagittarius, especially if it involves an active sport, such as skiing, cycling or mountain climbing. Give them enough space and encouragement, and their fiery spirit will propel them to achieve high goals.

Baby Sagittarius of 2009 has a natural generosity of spirit and an optimistic, expansive nature. They will also demand a great deal of freedom. They may need reality checks from time to time, since they may be risk takers, especially in the financial area. They should learn early in life how to handle money.

The Capricorn Child

These purposeful, goal-oriented children will work to capacity if they feel this will bring results. They're not ones who enjoy work for its own sake—there must be a goal in sight. Authority figures can do much to motivate these children, but once set on an upward path, young Capricorn will mobilize his energy and talent and work harder, and with more perseverance, than any other sign. Capricorn has built-in self-discipline that can achieve remarkable results, even if lacking the flashy personality, quick brainpower, or penetrating insight of others. Once involved, young Capricorn will stick to a task until it is mastered. This child also knows how to use others to his advantage and may well become the team captain or class president.

A wise parent will set realistic goals for the Capricorn child, paving the way for the early thrill of achievement. Youngsters should be encouraged to express their caring, feeling side to others, as well as their natural aptitude for leadership. Capricorn children may be especially fond of grandparents and older relatives, and will enjoy spending time with them and learning from them. It is not uncommon for young Capricorns to have an older mentor or teacher who guides them. With their great respect for authority, Capricorn children will take this influence very much to heart.

The Capricorn born in 2009 will have an upbeat cheerful personality. This child should have a generous, expansive nature, and be more outgoing than the usual member of this sign.

The Aquarius Child

The Aquarius child has a well-focused, innovative mind that often streaks so far ahead of peers that this child seems like an oddball. Routine studies never hold the restless youngster for long; he or she will look for another, more experimental place to try out his ideas and develop his inventions. Life is a laboratory to the inquiring Aquarius mind. School politics, sports, science, and the arts offer scope for their talents. But if there is no room for expression within approved social limits, Aquarius is sure to rebel. Questioning institutions and religions comes naturally, so these children may find an outlet elsewhere, becoming rebels with a cause. It is better not to force these children to conform, but rather to channel forward-thinking young minds into constructive group activities.

This year's Aquarius will have far-out glamour as well as charisma, thanks to his ruler, Uranus, in a friendly bond with Neptune. This could be a rock star, a statesman, or a scientist.

The Pisces Child

Give young Pisces praise, applause, and a gentle, but firm, push in the right direction. Lovable Pisces children may be abundantly talented, but may be hesitant to express themselves, because they are quite sensitive and easily hurt. It is a parent's challenge to help them gain self-esteem and self-confidence. However, this same sensitivity makes them trusted friends who'll have many confidants as they develop socially. It also endows many Pisces with spectacular creative talent.

Pisces adores drama and theatrics of all sorts; therefore, encourage them to channel their creativity into art forms rather than indulging in emotional dramas. Understand that they may need more solitude than other children may as they develop their creative ideas. But though daydreaming can be creative, it is important that these natural dreamers not dwell too long in the world of fantasy. Teach them practical coping skills for the real world.

Since Pisces are sensitive physically, parents should help them build strong bodies with proper diet and regular exercise. Young Pisces may gravitate to more individual sports, such as swimming, sailing, and skiing, rather than to team sports. Or they may prefer more artistic physical activities, like dance or ice-skating.

Born givers, these children are often drawn to the underdog (they quickly fall for sob stories) and attract those who might take advantage of their empathic nature. Teach them to choose friends wisely, to set boundaries in relationships, and to protect their emotional vulnerability—invaluable lessons in later life.

With the planet Uranus now in Pisces, the 2009 baby belongs to a generation of Pisces movers and shakers. This child may have a rebellious streak that rattles the status quo. But this generation also has a visionary nature, which will be much concerned with the welfare of the world at large.

♎ CHAPTER 9

Dive Deeper into Astrology with a Personal Reading

Ever wondered what a professional astrologer would have to say about the issues in your personal life? Then it might be worth your while to have a personal reading. A customized reading can deal with what matters most to you. It can help you sort out a problem, find and use the strengths in your horoscope, set you on a more fulfilling career path, or help you decide where to relocate. Many people consult astrologers to find the optimum time to schedule an important event such as a wedding or business meeting.

Another good reason for a reading is to refine your knowledge of astrology by consulting with someone who has years of experience analyzing charts. You might choose an astrologer with a specialty that intrigues you. Armed with the knowledge of your chart that you have acquired so far, you can then learn to interpret subtle nuances or gain insight into your talents and abilities.

How do you choose when there are so many different kinds of readings available, especially since the Internet has brought astrology into the mainstream? Besides individual one-on-one readings with a professional astrologer, there are personal readings by mail, telephone, Internet, and tape. Well-advertised computer-generated reports and celebrity-sponsored readings are sure to attract your attention on commercial Web sites and in magazines. You can even purchase a reading that is incorporated into an expensive handmade fine art book. Then there are astrologers who specialize in specific areas such as finance or medical astrology. And unfortunately, there are many questionable practitioners who range from streetwise Gypsy fortune-tellers to unscrupulous scam artists.

The following basic guidelines can help you sort out your options to find the reading that's right for you.

One-on-One Consultations with a Professional Astrologer

Nothing compares to a one-on-one consultation with a professional astrologer who has analyzed thousands of charts and can pinpoint the potential in yours. During your reading, you can get your specific questions answered and discuss possible paths you might take. There are many astrologers who now combine their skills with training in psychology and are well-suited to help you examine your alternatives.

To give you an accurate reading, an astrologer needs certain information from you: the date, time, and place where you were born. (A horoscope can be cast about anyone or anything that has a specific time and place.) Most astrologers will then enter this information into a computer, which will calculate a chart in seconds, and interpret the resulting chart.

If you don't know your exact birth time, you can usually locate it at the Bureau of Vital Statistics at the city hall of the town or the county seat in the state where you were born. If you still have no success in getting your time of birth, some astrologers can estimate an approximate birth time by using past events in your life to determine the chart. This technique is called rectification.

How to Find an Astrologer

Choose your astrologer with the same care as you would any trusted adviser, such as a doctor, lawyer, or banker. Unfortunately, anyone can claim to be an astrologer—to date, there is no licensing of astrologers or universally es-

tablished professional criteria. However, there are nation-
wide organizations of serious, committed astrologers that
can help you in your search.

Good places to start your investigation are organizations such as the American Federation of Astrologers
(AFA) or the National Council for Geocosmic Research
(NCGR), which offer a program of study and certification.
If you live near a major city, there is sure to be an active
NCGR chapter or astrology club in your area; many are
listed in astrology magazines available at your local news-
stand. In response to many requests for referrals, both
the AFA and the NCGR have directories of professional
astrologers listed on their Web sites; these directories include a glossary of terms and an explanation of specialties
within the astrological field. Contact the NCGR and AFA
headquarters for information. (See also Chapter 13.)

What Happens in a Reading

As a potentially lucrative freelance business, astrology has
always attracted self-styled experts who may not have the
knowledge or the counseling experience to give a helpful
reading. These astrologers can range from the well-meaning
amateur to the charlatan or street-corner Gypsy who has
for many years given astrology a bad name. Be very wary
of astrologers who claim to have occult powers or who
make pretentious claims of celebrated clients or miraculous
achievements. You can often tell from the initial phone
conversation if the astrologer is legitimate. He or she
should ask for your birthday time and place and then conduct the conversation in a professional manner. Any astrologer who gives a reading based only on your sun sign is
highly suspect.

When you arrive at the reading, the astrologer should be
prepared. The consultation should be conducted in a private, quiet place. The astrologer should be interested in
your problems of the moment. A good reading is inter-
active and involves feedback on your part, so if the reading
is not relating to your concerns, you should let the astrologer know. You should feel free to ask questions and get

clarifications of any technical terms. The more you actively participate, rather than expecting the astrologer to carry the reading or come forth with oracular predictions, the more meaningful your experience will be. An astrologer should help you validate your current experience and be frank about possible negative happenings, but also suggest a positive course of action.

In their approach to a reading, some astrologers may be more literal and others more intuitive. Those who have had counseling training may take a more psychological approach. Though some astrologers may seem to have an almost psychic ability, extrasensory perception or any other parapsychological talent is not essential. A very accurate picture can be drawn from the data in your horoscope chart.

An astrologer may do several charts for each client, including one for the time of birth and a progressed chart, showing the evolution from birth to the present time. According to your individual needs, there are many other possibilities, such as a chart for a different location if you are contemplating a change of place. Relationships between any two people, things, or events can be interpreted with a chart that compares one partner's horoscope with the other's. A composite chart, which uses the midpoint between planets in two individual charts to describe the relationship, is another commonly used device.

An astrologer will be particularly interested in transits, those times when cycling planets activate the planets or sensitive points in your birth chart. These indicate important events in your life.

Many astrologers offer readings recorded on tape or CD, which is another option to consider, especially if the astrologer you choose lives at a distance from you. In this case, you'll be mailed a recorded reading based on your birth chart. This type of reading is more personal than a computer printout and can give you valuable insights, though it is not equivalent to a live dialogue with the astrologer when you can discuss your specific interest and issues of the moment.

The Telephone Reading

Telephone readings come in two varieties: a dial-in taped reading, usually recorded in advance by an astrologer, or a live consultation with an "astrologer" on the other end of the line. The taped readings are general daily or weekly forecasts, applied to all members of your sign and charged by the minute. The quality depends on the astrologer. Be aware that these readings can run up quite a telephone bill, especially if you get into the habit of calling every day. Be sure that you are aware of the per-minute cost of each call beforehand.

Live telephone readings also vary with the expertise of the astrologer. Ideally, the astrologer at the other end of the line enters your birth data into a computer, which then quickly calculates your chart. This chart will be referred to during the consultation. The advantage of a live telephone reading is that your individual chart is used and you can ask about a specific problem. However, before you invest in any reading, be sure that your astrologer is qualified and that you fully understand in advance how much you will be charged. There should be no unpleasant financial surprises later. The best astrologer is one who is recommended to you by a friend or family member.

Computer-Generated Reports

Companies that offer computer programs (such as ACS, Matrix, and Astrolabe) also offer a variety of computer-generated horoscope readings. These can be quite comprehensive, offering a beautiful printout of the chart plus many pages of detailed information about each planet and aspect of the chart. You can then study it at your convenience. Of course, the interpretations will be general, since there is no personal input from you, and might not cover your immediate concerns. Since computer-generated horoscopes are much lower in cost than live consultations, you might consider them as either a supplement or a preparation for an eventual live reading You'll then be more familiar with your chart and able to plan specific questions in advance. They also make a terrific gift for astrology fans. In chapter 12, there are listed several companies that offer computerized readings prepared by reputable astrologers.

Whichever option you decide to pursue, may your reading be an empowering one!

☿ CHAPTER 10

The Key Role of Your Rising Sign

In order to interpret a chart accurately, an astrologer must know where in a person's life an activity will take place. That is determined by the rising sign, which is the degree of the zodiac ascending over the eastern horizon at the time you were born. (That's why it's often called the ascendant.) It marks the first point in the horoscope, the beginning of the first house. This house is one of twelve divisions of the horoscope, each of which represents a different area of life. After the rising sign, the other houses parade around the chart in sequence, with the following sign on the next house cusp.

Though you can learn much about a person by the signs and interactions of the sun, moon, and planets in the horoscope, without a valid rising sign, the collection of planets have no "homes." One would have no idea which area of life could be influenced by a particular planet. For example, you might know that a person has Mars in Aries, which will describe that person's dynamic fiery energy. But if you also know that the person has a Capricorn rising sign, this Mars will fall in the fourth house of home and family, so you know where that energy will operate.

Due to the earth's rotation, the rising sign changes every two hours, which means that babies born later or earlier on the same day in the same hospital will have most planets in the same signs, but may not have the same rising sign. Therefore, their planets may fall in different houses in the chart. For instance, if Mars is in Gemini and your rising sign is Taurus, Mars will most likely be active in the second or financial house of your chart. Someone born later in the same day when the rising sign is Virgo would have Mars positioned at the top of the chart, energizing the tenth house of career.

Most astrologers insist on knowing the exact time of a client's birth before they analyze a chart. The more accurate your birth time, the more accurately an astrologer can position the planets in your chart by determining the correct rising sign.

How Your Rising Sign Can Influence Your Sun Sign

Your rising sign has an important relationship with your sun sign. Some will complement the sun sign; others hide it under a totally different mask, as if playing an entirely different role, making it difficult to guess the person's sun sign from outer appearances. This may be the reason why you might not look or act like your sun sign's archetype. For example, a Leo with a conservative Capricorn ascendant would come across as much more serious than a Leo with a fiery Aries or Sagittarius ascendant.

Though the rising sign usually creates the first impression you make, there are exceptions. When the sun sign is reinforced by other planets in the same sign, this might overpower the impression of the rising sign. For instance, a Leo sun plus a Leo Venus and Leo Jupiter would counteract the more conservative image that would otherwise be conveyed by the person's Capricorn ascendant.

Those born early in the morning when the sun was on the horizon will be most likely to project the image of their sun sign. These people are often called a "double Aries" or a "double Virgo" because the same sun sign and ascendant reinforce each other.

Find Your Rising Sign

Look up your rising sign on the chart at the end of this chapter. Since rising signs change every two hours, it is important to know your birth time as close to the minute as possible. Even a few minutes' difference could change the rising sign and therefore the setup of your chart. If you are unsure about the exact time, but know within a few hours, check the following descriptions to see which is most like the personality you project.

Aries Rising: Alpha Energy

You are the most aggressive version of your sun sign, with boundless energy that can be used productively if it's channeled in the right direction. Watch a tendency to overreact emotionally and blow your top. You come across as openly competitive, a positive asset in business or sports. Be on guard against impatience, which could lead to head injuries. Your walk and bearing could have the telltale head-forward Aries posture. You may wear more bright colors, especially red, than others of your sign, or be a redhead. You may also have a tendency to drive your car faster.

Can you see the alpha Aries tendency in Barbra Streisand (a sun sign Taurus) and Bette Midler (a sun sign Sagittarius)?

Taurus Rising: Down-to-Earth

You're slow-moving, with a beautiful (or distinctive) speaking or singing voice. You probably surround yourself with comfort, good food, luxurious surroundings, and other sensual pleasures. You prefer welcoming others into your home to gadding about. You may have a talent for business,especially in trading, appraising, and real estate. A Taurus ascendant gives a well-padded physique that gains weight easily, like Liza Minnelli. This ascendant can also endow females with a curvaceous beauty.

Gemini Rising: A Way with Words

You're naturally sociable, with lighter, more ethereal mannerisms than others of your sign, especially if you're female. You love to communicate with people, and express your ideas easily, like former British prime minister Tony Blair. You may have a talent for writing or public speaking. You thrive on variety, a constantly changing scene, and a lively social life. However, you may relate to others at a deeper level than might be suspected. And you will be far more sympathetic and caring than you project. You will probably travel widely, changing partners and jobs several times (or juggle two at once). Physically, your nerves are quite sensitive. Occasionally, you would benefit from a calm, tranquil atmosphere away from your usual social scene.

Cancer Rising: Nurturing Instincts

You are naturally acquisitive, possessive, private, a moneymaker like Bill Gates or Michael Bloomberg. You easily pick up others' needs and feelings—a great gift in business, the arts, and personal relationships. But you must guard against overreacting or taking things too personally, especially during full-moon periods. Find creative outlets for your natural nurturing gifts, such as helping the less fortunate, particularly children. Your insights would be helpful in psychology. Your desire to feed and care for others would be useful in the restaurant, hotel, or child-care industries. You may be especially fond of wearing romantic old clothes, collecting antiques, and dining on exquisite food. Since your body may retain fluids, pay attention to your diet. To relax, escape to places near water.

Leo Rising: Diva Dazzle

You may come across as more poised than you really feel. However, you play it to the hilt, projecting a proud royal presence. A Leo ascendant gives you a natural flair for drama, like Marilyn Monroe, and you might be accused of stealing the spotlight. You'll also project a much more outgoing, optimistic, and sunny personality than others of your sign. You take care to please your public by always projecting star quality, probably tossing a luxuriant mane of hair, sporting a striking hairstyle, or dressing to impress. Females often dazzle with colorful clothing or spectacular jewelry. Since you may have a strong parental nature, you could well become a family matriarch or patriarch, like George H. W. Bush.

Virgo Rising: Hiqh Standards

Virgo rising endows you with a practical, analytical outer image. You seem neat, orderly, and more particular than others of your sign. Others in your life may feel they must live up to your high standards. Though at times you may be openly critical, this masks a well-meaning desire to have only the best for loved ones. Your sharp eye for details could be used in the financial world, or your literary skills could draw you to teaching or publishing. The healing arts, health care, and service-oriented professions attract many with a Virgo ascendant. You're likely to take good care of yourself, with great attention to health, diet, and exercise, like Madonna. You might even show some hypochondriac tendencies, like Woody Allen. Physically, you may have a very sensitive digestive system.

Libra Rising: The Charmer

Libra rising gives you a charming, social, and public persona, like John F. Kennedy and Bill Clinton. You tend to avoid confrontations in relationships, preferring to smooth the way or negotiate diplomatically rather than give in to an emotional reaction. Because you are interested in all aspects of a situation, you may be slow to reach decisions. Physically, you'll have good proportions and physical symmetry. You will move with natural grace and balance. You're likely to have pleasing, if not beautiful, facial features, with a winning smile, like Cary Grant. You'll show natural good taste and harmony in your clothes and home decor. Legal, diplomatic, or public relations professions could draw your interest.

Scorpio Rising: Air of Mystery

You project an intriguing air of mystery with this ascendant, as the Scorpio secretiveness and sense of underlying power combine with your sun sign. Like Jacqueline Kennedy Onassis, you convey that there's more to you than meets the eye. You seem like someone who is always in control and who can move comfortably in the world of power. Your physical look comes across as intense. Many of you have remarkable eyes, with a direct, penetrating gaze. But you'll never reveal your private agenda, and you tend to keep your true feelings under wraps (watch a tendency toward paranoia). You may have an interesting romantic history with secret love affairs, like Grace Kelly. Many of you heighten your air of mystery by wearing black. You're happiest near water; you should provide yourself with a seaside retreat.

Sagittarius Rising: The Explorer

You travel with this ascendant. You may also be a more outdoor, sportive type, with an athletic, casual, and outgoing air. Your moods are camouflaged with cheerful optimism or a philosophical attitude. Though you don't hesitate to speak your mind—like Ted Turner, who was called the Mouth of the South—you can also laugh at your troubles or crack a joke more easily than others of your sign. A Sagittarius ascendant can also draw you to the field of higher education or to spiritual life. You'll seem to have less attachment to things and people, and you may explore the globe. Your strong, fast legs are a physical bonus.

Capricorn Rising: Serious Business

This rising sign makes you come across as serious, goal-oriented, disciplined, and careful with cash. You are not one of the zodiac's big spenders, though you might splurge occasionally on items with good investment value. You're the conservative type in dress and environment, and you might come across as quite formal and businesslike, like Rupert Murdoch. You'll function well in a structured or corporate environment where you can climb to the top. (You are always aware of who's the boss.) In your personal life, you could be a loner or a single parent who is father and mother to your children.

Aquarius Rising: One of a Kind

You come across as less concerned about what others think and could even be a bit eccentric. Your appearance is sure to be unique and memorable. You're more at ease with groups of people than others in your sign, and you may be attracted to public life, like Jay Leno. Your appearance may be unique, either unconventional or unimportant to you. Those of you whose sun is in a water sign (Cancer, Scorpio, or Pisces) may exercise your nurturing qualities with a large group, an extended family, or a day-care or community center.

Pisces Rising: Romantic Roles

Your creative, nurturing talents are heightened and so is your ability to project emotional drama. And, like Antonio Banderas, your dreamy eyes and poetic air bring out the protective instinct in others. You could be attracted to the arts, especially theater, dance, film, and photography, or to psychology, spiritual practice, and charity work. You are happiest when you are using your creative ability to help others. Since you are vulnerable to mood swings, it is important for you to find interesting, creative work where you can express your talents and heighten your self-esteem. Accentuate the positive. Be wary of escapist tendencies, particularly involving alcohol or drugs to which you are supersensitive, like Whitney Houston.

RISING SIGNS—A.M. BIRTHS

	1 AM	2 AM	3 AM	4 AM	5 AM	6 AM	7 AM	8 AM	9 AM	10 AM	11 AM	12 NOON
Jan 1	Lib	Sc	Sc	Sc	Sag	Sag	Cap	Cap	Aq	Aq	Pis	Ar
Jan 9	Lib	Sc	Sc	Sag	Sag	Sag	Cap	Cap	Aq	Pis	Ar	Tau
Jan 17	Sc	Sc	Sc	Sag	Sag	Cap	Cap	Aq	Aq	Pis	Ar	Tau
Jan 25	Sc	Sc	Sag	Sag	Sag	Cap	Cap	Aq	Pis	Ar	Tau	Tau
Feb 2	Sc	Sc	Sag	Sag	Cap	Cap	Aq	Pis	Pis	Ar	Tau	Gem
Feb 10	Sc	Sag	Sag	Sag	Cap	Cap	Aq	Pis	Ar	Tau	Tau	Gem
Feb 18	Sc	Sag	Sag	Cap	Cap	Aq	Pis	Pis	Ar	Tau	Gem	Gem
Feb 26	Sag	Sag	Sag	Cap	Aq	Aq	Pis	Ar	Tau	Tau	Gem	Gem
Mar 6	Sag	Sag	Cap	Cap	Aq	Pis	Pis	Ar	Tau	Gem	Gem	Can
Mar 14	Sag	Cap	Cap	Aq	Aq	Pis	Ar	Tau	Tau	Gem	Gem	Can
Mar 22	Sag	Cap	Cap	Aq	Pis	Ar	Ar	Tau	Gem	Gem	Can	Can
Mar 30	Cap	Cap	Aq	Pis	Pis	Ar	Tau	Tau	Gem	Can	Can	Can
Apr 7	Cap	Cap	Aq	Pis	Ar	Ar	Tau	Gem	Gem	Can	Can	Leo
Apr 14	Cap	Aq	Aq	Pis	Ar	Tau	Tau	Gem	Gem	Can	Can	Leo
Apr 22	Cap	Aq	Pis	Ar	Ar	Tau	Gem	Gem	Gem	Can	Leo	Leo
Apr 30	Aq	Aq	Pis	Ar	Tau	Tau	Gem	Can	Can	Can	Leo	Leo
May 8	Aq	Pis	Ar	Ar	Tau	Gem	Gem	Can	Can	Leo	Leo	Leo
May 16	Aq	Pis	Ar	Tau	Gem	Gem	Can	Can	Can	Leo	Leo	Vir
May 24	Pis	Ar	Ar	Tau	Gem	Gem	Can	Can	Leo	Leo	Leo	Vir
June 1	Pis	Ar	Tau	Gem	Gem	Can	Can	Can	Leo	Leo	Vir	Vir
June 9	Ar	Ar	Tau	Gem	Gem	Can	Can	Leo	Leo	Leo	Vir	Vir
June 17	Ar	Tau	Gem	Gem	Can	Can	Can	Leo	Leo	Vir	Vir	Vir
June 25	Tau	Tau	Gem	Gem	Can	Can	Leo	Leo	Leo	Vir	Vir	Lib
July 3	Tau	Gem	Gem	Can	Can	Can	Leo	Leo	Vir	Vir	Vir	Lib
July 11	Tau	Gem	Gem	Can	Can	Leo	Leo	Leo	Vir	Vir	Lib	Lib
July 18	Gem	Gem	Can	Can	Can	Leo	Leo	Vir	Vir	Vir	Lib	Lib
July 26	Gem	Gem	Can	Can	Leo	Leo	Vir	Vir	Vir	Lib	Lib	Lib
Aug 3	Gem	Can	Can	Can	Leo	Leo	Vir	Vir	Vir	Lib	Lib	Sc
Aug 11	Gem	Can	Can	Leo	Leo	Leo	Vir	Vir	Lib	Lib	Lib	Sc
Aug 18	Can	Can	Can	Leo	Leo	Vir	Vir	Vir	Lib	Lib	Sc	Sc
Aug 27	Can	Can	Leo	Leo	Leo	Vir	Vir	Lib	Lib	Lib	Sc	Sc
Sept 4	Can	Can	Leo	Leo	Leo	Vir	Vir	Vir	Lib	Lib	Sc	Sc
Sept 12	Can	Leo	Leo	Leo	Vir	Vir	Lib	Lib	Lib	Sc	Sc	Sag
Sept 20	Leo	Leo	Leo	Vir	Vir	Vir	Lib	Lib	Sc	Sc	Sc	Sag
Sept 28	Leo	Leo	Leo	Vir	Vir	Lib	Lib	Lib	Sc	Sc	Sag	Sag
Oct 6	Leo	Leo	Vir	Vir	Vir	Lib	Lib	Sc	Sc	Sc	Sag	Sag
Oct 14	Leo	Vir	Vir	Vir	Lib	Lib	Lib	Sc	Sc	Sag	Sag	Cap
Oct 22	Leo	Vir	Vir	Lib	Lib	Lib	Sc	Sc	Sc	Sag	Sag	Cap
Oct 30	Vir	Vir	Vir	Lib	Lib	Sc	Sc	Sc	Sag	Sag	Cap	Cap
Nov 7	Vir	Vir	Lib	Lib	Lib	Sc	Sc	Sc	Sag	Sag	Cap	Cap
Nov 15	Vir	Vir	Lib	Lib	Sc	Sc	Sc	Sag	Sag	Cap	Cap	Aq
Nov 23	Vir	Lib	Lib	Lib	Sc	Sc	Sag	Sag	Sag	Cap	Cap	Aq
Dec 1	Vir	Lib	Lib	Sc	Sc	Sc	Sag	Sag	Cap	Cap	Aq	Aq
Dec 9	Lib	Lib	Lib	Sc	Sc	Sag	Sag	Sag	Cap	Cap	Aq	Pis
Dec 18	Lib	Lib	Sc	Sc	Sc	Sag	Sag	Cap	Cap	Aq	Aq	Pis
Dec 28	Lib	Lib	Sc	Sc	Sag	Sag	Sag	Cap	Aq	Aq	Pis	Ar

134

RISING SIGNS—P.M. BIRTHS

	1 PM	2 PM	3 PM	4 PM	5 PM	6 PM	7 PM	8 PM	9 PM	10 PM	11 PM	12 MIDNIGHT
Jan 1	Tau	Gem	Gem	Can	Can	Can	Leo	Leo	Vir	Vir	Vir	Lib
Jan 9	Tau	Gem	Gem	Can	Can	Leo	Leo	Leo	Vir	Vir	Vir	Lib
Jan 17	Gem	Gem	Gem	Can	Can	Leo	Leo	Leo	Vir	Vir	Lib	Lib
Jan 25	Gem	Gem	Can	Can	Leo	Leo	Leo	Vir	Vir	Lib	Lib	Lib
Feb 2	Gem	Can	Can	Can	Leo	Leo	Vir	Vir	Vir	Lib	Lib	Sc
Feb 10	Gem	Can	Can	Leo	Leo	Leo	Vir	Vir	Lib	Lib	Lib	Sc
Feb 18	Can	Can	Can	Leo	Leo	Vir	Vir	Vir	Lib	Lib	Sc	Sc
Feb 26	Can	Can	Leo	Leo	Leo	Vir	Vir	Lib	Lib	Lib	Sc	Sc
Mar 6	Can	Leo	Leo	Leo	Vir	Vir	Vir	Lib	Lib	Lib	Sc	Sc
Mar 14	Can	Leo	Leo	Vir	Vir	Vir	Lib	Lib	Lib	Sc	Sc	Sag
Mar 22	Leo	Leo	Leo	Vir	Vir	Lib	Lib	Lib	Sc	Sc	Sc	Sag
Mar 30	Leo	Leo	Vir	Vir	Vir	Lib	Lib	Sc	Sc	Sc	Sag	Sag
Apr 7	Leo	Leo	Vir	Vir	Vir	Lib	Lib	Lib	Sc	Sc	Sag	Sag
Apr 14	Leo	Vir	Vir	Vir	Lib	Lib	Sc	Sc	Sc	Sag	Sag	Cap
Apr 22	Leo	Vir	Vir	Lib	Lib	Lib	Sc	Sc	Sc	Sag	Sag	Cap
Apr 30	Vir	Vir	Vir	Lib	Lib	Sc	Sc	Sc	Sag	Sag	Cap	Cap
May 8	Vir	Vir	Lib	Lib	Lib	Sc	Sc	Sag	Sag	Sag	Cap	Cap
May 16	Vir	Vir	Lib	Lib	Sc	Sc	Sc	Sag	Sag	Cap	Cap	Aq
May 24	Vir	Lib	Lib	Lib	Sc	Sc	Sag	Sag	Sag	Cap	Cap	Aq
June 1	Vir	Lib	Lib	Sc	Sc	Sc	Sag	Sag	Cap	Cap	Aq	Aq
June 9	Lib	Lib	Lib	Sc	Sc	Sag	Sag	Sag	Cap	Cap	Aq	Pis
June 17	Lib	Lib	Sc	Sc	Sc	Sag	Sag	Cap	Cap	Aq	Aq	Pis
June 25	Lib	Lib	Sc	Sc	Sag	Sag	Sag	Cap	Cap	Aq	Pis	Ar
July 3	Lib	Sc	Sc	Sc	Sag	Sag	Cap	Cap	Aq	Aq	Pis	Ar
July 11	Lib	Sc	Sc	Sag	Sag	Sag	Cap	Cap	Aq	Pis	Ar	Tau
July 18	Sc	Sc	Sc	Sag	Sag	Cap	Cap	Aq	Aq	Pis	Ar	Tau
July 26	Sc	Sc	Sag	Sag	Sag	Cap	Cap	Aq	Pis	Ar	Tau	Tau
Aug 3	Sc	Sc	Sag	Sag	Cap	Cap	Aq	Aq	Pis	Ar	Tau	Gem
Aug 11	Sc	Sag	Sag	Sag	Cap	Cap	Aq	Pis	Ar	Tau	Tau	Gem
Aug 18	Sc	Sag	Sag	Sag	Cap	Cap	Aq	Pis	Pis	Ar	Tau	Gem
Aug 27	Sag	Sag	Sag	Cap	Cap	Aq	Pis	Ar	Tau	Tau	Gem	Gem
Sept 4	Sag	Sag	Cap	Cap	Aq	Pis	Pis	Ar	Tau	Gem	Gem	Can
Sept 12	Sag	Sag	Cap	Aq	Aq	Pis	Ar	Tau	Tau	Gem	Gem	Can
Sept 20	Sag	Cap	Cap	Aq	Pis	Pis	Ar	Tau	Gem	Gem	Can	Can
Sept 28	Cap	Cap	Aq	Aq	Pis	Ar	Tau	Tau	Gem	Gem	Can	Can
Oct 6	Cap	Cap	Aq	Pis	Ar	Ar	Tau	Gem	Gem	Can	Can	Leo
Oct 14	Cap	Aq	Aq	Pis	Ar	Tau	Tau	Gem	Gem	Can	Can	Leo
Oct 22	Cap	Aq	Pis	Ar	Ar	Tau	Gem	Gem	Can	Can	Leo	Leo
Oct 30	Aq	Aq	Pis	Ar	Tau	Tau	Gem	Can	Can	Can	Leo	Leo
Nov 7	Aq	Aq	Pis	Ar	Tau	Tau	Gem	Can	Can	Can	Leo	Leo
Nov 15	Aq	Pis	Ar	Tau	Gem	Gem	Can	Can	Can	Leo	Leo	Vir
Nov 23	Pis	Ar	Ar	Tau	Gem	Gem	Can	Can	Leo	Leo	Leo	Vir
Dec 1	Pis	Ar	Tau	Gem	Gem	Can	Can	Can	Leo	Leo	Vir	Vir
Dec 9	Ar	Tau	Tau	Gem	Gem	Can	Can	Leo	Leo	Leo	Vir	Vir
Dec 18	Ar	Tau	Gem	Gem	Can	Can	Can	Leo	Leo	Vir	Vir	Vir
Dec 28	Tau	Tau	Gem	Gem	Can	Can	Leo	Leo	Vir	Vir	Vir	Lib

♎ CHAPTER 11

The Secret Language of Astrology: What the Glyphs Reveal About the Signs and Planets

At last, you've got your very first horoscope chart. Perhaps you've downloaded it from one of the many Internet sites that offer free charts, or you're trying out new astrology software. But then you find that the chart is covered with strange symbols that look like an exotic language, indecipherable by a neophyte astrology fan. Reading a horoscope chart can be a daunting task if you don't understand the meaning of the mysterious symbols, called glyphs, used as a kind of universal shorthand on the horoscope chart. There's no avoiding it—if you want to read an astrology chart, you've got to learn the glyphs!

The glyphs are more than just pictographs. They contain a kind of code, with built-in clues that will tell you not only which sign or planet each represents, but what the symbol means in a deeper, more esoteric sense. Actually the physical act of writing the symbol is a mystical experience in itself, a way to invoke the deeper meaning of the sign or planet through age-old visual elements that have been with us since time began.

Since there are only twelve signs and ten planets (not counting a few asteroids and other space objects some astrologers use), it's a lot easier than learning to read a foreign language. Here's a code cracker for the glyphs, beginning with the glyphs for the planets. To those who already know their glyphs, don't just skim over the chapter.

These familiar graphics have hidden meanings you will discover!

The Glyphs for the Planets

The glyphs for the planets are easy to learn. They're simple combinations of the most basic visual elements: the circle, the semicircle or arc, and the cross. However, each component of a glyph has a special meaning in relation to the other parts of the symbol.

The circle, which has no beginning or end, is one of the oldest symbols of spirit or spiritual forces. Early diagrams of the heavens—spiritual territory—are shown in circular form. The never-ending line of the circle is the perfect symbol for eternity. The semicircle or arc is an incomplete circle, symbolizing the receptive, finite soul, which contains spiritual potential in the curving line.

The vertical line of the cross symbolizes movement from heaven to earth. The horizontal line describes temporal movement, here and now, in time and space. Combined in a cross, the vertical and horizontal planes symbolize manifestation in the material world.

The Sun Glyph ☉

The sun is always shown by this powerful solar symbol, a circle with a point in the center. The center point is you, your spiritual center, and the symbol represents your infinite personality incarnating (the point) into the finite cycles of birth and death.

The sun has been represented by a circle or disk since ancient Egyptian times when the solar disk represented the sun god, Ra. Some archaeologists believe the great stone circles found in England were centers of sun worship. This particular version of the symbol was brought into common use in the sixteenth century after German occultist and scholar Cornelius Agrippa (1486–1535) wrote a book called *Die Occulta Philosophia,* which became accepted as the authority in the field. Agrippa collected many of the medieval astrological and magical symbols in this book, which have been used by astrologers since then.

The Moon Glyph ☽

The moon glyph is the most recognizable symbol on a chart, a left-facing arc stylized into the crescent moon. As part of a circle, the arc symbolizes the potential fulfillment of the entire circle, the life force that is still incomplete. Therefore, it is the ideal representation of the reactive, receptive, emotional nature of the moon.

The Mercury Glyph ☿

Mercury contains all three elemental symbols: the crescent, the circle, and the cross in vertical order. This is the "Venus with a hat" glyph (compare with the symbol of Venus). With another stretch of the imagination, can't you see the winged cap of Mercury the messenger? Think of the upturned crescent as antennae that tune in and transmit messages from the sun, reminding you that Mercury is the way you communicate, the way your mind works. The upturned arc is receiving energy into the spirit or solar circle, which will later be translated into action on the material plane, symbolized by the cross. All the elements are equally sized because Mercury is neutral; it doesn't play favorites! This planet symbolizes objective, detached, unemotional thinking.

The Venus Glyph ♀

Here the relationship is between two components: the circle of spirit and the cross of matter. Spirit is elevated over matter, pulling it upward. Venus asks, "What is beautiful? What do you like best? What do you love to have done to you?" Consequently, Venus determines both your ideal of beauty and what feels good sensually. It governs your own allure and power to attract, as well as what attracts and pleases you.

The Mars Glyph ♂

In this glyph, the cross of matter is stylized into an arrowhead pointed up and outward, propelled by the circle of spirit. With a little imagination, you can visualize it as the shield and spear of Mars, the ancient god of war. You can deduce that Mars embodies your spiritual energy projected into the outer world. It's your assertiveness, your initiative, your aggressive drive, what you like to do to others, your temper. If you know someone's Mars, you know whether they'll blow up when angry or do a slow burn. Your task is to use your outgoing Mars energy wisely and well.

The Jupiter Glyph ♃

Jupiter is the basic cross of matter, with a large stylized crescent perched on the left side of the horizontal, temporal plane. You might think of the crescent as an open hand, because one meaning of Jupiter is "luck," what's handed to you. You don't have to work for what you get from Jupiter; it comes to you, if you're open to it.

The Jupiter glyph might also remind you of a jumbo jet plane, with a huge tail fin, about to take off. This is the planet of travel, mental and spiritual, of expanding your horizons via new ideas, new spiritual dimensions, and new places. Jupiter embodies the optimism and enthusiasm of the traveler about to embark on an exciting adventure.

The Saturn Glyph ♄

Flip Jupiter over, and you've got Saturn. This might not be immediately apparent because Saturn is usually stylized into an "h" form like the one shown here. The principle it expresses is the opposite of Jupiter's expansive tendencies. Saturn pulls you back to earth: the receptive arc is pushed down underneath the cross of matter. Before there are any rewards or expansion, the duties and obligations of the material world must be considered. Saturn says, "Stop, wait, finish your chores before you take off!"

Saturn's glyph also resembles the sickle of old "Father Time." Saturn was first known as Chronos, the Greek god of time, for time brings all matter to an end. When it was the most distant planet (before the discovery of Uranus), Saturn was believed to be the place where time stopped. After the soul departed from earth, it journeyed back to the outer reaches of the universe and finally stopped at Saturn, or at "the end of time."

The Uranus Glyph ♅

The glyph for Uranus is often stylized to form a capital *H* after Sir William Herschel, who discovered the planet. But the more esoteric version curves the two pillars of the H into crescent antennae, or "ears," like satellite disks receiving signals from space. These are perched on the horizontal material line of the cross of matter and pushed from below by the circle of the spirit. To many sci-fi fans, Uranus looks like an orbiting satellite.

Uranus channels the highest energy of all, the white electrical light of the universal spiritual force that holds the cosmos together. This pure electrical energy is gathered from all over the universe. Because Uranus energy doesn't follow any ordinary celestial drumbeat, it can't be controlled or predicted (which is also true of those who are strongly influenced by this eccentric planet). In the symbol, this energy is manifested through the balance of polarities (the two opposite arms of the glyph) like the two polarized wires of a lightbulb.

The Neptune Glyph ♆

Neptune's glyph is usually stylized to look like a trident, the weapon of the Roman god Neptune. However, on a more esoteric level, it shows the large upturned crescent of the soul pierced through by the cross of matter. Neptune nails down, or materializes, soul energy, bringing impulses from the soul level into manifestation. That is why Neptune is associated with imagination or "imagining in," making an image of the soul. Neptune works through feelings, sensitivity, and the mystical capacity to bring the divine into the earthly realm.

The Pluto Glyph ♇

Pluto is written two ways. One is a composite of the letters *PL,* the first two letters of the word Pluto and coincidentally the initials of Percival Lowell, one of the planet's discoverers. The other, more esoteric symbol is a small circle above a large open crescent that surmounts the cross of matter. This depicts Pluto's power to regenerate. Imagine a new little spirit emerging from the sheltering cup of the soul. Pluto rules the forces of life and death. After this planet has passed a sensitive point in your chart, you are transformed, reborn in some way.

Sci-fi fans might visualize this glyph as a small satellite (the circle) being launched. It was shortly after Pluto's discovery that we learned how to harness the nuclear forces that made space exploration possible. Pluto rules the transformative power of atomic energy, which totally changed our lives and from which there is no turning back.

The Glyphs for the Signs

On an astrology chart, the glyph for the sign will appear after that of the planet. For example, when you see the moon glyph followed first by a number and then by another glyph representing the sign, this means that the moon was passing over a certain degree of that astrological sign at the time of the chart. On the dividing lines between the houses on your chart, you'll find the symbol for the sign that rules the house.

Because sun sign symbols do not contain the same basic geometric components of the planetary glyphs, we must look elsewhere for clues to their meanings. Many have been passed down from ancient Egyptian and Chaldean civilizations with few modifications. Others have been adapted over the centuries.

In deciphering many of the glyphs, you'll often find that the symbols reveal a dual nature of the sign, which is not always apparent in the usual sun sign descriptions. For instance, the Gemini glyph is similar to the Roman numeral for two, and reveals this sign's longing to discover a twin soul. The Cancer glyph may be interpreted as resembling either the nurturing breasts or the self-protective claws of a crab, both symbols associated with the contrasting qualities of this sign. Libra's glyph embodies the duality of the spirit balanced with material reality. The Sagittarius glyph shows that the aspirant must also carry along the earthly animal nature in his quest. The Capricorn sea goat is another symbol with dual emphasis. The goat climbs high, yet is always pulled back by the deep waters of the unconscious. Aquarius embodies the double waves of mental detachment, balanced by the desire for connection with others, in a friendly way. Finally, the two fishes of Pisces, which are forever tied together, show the duality of the soul and the spirit that must be reconciled.

The Aries Glyph ♈

Since the symbol for Aries is the Ram, this glyph is obviously associated with a ram's horns, which characterize one aspect of the Aries personality—an aggressive, me-first, leaping-headfirst attitude. But the symbol can be interpreted in other ways as well. Some astrologers liken it to a fountain of energy, which Aries people also embody. The first sign of the zodiac bursts on the scene eagerly, ready to go. Another analogy is to the eyebrows and nose of the human head, which Aries rules, and the thinking power that is initiated by the brain.

One theory of this symbol links it to the Egyptian god Amun, represented by a ram in ancient times. As Amun-Ra, this god was believed to embody the creator of the universe, the leader of all the other gods. This relates easily to the position of Aries as the leader (or first sign) of the zodiac, which begins at the spring equinox, a time of the year when nature is renewed.

The Taurus Glyph ♉

This is another easy glyph to draw and identify. It takes little imagination to decipher the bull's head with long curving horns. Like its symbol the Bull, the archetypal Taurus is slow to anger but ferocious when provoked, as well as stubborn, steady, and sensual. Another association is the larynx (and thyroid) of the throat area (ruled by Taurus) and the eustachian tubes running up to the ears, which coincides with the relationship of Taurus to the voice, song, and music. Many famous singers, musicians, and composers have prominent Taurus influences.

Many ancient religions involved a bull as the central figure in fertility rites or initiations, usually symbolizing the victory of man over his animal nature. Another possible origin is in the sacred bull of Egypt, who embodied the incarnate form of Osiris, god of death and resurrection. In early Christian imagery, the Taurus Bull represented St. Luke.

The Gemini Glyph ♊

The standard glyph immediately calls to mind the Roman numeral for two (II) and the Twins symbol, as it is called, for Gemini. In almost all drawings and images used for this sign, the relationship between two persons is emphasized. Usually one twin will be touching the other, which signifies communication, human contact, the desire to share.

The top line of the Gemini glyph indicates mental communication, while the bottom line indicates shared physical space.

The most famous Gemini legend is that of the twin sons, Castor and Pollux, one of whom had a mortal father while the other was the son of Zeus, king of the gods. When it came time for the mortal twin to die, his grief-stricken brother pleaded with Zeus, who agreed to let them spend half the year on earth in mortal form and half in immortal life, with the gods on Mount Olympus. This reflects a basic duality of humankind, which possesses an immortal soul yet is also subject to the limits of mortality.

The Cancer Glyph ♋

Two convenient images relate to the Cancer glyph. It is easiest to decode the curving claws of the Cancer symbol, the Crab. Like the crab's, Cancer's element is water. This sensitive sign also has a hard protective shell to protect its tender interior. The crab must be wily to escape predators, scampering sideways and hiding under rocks. The crab also responds to the cycles of the moon, as do all shellfish. The other image is that of two female breasts, which Cancer rules, showing that this is a sign that nurtures and protects others as well as itself.

In ancient Egypt, Cancer was also represented by the scarab beetle, a symbol of regeneration and eternal life.

The Leo Glyph ♌

Notice that the Leo glyph seems to be an extension of Cancer's glyph, with a significant difference. In the Cancer glyph, the lines curve inward protectively. The Leo glyph expresses energy outwardly. And there is no duality in the symbol, the Lion, or in Leo, the sign.

Lions have belonged to the sign of Leo since earliest times. It is not difficult to imagine the king of beasts with his sweeping mane and curling tail from this glyph. The upward sweep of the glyph easily describes the positive energy of Leo: the flourishing tail, the flamboyant qualities. Anther analogy, perhaps a stretch of the imagination, is that of a heart leaping up with joy and enthusiasm, also very typical of Leo, which also rules the heart. In early Christian imagery, the Leo Lion represented St. Mark.

The Virgo Glyph ♍

You can read much into this mysterious glyph. For instance, it could represent the initials of "Mary Virgin," or a young woman holding a staff of wheat, or stylized female genitalia, all common interpretations. The M shape might also remind you that Virgo is ruled by Mercury. The cross beneath the symbol reveals the grounded, practical nature of this earth sign.

The earliest zodiacs link Virgo with the Egyptian goddess Isis, who gave birth to the god Horus after her husband Osiris had been killed, in the archetype of a miraculous conception. There are many ancient statues of Isis nursing her baby son, which are reminiscent of medieval Virgin and Child motifs. This sign has also been associated with the image of the Holy Grail, when the Virgo symbol was substituted with a chalice.

The Libra Glyph ♎

It is not difficult to read the standard image for Libra, the Scales, into this glyph. There is another meaning, however, that is equally relevant: the setting sun as it descends over the horizon. Libra's natural position on the zodiac wheel is the descendant, or sunset position (as the Aries natural position is the ascendant, or rising sign). Both images relate to Libra's personality. Libra is always weighing pros and cons for a balanced decision. In the sunset image, the sun (male) hovers over the horizontal earth (female) before setting. Libra is the space between these lines, harmonizing yin and yang, spiritual and material, male and female, ideal and real worlds. The glyph has also been linked to the kidneys, which are associated with Libra.

The Scorpio Glyph ♏

With its barbed tail, this glyph is easy to identify as the Scorpion for the sign of Scorpio. It also represents the male sexual parts, over which the sign rules. From the arrowhead, you can draw the conclusion that Mars was once its ruler. Some earlier Egyptian glyphs for Scorpio represent it as an erect serpent, so the Serpent is an alternate symbol.

Another symbol for Scorpio, which is not identifiable in this glyph, is the Eagle. Scorpios can go to extremes, either in soaring like the eagle or self-destructing like the scorpion. In early Christian imagery, which often used zodiacal symbols, the Scorpio Eagle was chosen to symbolize the intense apostle St. John the Evangelist.

The Sagittarius Glyph ♐

This is one of the easiest to spot and draw: an upward pointing arrow lifting up a cross. The arrow is pointing skyward, while the cross represents the four elements of the material world, which the arrow must convey. Elevating materiality into spirituality is an important Sagittarius quality, which explains why this sign is associated with higher learning, religion, philosophy, travel—the aspiring professions. Sagittarius can also send barbed arrows of frankness in the pursuit of truth, so the Archer symbol for Sagittarius is apt. (Sagittarius is also the sign of the supersalesman.)

Sagittarius is symbolically represented by the centaur, a mythological creature who is half man, half horse, aiming his arrow toward the skies. Though Sagittarius is motivated by spiritual aspiration, it also must balance the powerful appetites of the animal nature. The centaur Chiron, a figure in Greek mythology, became a wise teacher who, after many adventures and world travels, was killed by a poisoned arrow.

The Capricorn Glyph ♑

One of the most difficult symbols to draw, this glyph may take some practice. It is a representation of the sea goat: a mythical animal that is a goat with a curving fish's tail. The goat part of Capricorn wants to leave the waters of the emotions and climb to the elevated areas of life. But the fish tail is the unconscious, the deep chaotic psychic level that draws the goat back. Capricorn is often trying to escape the deep, feeling part of life by submerging himself in work, steadily ascending to the top. To some people, the glyph represents a seated figure with a bent knee, a reminder that Capricorn governs the knee area of the body.

An interesting aspect of this glyph is the contrast of the sharp pointed horns—which represent the penetrating, shrewd, conscious side of Capricorn—with the swishing tail—which represents its serpentine, unconscious, emotional force. One Capricorn legend, which dates from Roman times, tells of the earthy fertility god, Pan, who tried to save himself from uncontrollable sexual desires by jumping into the Nile. His upper body then turned into a goat, while the lower part became a fish. Later, Jupiter gave him a safe haven as a constellation in the skies.

The Aquarius Glyph ♒

This ancient water symbol can be traced back to an Egyptian hieroglyph representing streams of life force. Symbolized by the Water Bearer, Aquarius is distributor of the waters of life—the magic liquid of regeneration. The two waves can also be linked to the positive and negative charges of the electrical energy that Aquarius rules, a sort of universal wavelength. Aquarius is tuned in intuitively to higher forces via this electrical force. The duality of the glyph could also refer to the dual nature of Aquarius, a sign that runs hot and cold and that is friendly but also detached in the mental world of air signs.

In Greek legends, Aquarius is represented by Ganymede, who was carried to heaven by an eagle in order to become the cupbearer of Zeus and to supervise the annual flooding of the Nile. The sign later became associated with aviation and notions of flight. Like the other fixed signs (Taurus, Scorpio, and Leo), Aquarius is associated with an apostle, in this case St. Matthew.

The Pisces Glyph)(

Here is an abstraction of the familiar image of Pisces, two Fishes swimming in opposite directions yet bound together by a cord. The Fishes represent the spirit—which yearns for the freedom of heaven—and the soul—which remains attached to the desires of the temporal world. During life on earth, the spirit and the soul are bound together. When they complement each other, instead of pulling in opposite directions, they facilitate the Pisces creativity. The ancient version of this glyph, taken from the Egyptians, had no connecting line, which was added in the fourteenth century.

In another interpretation, it is said that the left fish indicates the direction of involution or the beginning of a cycle, while the right fish signifies the direction of evolution, the way to completion of a cycle. It's an appropriate grand finale for Pisces, the last sign of the zodiac.

CHAPTER 12

The Astrology Software Shop

Once upon a time, casting a horoscope required consulting thick books of tables, poring over atlases, and punching numbers on a calculator. Now a few clicks of the computer mouse can provide an accurate and beautifully drawn chart that's equal to any a professional astrologer could cast. A few more clicks will give you a professional interpretation by a world-famous astrologer. How easy is that?

Astrology technology has advanced to the point where even a computerphobe can put a chart on the screen in seconds. It does help to have some basic knowledge of the signs, houses, planets, and especially, the glyphs for the planets and the signs. Then you can practice reading charts and relating the planets to the lives of friends, relatives, and daily events, the ideal way to get more involved with astrology.

When it comes to choosing your astrology software, there are endless options. How do you make the right choice? First, define your goals. Do you want to do charts of friends and family, study celebrity charts, or check the aspects every day on your Palm Pilot? Do you want to invest in a more comprehensive program that adapts to your changing needs as you learn astrology?

The good news is that there's a program for every level of interest at all price points—starting with free. For the dabbler, there is the affordable Winstar Express, Know, and Time Passages. For the serious student, there's Astrolog (free), Solar Fire, Kepler, Winstar Plus—software that does every technique on the planet and gives you beautiful chart printouts. You can do a chart of someone you've just met on your PDA with Astracadabra. If you're a Mac user, you'll be satisfied with the wonderful IO and Time Passages software.

However, since all the programs use the astrology symbols, or glyphs, for planets and signs, rather than written words, you should learn the glyphs before you purchase your software. Chapter 11 will help you do just that. Here are some software options for you to explore.

Easy for Beginners

Time Passages

Designed for either a Macintosh or Windows computer, Time Passages is straightforward and easy to use. It allows you to generate charts and interpretation reports for yourself or friends and loved ones at the touch of a button. If you haven't yet learned the astrology symbols, this might be the program for you. Just roll your mouse over any symbols of the planets, signs, or house cusps, and you'll be shown a description in plain English below the chart. Then click on the planet, sign, or house cusp and up pops a detailed interpretation. Couldn't be easier. A new Basic Edition, under fifty dollars at this writing, is bargain priced and ideal for beginners.

Time Passages
(866) 772-7876 (866-77-ASTRO)
Web site: www.astrograph.com

The "Know Thru Astrology" Series

This new series is designed especially for the nonastrologer. There are four programs in the series: KNOW Your Self, KNOW your future, KNOW Your Lover, and KNOW Your Child, each priced at an affordable $49.95 (at this writing). Though it is billed as beginner software, the KNOW series offers many sophisticated options, such as a calendar to let you navigate future or past influences, detailed chart interpretations, built-in pop-ups to show you what everything means. You'll need a PC running current

Windows versions starting with Windows 98 SE, with 64 Mb RAM, and a hard drive with 170–300 Mb free space.

Matrix Software
126 South Michigan Avenue
Big Rapids, MI 49307
(800) 416-3924
Web site: www.astrologysoftware.com

Growth Opportunities

Astrolabe

Astrolabe is one of the top astrology software resources. Check out the latest version of their powerful Solar Fire software for Windows. It's a breeze to use and will grow with your increasing knowledge of astrology to the most sophisticated levels. This company also markets a variety of programs for all levels of expertise and a wide selection of computer-generated astrology readings. This is a good resource for innovative software as well as applications for older computers.

The Astrolabe Web site is a great place to start your astrology tour of the Internet. Visitors to the site are greeted with a chart of the time you log on. And you can get your chart calculated, also free, with a mini interpretation e-mailed to you.

Astrolabe
Box 1750-R
Brewster, MA 02631
Phone: (800) 843-6682
Web site: www.alabe.com

Matrix Software

You'll find a wide variety of software at student and advanced levels in all price ranges, demo disks, lots of interesting readings. Check out Winstar Express, a powerful but reasonably priced program suitable for all skill levels. The

Matrix Web site offers lots of fun activities for Web surfers, such as free readings from the I Ching, the runes, and the tarot. There are many free desktop backgrounds with astrology themes. Here's where to connect with news groups and online discussions. Their online almanac helps you schedule the best day to sign on the dotted line, ask for a raise, or plant your tomatoes.

Matrix Software
126 South Michigan Avenue
Big Rapids, MI 49307
Phone: (800) 416-3924
Web site: www.astrologysoftware.com

Astro Communications Services (ACS)

Books, software, individual charts, and telephone readings are offered by this California company. Their freebies include astrology greeting cards and new moon reports. Find technical astrology materials here such as *The American Ephemeris* and PC atlases. ACS will calculate and send charts to you, a valuable service if you do not have a computer.

ACS Publications
P.O. Box 1646
El Cajon, CA 92022-1646
Phone: (800) 514-5070
Fax: (619) 631-0180
Web site: www.astrocom.com

Air Software

Here you'll find powerful, creative astrology software, plus current stock market analysis. Financial astrology programs for stock market traders are a specialty. There are some interesting freebees at this site. Check out the maps of eclipse paths for any year and a free astrology clock program.

Air Software
115 Caya Avenue

West Hartford, CT 06110
Phone: (800) 659-1247
Web site: www.alphee.com

Kepler: State of the Art

Here's a program that's got everything. Gorgeous graphic images, audio-visual effects, and myriad sophisticated chart options are built into this fascinating software. It's even got an astrological encyclopedia, plus diagrams and images to help you understand advanced concepts. This program is pricey, but if you're serious about learning astrology, it's an investment that will grow with you! Check out its features at www.astrologysoftwareshop.com.

Timecycles Research: For Mac Users

Here's where Mac users can find astrology software that's as sophisticated as it gets. If you have a Mac, you'll love their beautiful graphic IO Series programs.

Time Cycles Research
P.O. Box 797
Waterford, CT 06385
(800) 827-2240
Web site: www.timecycles.com

Shareware and Freeware: The Price Is Right!

Halloran Software: A Super Shareware Program

Check out Halloran Software's Web site, which offers several levels of Windows astrology software. Beginners should consider their Astrology for Windows shareware program, which is available in unregistered demo form as a free download and in registered form for a very reasonable price.

Halloran Software
P.O. Box 75713
Los Angeles, CA 90075
(800) 732-4628
Web site: www.halloran.com

ASTROLOG

If you're computer-savvy, you can't go wrong with Walter Pullen's amazingly complete Astrology program, which is offered absolutely free at the site. The Web address is www.astrolog.org/astrolog.htm.

Astrolog is an ultrasophisticated program with all the features of much more expensive programs. It comes in versions for all formats: DOS, Windows, Mac, and UNIX. It has some cool features, such as a revolving globe and a constellation map. If you are looking for astrology software with all the bells and whistles that doesn't cost big bucks, this program has it all!

Software for the Pocket PDA and Palm Pilot

Would you like to have astrology at your fingertips everywhere you go? No need to drag along your laptop. You can now check the chart of the moment or of someone you've just met on your Pocket PDA or Palm Pilot. As with most other astrology software, you'll need to know the astrological symbols in order to read the charts.

For the pocket PC that has the Microsoft Windows Mobile operating system, there is the versatile Astracadabra, which can interchange charts with the popular Solar Fire software. It can be ordered at www.leelehman.com or www.astrology softwareshop.com.

For the Palm OSS and compatible handheld devices, there is Astropocket from www.astropocket.com. This is a shareware program that allows you to use all the features free. However, you cannot store more than one chart at a time until you pay a mere 28-dollar registration fee for the complete version.

Buying a Computer with Astrology in Mind?

The good news is that astrology software is becoming more sophisticated and fun to use. It won't be long before there are programs for the iPhone and BlackBerry. However, if you've inherited an old computer, don't despair. You don't need the fastest processor and all the newest bells and whistles to run perfectly adequate astrology software. It is still possible to find programs for elder systems, including many new exciting programs.

To take full advantage of all the options, however, it is best to have a system that runs versions of Windows starting with Windows 98 SE. If you're buying a new computer, invest in one with as much RAM as possible, at least 1 GB. A CD drive will be necessary to load programs or an Internet connection, if you prefer to download programs online.

Mac fans who want to run Windows astrology software should invest in the new dual boot computers that will operate both the Mac and the Windows XP and Vista platforms.

♎ CHAPTER 13

Join the Astrology Community

If you've become hooked on astrology, you'll want to share your enthusiasm with others, and perhaps join an astrology club in your city or go to a conference where you can meet the world's top astrologers. Connecting with astrology fans and learning more about this fascinating subject has never been easier. In fact the many options available with just a click of your computer are mind-boggling.

You need only type the word *astrology* into any Internet search engine and watch hundreds of listing of astrology-related sites pop up. There are local meetings and international conferences where you can meet and study with other astrologers, and books and tapes to help you learn at home. You could even combine your vacation with an astrological workshop in an exotic locale, such as Bali or Mexico.

To help you sort out the variety of options available, here are our top picks of the Internet and the astrological community at large.

National Council for Geocosmic Research (NCGR)

Whether you'd like to know more about such specialties as financial astrology or techniques for timing events, or if you'd prefer the psychological or mythological approach, you'll meet the top astrologers at conferences sponsored by the National Council for Geocosmic Research. NCGR is dedicated to providing quality education, bringing astrologers and astrology fans together at conferences, and promoting fellowship. Their course structure provides a systematized study of the many facets of astrology. The organization sponsors educational workshops, taped lectures, conferences, and a directory of professional astrologers.

For an annual membership fee, you get their excellent publications and newsletters, plus the opportunity to network with other astrology buffs at local chapter events. At this writing there are chapters in twenty-six states and four countries.

To join NCGR and for the latest information on upcoming events and chapters in your city, consult their Web site: www.geocosmic.org.

American Federation of Astrologers (AFA)

Established in 1938, this is one of the oldest astrological organizations in the United States. AFA offers conferences, conventions, and a correspondence course. If you are looking for a reading, their interesting Web site will refer you to an accredited AFA astrologer.

6535 South Rural Road
Tempe, AZ 85283
Phone: (888) 301-7630 or (480) 838-1751
Fax: (480) 838-8293
Web site: www.astrologers.com

Association for Astrological Networking (AFAN)

Did you know that astrologers are still being harassed for practicing astrology? AFAN provides support and legal information, and works toward improving the public image of astrology. AFAN's network of local astrologers links with the international astrological community. Here are the people who will go to bat for astrology when it is attacked in the media. Everyone who cares about astrology should join!

8306 Wilshire Boulevard
PMB 537

Beverly Hills, CA 90211
Phone: (800) 578-2326
E-mail: info@afan.org
Web site: www.afan.org

International Society for Astrology Research (ISAR)

An international organization of professional astrologers dedicated to encouraging the highest standards of quality in the field of astrology with an emphasis on research. Among ISAR's benefits are quarterly journals, a weekly e-mail newsletter, and a free membership directory.

P.O. Box 38613
Los Angeles, CA 90038
Fax: (800) 933-0301
Web site: www.isarastrology.com

Astrology Magazines

In addition to articles by top astrologers, most have listings of astrology conferences, events, and local happenings.

Horoscope Guide
Kappa Publishing Group
6198 Butler Pike
Suite 200
Blue Bell, PA 19422-2600
Web site: www.kappapublishing.com/astrology

Dell Horoscope
Their Web site features a listing of local astrological meetings.

Customer Service
6 Prowitt Street
Norwalk, CT 06855
Phone: (800) 220-7443
Web site: www.dellhoroscope.com

The Mountain Astrologer
A favorite magazine of astrology fans, *The Mountain Astrologer* also has an interesting Web site featuring the latest news from an astrological point of view, plus feature articles from the magazine.

P.O. Box 970
Cedar Ridge, CA 95924
Web site: www.mountainastrologer.com

Astrology College

Kepler College of Astrological Arts and Sciences

A degree-granting college, which is also a center of astrology, has long been the dream of the astrological community and is a giant step forward in providing credibility to the profession. Therefore, the opening of Kepler College in 2000 was a historical event for astrology. It is the only college in the United States authorized to issue BA and MA degrees in astrological studies. Here is where to study with the best scholars, teachers, and communicators in the field. A long-distance study program is available for those interested.

4630 200th Street SW
Suite P
Lynnwood, WA 98036
Phone: (425) 673-4292
Fax: (425) 673-4983
Web site: www.kepler.edu

Our Favorite Websites

Of the thousands of astrological Web sites that come and go on the Internet, these have stood the test of time and are likely to still be operating when this book is published.

Astrodienst (www.astro.com)

Don't miss this fabulous international site, which has long been one of the best astrology resources on the Internet. It's a great place to view your own astrology chart. The world atlas on this site will give you the accurate longitude and latitude of your birthplace for setting up your horoscope. Then you can print out your free chart in a range of easy-to-read formats. Other attractions: a list of famous people born on your birth date, a feature that helps you choose the best vacation spot, and articles by world-famous astrologers.

AstroDatabank (www.astrodatabank.com)

When the news is breaking, you can bet this site will be the first to get accurate birthdays of the headliners. The late astrologer Lois Rodden was a stickler for factual information and her meticulous research is being continued, much to the benefit of the astrological community. The Web site specializes in charts of current newsmakers, political figures, and international celebrities. You can also participate in discussions and analysis of the charts and see what some of the world's best astrologers have to say about them. Their AstroDatabank program, which you can purchase at the site, provides thousands of birthdays sorted into categories. It's an excellent research tool.

StarIQ (www.stariq.com)

Find out how top astrologers view the latest headlines at the must-see StarIQ site. Many of the best minds in astrology comment on the latest news, stock market ups and downs, and political contenders. You can sign up to receive e-mail forecasts at the most important times keyed to your individual chart. (This is one of the best of the online forecasts.)

Astro-Noetics (www.astro-noetics.com)

For those who are ready to explore astrology's interface with politics, popular culture, and current events, here is a sophisticated site with in-depth articles and personality profiles. Lots of depth and content here for the astrology-savvy surfer.

Astrology Books (www.astroamerica.com)

The Astrology Center of America sells a wide selection of books on all aspects of astrology, from the basics to the most advanced, at this online bookstore. Also available are many hard-to-find and used books.

Astrology Scholars' Sites:

See what Robert Hand, one of astrology's great teachers, has to offer on his site at www.robhand.com. A leading expert on the history of astrology, he's on the cutting edge of the latest research.

The Project Hindsight group of astrologers is devoted to restoring the astrology of the Hellenistic period, the primary source for all later Western astrology. There are fascinating articles for astrology fans on this site at www.projecthindsight.com.

Financial Astrology Sites

Financial astrology is a hot specialty, with many tipsters, players, and theorists. There are online columns, newsletters, specialized financial astrology software, and mutual funds run by astrology seers. One of the more respected financial astrologers is Ray Merriman, whose market comments on www.mmacycles.com are a must for those following the bulls and bears.

How to Zoom Around the Sky

If you haven't already discovered the wonders of Google Earth (www.earth.google.com), then you've been missing close-up aerial views of anyplace on the planet from your old hometown to the beaches of Hawaii. Even more fascinating for astrology buffs is the newest feature called Google Sky, a marvel of computer technology that lets you view the sky overhead from anyplace you choose. Want to see the stars over Paris at the moment? A few clicks of your mouse will take you there. Then you can follow the tracks of the sun, moon, and planets or check astronomical information and beautiful Hubble images. Go to the Google Web site to download this free program. Then get ready to take a cosmic tour around the earth and sky.

Listen to the Sounds of Your Sign

Astrology Weekly (www.astrologyweekly.com) is a Web site from Romania, with lots to offer astro surfers. Here you can check all the planetary placements for the week, get free charts, join an international discussion group, and check out charts for countries and world leaders. Of special interest is the chart generator, an easy-to-use feature that will create a natal chart. Just click on *new chart* and enter the year, month, day, time, longitude, and latitude of your birth place. Select the Placidus or Koch house system and click on *show it*. Your chart should come right up on the screen. You can then copy the link to your astrology chart, store it, and later share your chart with friends. If you don't have astrology software, this is a good way to view charts instantly. This site also has some fun ways to pass the time, such as listening to music especially chosen for your sun sign.

Stellar Gifts

If you've ever wondered what to give your astrology buddies, here's the place to find foolproof gifts. How about a mug, mouse pad, or plaque decorated with someone's chart? Would a special person like a pendant personalized with their planets? Check out www.milestonegifts.co.uk for some great ideas for putting those astrology charts to decorative use.

⚖ CHAPTER 14

Going Green in 2009: How to Help Save the Planet

Living a sustainable life is a high priority in 2009, as ecological concerns continue to dominate the news, and the media devote more resources to educating consumers in how to help the planet. Astrologically, this corresponds to the joining of Jupiter (expansion) and Neptune (creativity) in socially conscious Aquarius, which will influence us to move beyond differences as we share responsibility for the future of the environment.

Whether you're choosing to commit to the green movement, or wondering how you can do something about this critical situation by making lifestyle changes or helping local efforts, astrology can help you decide where to make a difference. Here are some suggestions for each sign.

Aries: The Eco-Warrior

What could be a more appropriate cause for fire sign Aries than taking up the cause of global warming? Pioneering Aries such as Al Gore and Jane Goodall were among the first to give the world wake-up calls, bringing environmental concerns to the public's attention with great urgency. Now is the time to research the new options in fuel-efficient cars and prod local dealers to offer them to consumers. Be the first in your town to drive a hot new electric sports car. Some of you may opt for low-tech solutions by taking bikes to work or crusading for better public transportation. Energy-saving appliances and lightbulbs should be on your

162

shopping list. For a complete list of green energy utilities across the country, visit the U.S. Department of Energy's Web site, and use a clickable map to find options in your state.

Taurus: The Nurturer of Nature

Nature-loving Taurus is ideally suited to protecting our parks and wildlife, as well as promoting the humane treatment of animals. Supporting your local farmers by buying organic produce at farmers' markets gives you the pleasure of superior food and drink while you nurture local agriculture. You can participate in creating gardens and beautifying the landscape in your area, or perhaps raise your own organic produce using compost and nontoxic fertilizers. Taurus is a natural fund-raiser for worthy causes, so how about starting a thrift shop or conducting yard sales for your favorite charity?

Gemini: Media Savvy

There are many ways to use your Gemini communications skills in the service of sustainable living. Beat the drum loudly to bring local environmental problems to the attention of the public. For inspiration, there's Gemini beauty Angelina Jolie, who has crusaded for the underprivileged around the world. Write a newsletter for your favorite cause, contribute to the op-ed page, call in to talk shows. Use your way with words to sway the public. Since you love to socialize, why not throw a fund-raising party for a local charity?

Cancer: Home Remedies

Green living begins at home, so start by using eco-friendly cleaning products and buy furniture made of nontoxic materials. If you are building a home, use recycled or green materials as much as possible. Volunteer to help food-based charities like Meals on Wheels, which provide food to the elderly, ill, or homeless. Offer help and visits to the elderly in your neighborhood so they can remain in their own homes. A Cancer-ruled area is the hospitality industry—one that should pay special attention to its impact on the environment. Campaign for regulation of cruise boats and hotels, which have been major polluters. Vacation in eco-friendly resorts, like Maho Bay in the Caribbean and Central America, for a beautiful healthy alternative.

Leo: Change a Child's Life

Child-oriented charities are naturally attuned to Leo's generous nature. Bill Clinton and Arnold Schwarzenegger, both Leos, have collaborated to focus on fighting one of our nation's leading health threats—childhood obesity—and to inspire young people to form lifelong healthy habits. You could join their efforts or sponsor a child in a third-world country. You can make a big difference in a child's life by supporting organizations that provide health care, education, and social services. Publicize your favorite causes by organizing charity events, fashion shows, and fund-raisers with entertainment.

Virgo: The Activist Educator

Virgo has a special affinity for health and education issues, promoting literacy, raising educational standards, and supporting schools and libraries. Why not volunteer at a local school or hospital, to promote change from within these institutions, such as implementing sustainable energy policies, reducing carbon emissions, and teaching children to recycle? Support local programs that bring health care to the underinsured or international projects such as Doctors Without Borders or the Smile Train, which transforms the lives of children with cleft palates.

Libra: Fair Trading

Libra's concern for fairness extends to purchasing products made by sustainable methods—ones that also ensure that the farmer or worker is paid a fair wage. Your love of the arts and beautiful objects could inspire you to promote native handicrafts in undeveloped countries and rescue ancient artistic techniques from becoming obsolete. We also need to pay attention to where and how our fashionable clothing is made and to encourage the use of nontoxic materials and finishes, as well as humane working conditions in third-world factories.

Scorpio: Creating Transformation

As a water sign and the sign of transformation, Scorpio has a special affinity for recycling, waste treatment, and water purification. Support the fight against pollution of the oceans and destruction of coral reefs. Join your local eco-warriors to clean up toxic waste in bays and rivers. With your detective skills, find the local toxic waste dumps and help to bring polluters to justice. Preventing the spread of AIDs and supporting organizations that fight deadly diseases are other special interests of your sign. Locally, you could organize recycling events for used electronics and clothing.

Sagittarius: The Outdoor Activist

You're a natural motivator, so why not turn this talent to a green cause? Get involved in local activities that encourage young people to live a healthy lifestyle. Coach a local team, take a group of children to a ball game, or help maintain athletic facilities in your area. Animal rescue and welfare is another Sagittarius concern. Volunteering at a local animal shelter, adopting a rescued pet, or fostering local wildlife would be rewarding. Like Bette Midler, you could form an organization to clean up local parks and green areas, creating hiking trails and picnic areas for outdoor family fun.

Capricorn: Green Business Opportunities

Capricorn is destined to play a transformative role in preserving the environment, especially the endangered forests and jungles around the world, as well as helping to build a green economy. As an investor, insist on corporate responsibility to the environment and employees. Lend your organizing skills to create a healthier workplace, with better air quality and lighting, use of recycled or natural materials, and energy control. Consider business opportunities in underdeveloped countries, such as providing microloans that help local people become self-sufficient. Be a mentor to a young entrepreneur who is starting a green business.

Aquarius: The Eco-Politician

Aquarius is a visionary thinker, ideally suited to influence politicians in your local area and campaign for causes that promote green enterprises, social welfare, and environmental action. Organize green festivals for a lively exchange of ideas, commerce, and movement building in your local area, with educational workshops, speakers, and networking opportunities for people looking to work together for change at the local, national, and global level. Address air pollution, toxins in the environment, and mold in buildings. Start a Web site devoted to improving your local environment.

Pisces: The art of Change

Green concerns can combine with the creative arts to make the world a more beautiful and livable place. Pisces is endowed with imaginative gifts that can find new ways to use recycled materials or design products and homes that complement the environment. Support your local arts, especially organizations that bring music, theater, and dance expression to underprivileged children. We live on a water-dependent planet on which access to clean water is denied to many people. You can help the severe water-pollution problem by joining an organization devoted to protecting our oceans, fisheries, and water supply.

⚖ CHAPTER 15

Rock Stars: Empower Yourself with Zodiac Gems

Could a ruby bring you luck on Tuesday, or how about wearing a rainbow moonstone during the full moon? When we think of wearing astrological jewelry, we usually think of birthstones, but did you know that there are planetary fingers and that your hands transmit solar and lunar energy? Jewelry can be much more meaningful, as well as fun to wear, when it is believed to resonate with our personalities or empower us in some way. With the current earthy Capricorn influence in the cosmos, we'll be examing all the value-added ways to wear our favorite gems, so let's take a look in our jewelry box for some astrological benefits.

Since ancient times, gems have been used to empower as well as decorate the wearer. In India, Egypt, and Babylonia, rare and beautiful gemstones were thought to have magical properties. People are said to have consulted astrologers for advice on wearing the appropriate gem for each occasion. Ancient Egyptians carried scarabs and tiny figures of their gods for protection and luck. These were carved in semiprecious stones like lapis lazuli, carnelian, and turquoise. In India, one of the most powerful talismans was the Nava Ratna, an amulet designed with precious stones representing the known planets at the time. This very talisman is still being worn today.

Another astrological connection was the wearing of gems associated with a planet on that planet's special day. Mars-ruled rubies would be worn on the Mars day, Tuesday, or moonstones on Monday. You could cover the bases by wearing *all* the gems in your horoscope at once. There are astrologer jewelers who will make up a special pendant or necklace that displays all your horoscope's special stones in a beautiful design.

To complicate matters when deciding when and how to wear your gems, there is the belief that each finger of the hand corresponds to a certain planet. So wearing that beautiful turquoise ring on your pointer or lucky Jupiter finger would be especially auspicious, according to ancient wisdom. The middle finger invokes the wisdom and discipline of Saturn, so try a garnet there. The Venus or third finger is the finger of love, which is why we wear wedding bands there. A stone associated with Libra or Taurus, the Venus-ruled signs, worn on that digit might help you attract a soul mate. The little finger enhances Mercury, the planet of communication, so pull out your Gemini or Virgo jewels and decorate your pinky when you have something special to say.

Then there's the question of which hand to wear your rings on. The right hand is associated with masculine outgoing energy and the left with female, receptive energy. Perhaps that is one reason why empowered young women are celebrating their career success by purchasing diamonds to wear proudly on the right hand.

In the Judeo-Christian tradition, the astrological association with gemstones dates from the sacred twelve-gem breastplate of Aaron, recorded in Exodus. Each gem symbolized one of the twelve tribes of Israel. Later these gems became connected with the twelve signs of the zodiac. However, it was not until the eighteenth century that people began to wear their special birthstones. For more information on the history and mystery of gemstones, including their astrological use, read *The Curious Lore of Precious Stones* by George Frederick Kunz, written in 1913 and still consulted today.

There is quite a bit of confusion over which stone is best for each sign, because we are often given birthstones according to the month of our birthday rather than our zodiac sign. You may be wondering if the amethyst is more suitable than the aquamarine for a February-born Pisces, or you might prefer the gems associated with your moon sign because they resonate with your emotional nature, or your Venus sign, which appeals to your sense of fashion and good taste. Lovers of precious gems could choose one that reflects the element of their sun sign. Earth signs (Taurus, Virgo, Capricorn) resonate to the bright green emerald, fire signs (Aries, Leo, Sagittarius) belong to the flaming ruby, water signs (Cancer, Scorpio, Pisces) might prefer the deep blue sapphire, and air signs (Gemini, Libra, Aquarius) may gravitate to the clear, brilliant diamond.

If you don't care for your birthstone, you could choose a talisman by color—one that is associated with your sun, moon, or Venus sign. An Aries with a moon in Cancer might prefer a pale lunar jewel like the pearl or moonstone. A Pisces with Venus in Aries might love to wear bright red stones like ruby or spinel.

Here are some suggestions for choosing stones associated with a given zodiac sign. Bear in mind that there are no hard and fast rules; you might find yourself attracted to a certain gem without fully understanding why. That might well be the gem you are supposed to wear, regardless of your sign. The bottom line is, wear whatever you love!

Aries

Though most sources give the birthstone for April as the diamond, Aries may feel more affinity for Mars-ruled stones with red hues, such as ruby, spinels, fire opals, garnets, coral, and carnelian. Go for the flash and fire!

Taurus

Emeralds are most associated with Taurus. However, Taurus might gravitate toward some of the earthy agates and green stones such as tourmaline, jade, serpentine (which is believed to draw good fortune), green quartz, or green turquoise. Try a newly available gem, like pale sage prasiolite, subtle glowing prenite, and the lustrous green seraphinite, flickering with white "angel wings," newly available from Russia.

Gemini

Pearls and agates are associated with Gemini, but you might prefer fascinating gems like alexandrite or tanzanite, which change color according to the angle of light. Or watermelon tourmaline, which has dual colorations. Interesting rutilated quartzes with fine hairlike inclusions are associated with communication and might be perfect for your sign.

Cancer

July has often been linked with the ruby; however, that fiery stone might be better suited to Leos born in late July than to early-July birthdays. Cancer seems to resonate more with the elegant blue sapphire, moonstone, and chalcedony, and the deep blue flashes of labradorite and rainbow moonstone.

Leo

The yellow-green peridot and all golden stones belong to sun-ruled Leos. You may also love the ruby, yellow diamonds, amber, and citrine. Go for the golden tones!

Virgo

Sapphires, which come in many colors, carnelian, onyx, and pink jasper are associated with Virgo. You may also respond to the earthy agates and the green tones of emerald and jade.

Libra

Opal was once considered exclusive to Libra and comes in many variations. In fact, the opal was deemed unlucky for any other sign. This beautiful stone comes in many color variations, from the deeper Australian opals to the pale Russian opals. You might try the blue or pink Peruvian opal or the mysterious earthy boulder opal. Libra is also associated with the color pink, as in rose quartz, rhodonite, pink sapphires, pink diamonds, and kunzite. Apple green chrysoprase is another beautiful choice.

Scorpio

This mysterious sign was given the topaz, which comes in blue or golden variations. You might also respond to the deep tones of smoky quartz, tigereye, black onyx, rainbow obsidian, black diamonds, or black South Sea pearls. You could be attracted to the deep multihued Pietersite, a mysterious stone that flickers with color.

Sagittarius

Visionary Sagittarius respond to turquoise, the mystical stone of Native Americans and Tibetans. No medicine man's outfit was complete without a turquoise. It was treasured by the Persians, who believed that turquoise could protect from evil and bring good fortune. Also consider lapis lazuli, blue topaz, and ruby.

Capricorn

The burgundy red garnet is the usual stone for Capricorn, but garnets are now available in many other colors, such as the green Tsavorite garnet and the orange hessionite garnet. Also consider the beautifully marked green malachite. Onyx in all its color variations is especially compatible with Capricorn.

Aquarius

Aquarius is associated with the purple amethyst, a type of quartz that was once thought to prevent drunkenness. This sign might respond to some of the newer stones on the market, such as labradorite, a gray stone that flashes electric blue, or to some of the other purple stones such as sugilite, tanzanite, or purple jade. Choose an unusual stone to highlight your originality, like Russian charoite, a gorgeous purple gem now being used in rings and pendants. Dumortuite, with a subtle glow, is also terrific for lovers of the color purple. The colorful quartzes, which are able to conduct electricity, could be your gem. Diamonds of all kinds also resonate with Aquarius, according to the glamorous Aquarius Gabor sisters and Carol Channing, who sang "Diamonds Are a Girl's Best Friend."

Pisces

The blue-green aquamarine and the earthy bloodstone are usually associated with Pisces. During the sixteenth century, bloodstone was believed to cure hemorrhages caused by the plague. Jasper is also a Pisces stone, now available in many beautiful colors such as picture jasper and poppy jasper, which look like miniature paintings. Pisces also responds to jewels from the sea: pearls, coral, and ocean blue sapphires. Elizabeth Taylor, a great Pisces jewel collector, owns the famous Peregrina pearl as well as many deep blue sapphires.

♎ CHAPTER 16

The Year to Get Organized

With Saturn in Virgo and Pluto in Capricorn, both signs of organization, neatness, and efficiency, there couldn't be a better time to put your life in order. If you haven't conquered clutter, if your to-do list has become overwhelming, and if your schedule is overloaded, why not use your sign's natural inclinations to help you get things done and restore peace of mind?

Here are some strategies tailored to each sun sign to help you get life under control again.

Aries

Do you have the common Aries trait of wanting to get things done immediately? If a task can't be crossed off the list right away, Aries tends to put it out of sight and out of mind. With your amazing energy, you can forge through a project until it is completed, so make it fast and fun. Think of your task as a military campaign you're sure to win. Divide long, complicated cleanup or fix-up projects into several (or many) small portions, each of which can be completed within a time limit—no lingering or postponing. Then attack each segment until it is done. Afterward, reward yourself! Give yourself a bright, colorful, fashionable place to work, so you'll feel like captain of the ship.

Taurus

Taurus often needs to take some weight off your shoulders, in terms of too many possessions. But your sign finds it so difficult to part with your treasures. After all, you're one of the zodiac's great collectors, and you value each and every item you've accumulated. However, there are sure to be piles of things you haven't seen or enjoyed for a while. You may also have piled up in the attic or garage boxes of possessions—ones you haven't opened in years. Sharing your possessions with others can bring you great joy, so consider donating some to charity. Out-of-style clothing could be dropped off at your local thrift shop. You could sell some of the clothes you've been saving from former sizes in case you lose weight. Taking a temporary booth in a local flea market could be a fun weekend activity and bring you in extra money, as well as freeing up space in your home.

Gemini

Busy, multitasking Gemini often forgets to organize their living space. Gemini accumulates paper and books, communications devices, party-giving clutter. You may have half-completed projects piled up in hopes that one day you'll get around to finishing them. A good storage system could help you keep track of your projects, even complete those you've abandoned or put aside. Invest in shelving, bookcases, and file cabinets to keep the clutter at bay and help you find things instead of wasting time searching for them. A cabinet or armoire dedicated to entertainment supplies would be ready for an instant party. To find important papers fast, Gemini financial counselor Suze Orman keeps them in a separate waterproof case, ready for any emergency. There's never any doubt where to find wills, insurance policies, or birth certificates.

Cancer

Cancer is another sign that has difficulty letting go of possessions, especially if there is some sentimental value attached. Be sure that you are not just hoarding items for a feeling of security. You'll be more serene emotionally and creative in a tranquil, ordered environment. Turn clutter into art by editing your favorites to the most special ones and then arranging them in a beautiful display. Choose your organization items for their decorative value as well as functionality. Antique armoires and chests of drawers or vintage trunks could provide storage while adding character to your room. Consider photographing your possessions for inventory purposes, and invest in one of the many inventory computer applications to keep track of what you own and its value.

Leo

Leo loves a well-ordered lair where you can proudly entertain friends, but your busy lifestyle can leave clutter in its wake and closets overflowing with fashionable clothing. Do what Leo does best—delegate the organization to someone else. Consult a store with a resident expert who could design a custom closet with colorful hangers to store your wardrobe in style and expand your space. Well-stocked makeup tables and cosmetics cabinets are also Leo musts. You're sure to have a good entertainment system. Invest in special shelving for your DVD and CD collection so your favorite video games, shows, and music are available when the right mood strikes.

Virgo

Desiring to be of service to others, Virgo can take on too many tasks. Learn to say no, and choose your commitments wisely. That way you'll avoid becoming overwhelmed and be better able to give quality time to the most important projects and people in your life. Virgo is supposed to be one of the most organized signs; however, too many to-do lists could be counterproductive. The task for many Virgos is to simplify your systems. Take advantage of the many computer programs that can help organize your finances and catalog possessions.

Libra

For beauty-loving Libra, storage solutions should be aesthetically pleasing as well as efficient. Color-coordinated hangers and storage boxes make keeping neat closets a pleasure. Since you often have large wardrobes, invest in a beautiful armoire or mirrored closet. Disguise a rolling garment rack with decorator fabric. Office armoires that can hide your work area are a good solution for Libras who work at home.

Scorpio

Whether choosing minimal or maximal decorating effects, all-or-nothing Scorpio likes to keep his environment under control. You often have a secret closet or storage room to stash possessions. A well-organized filing system and furniture that does double duty—such as an ottoman that hides a storage bin—are perfect for Scorpio. This sign, not usually a clutterer, has no problem tossing away what is no longer useful. Make digital photographs of your rooms or valuable objects for insurance purposes and also for your will. Hide your file cabinets and storage containers behind a beautiful screen or curtain on a ceiling track.

Sagittarius

On-the-go Sagittarius usually accumulates luggage, sporting goods, and travel items. You need these items to be easily accessible when you decide to take off on a spur-of-the-moment adventure or pile the family into the car for a road trip. A good backseat organizer is a must for conquering car clutter. A garage storage system could maximize space by getting sports equipment off the floor and onto elevated shelving. Frequent flyers might keep a small bag of necessary items in travel sizes and travel documents packed in a suitcase.

Capricorn

The most naturally organized of all the signs, Capricorn is quick to latch on to new techniques and shortcuts to utilize every bit of living and working space. And you can be coolly objective when it comes to throwing out what is no longer useful. A good recycling station is a must for Capricorn, who dislikes waste of any kind. Schedule regular times to go through your wardrobe and possessions to weed out what you don't need and donate items to charity. Put your affairs in order with an up-to-date filing system, which can be disguised in an attractive cabinet. Be careful not to overorganize—keep your system simple and easy to remember.

Aquarius

So many things, so little time could be the complaint of Aquarius, whose active lifestyle is often order-challenged. This sign dislikes anything that infringes on freedom and independence, such as too much structure and a rigid schedule. However, you and everyone around you will function much better in an ordered environment. When things get out of control, call in the troups, enlist help, or hire a professional organizer. Make cleanup time fun by throwing a party. Invite friends to help you with specific tasks, and then reward them with a terrific meal. Or barter one of your many talents for some cleanup skills. Take advantage of computer technology to pay bills and keep records up-to-date.

Pisces

Most Pisces avoid tackling clutter until it threatens to take over their space. However, taking charge of your environment is not only empowering, but it can free you up for the creative activities you love. Who needs to waste time looking for important papers? Get an attractive container and assemble your passport, credit cards, lease, and tax information where you can easily find them. Scan key documents into your computer so you'll have duplicates handy. Keep things where you'd naturally look for them (keys in a pretty container by the door, clothes you wear most often in the front of the closet). Pay special attention to organization of footwear, perhaps dedicating a closet or small cabinet to your shoe and boot collection. Sentimental Pisces also needs to learn to let go of gifts that will never be used. Don't feel guilty. Remember the good feelings, and then embrace your freed-up space!

♎ CHAPTER 17

Your Libra Close-Up: Introduction to Man, Woman, and Child

Did you know that your Libra sun sign can enhance all areas of your life? That includes what and whom you like, your family relationships, your strengths on the job, and even the way you furnish your home. The more you understand your Libra personality and potential, the more you'll benefit from using your special solar power to help you make good decisions. You might use it for something as basic as choosing what to wear or the color to paint a room. Or you could tap into your Libra power to deal with more important issues, such as getting along with your boss or spicing up your love life.

Let the following chapters empower you with the confidence that you're moving in harmony with your natural Libra inclinations. As the ancient oracle advised, "Know thyself." To know yourself, as astrology helps you do, is to gain confidence and strength.

So let's get up close and personal with Libra. You may wonder how astrologers determine what a Libra personality is like. To begin with, we use a type of recipe, blending several ingredients. The first is your element, air, which indicates that you are mentally oriented. You're a doer, like the other active, cardinal signs (Aries and Capricorn). Libra has a positive masculine yang polarity, which adds yet another dimension. Then there's the influence of your planetary ruler, Venus, the planet of attraction, love, beauty, relationships. Add your sign's place in the zodiac: seventh, in the house of partnership, the place of relating. Finally, stir in your symbol: the Scales of Justice, balance.

This recipe influences everything we say about Libra. For example, you could deduce that a mentally oriented, Venus-ruled sign would thrive in an atmosphere of beauty and harmony and tend to avoid confrontations. You would be likely to enjoy relationships, seek marriage and partnerships, rather than going it alone. Your favorite colors might be flattering pastels. You may have a charming, diplomatic manner with others. But remember that your total astrological personality contains a blend of many other planets, colored by the signs they occupy, plus factors such as the sign coming over the horizon at the exact moment of your birth. The more planets in Libra in your horoscope, the more likely you'll follow your sun sign's prototype. On the other hand, if planets are grouped together in a different sign, they will color your horoscope accordingly, sometimes making a low-key, mellow sun sign come on much stronger. So if the Libra traits mentioned here don't describe you, there could be other factors flavoring your cosmic stew. (Look up your planets in the tables in this book to find out what they might be!)

The Libra Man: Well-Balanced

The typical Libra man appears charming, cool, and well mannered at all times. But your delicately balanced nervous system is highly sensitive to disharmony of any sort. Whether the cause is blatantly rude behavior or simply a picture tilted out of alignment or a color mismatched, you will pick it up instantly. And when you are seriously offended, you will vanish into thin air, often before airing your grievances.

The Libra man appreciates (some might say, worships) style. Beauty of ideas and beauty of form are priorities, and you'd scrimp on mundane necessities to buy a beautiful object. You always look put together, even in the most casual clothes. It took a Libra designer like Ralph Lauren to make coveted items of Indian blankets, blue jeans, and polo shirts. But Libra is not easy to please. You are never truly satisfied until you've achieved perfect balance.

Striving for harmony at all costs, Libra often retreats into an ivory tower to avoid the messy world of emotions. Your real potential lies in blending the two, bringing the ideals of your ivory tower down to the human earthly level.

You need companionship to exchange ideas and to help you define what you really think. Libras have been known to infuriate others by not offering an opinion until they have weighed the pros and cons and considered every possible angle. Too many alternatives could leave you suspended in a quandary. But, like Vaclav Havel or Jesse Jackson, you'll find a strong authoritative voice quickly when there is obvious injustice.

The Libra man functions better when performing the role of mediator or moderator than in a situation where you must make quick decisions. You are scrupulously fair when it comes to presenting each side of a question, but you can debate endlessly before taking action. Usually you excel on a team where others make the final decisions based on your evaluation.

In a Relationship

Partnerships are necessary for you; they make you feel complete. You'll truly enjoy sharing all the happenings in your life and participating in lots of outside activities with your partner on your arm.

Unlike many other men, the Libra man is a perennial romantic who truly enjoys the company of women, especially if they are lovely to look at and stylishly dressed. You'll be quick to notice details of dress and grooming. If your mate changes her hairstyle or the length of her skirts, you'll have a strong opinion pro or con. You love to see your mate looking beautiful, and may even pick out or design her clothes. You have probably searched long and hard to find the perfect partner, one who shares your aesthetic values, appeals to your tastes, and balances out your other qualities. Though it is difficult for you to express dissatisfaction openly (or tell your mate how you dislike the color of the new sofa), you'll do your best to encourage calm discussion of problems. However, you'll avoid emotional scenes and any confrontation that throws you off balance.

The Libra Woman: A Fair Lady

The balance of masculine and feminine energies is nowhere more evident than in the Libra woman. Strikingly feminine, elegant, and stylish in appearance, you are oft idealized as a love goddess or a fashion plate. But anyone who thinks of the Libra woman as a frivolous beauty should carefully study Eleanor Roosevelt or England's former Prime Minister Margaret Thatcher. Libra women, under their elegant facade, are active and strong-willed, with considerable drive. The Libra woman is busy, energetic, and involved in life around her. She often prefers the company of men, which allows her to balance her femininity with the other, masculine, side of her nature.

One of the most charming and social beings, Libras such as Brigitte Bardot, Catherine Deneuve, Rita Hayworth, and Gwyneth Paltrow have often been the love goddess of their time. But your feminine appearance usually hides a cool intellect, which is at ease working with abstract concepts. The logical side to your personality often surprises those who perceive you as a woman preoccupied with superficialities, who happily spends the day at the mall or the beauty salon.

Because you are constantly searching for balance in your life, you usually get involved in a variety of activities, rarely focusing on one aspect of anything to the exclusion of other interests. You can be most successful in a career that blends your artistic and social skills and that involves either a partner or teamwork. You are a talented peacemaker or strategist, guiding others to the right course. Your good looks, style, and diplomacy are great social assets, making you popular with a wide scope of friends.

In a Relationship

Born under the sign that rules relationships of all sorts, the Libra woman is naturally geared for marriage. You thrive on a committed partnership because you need someone who complements your energies and shares your experiences. To the right mate, you offer support and well-considered advice, as well as a beautiful home where you can entertain friends and business associates.

Since your major challenge is indecisiveness, you must find a partner who is not only compatible but who also helps balance the male and female elements within yourself. To do this, Libra women cultivate male attention (sometimes at the expense of female friends). Most Libra women will have a group of male courtiers who offer flattering, romantic attention and with whom she can flirt. But your real goal in a male-female relationship is an equal partnership where each supplies what the other lacks.

Once married, the other side of your personality that demands an active public life comes to the fore. Again, you'll find yourself balancing the scales between two polarities—in this case, your home and the outside world. Though your home will be in exquisite taste, you're not the stay-at-home type and will get involved in social life as soon as possible. If the marriage is lacking, Libra will compensate with a full schedule of outside activities, artistic pursuits, political or charitable activities, or an engrossing career.

Libra in the Family

The Libra Parent

Ideally, your family group will contain attractive, intelligent, well-mannered children raised in a calm, rational, harmonious environment. The reality, however, may set your scales swinging, especially if your children are strong-willed, competitive, and aggressive. Discipline by discussion is more your style than confrontation or a show of power. You'll coolly withdraw from emotional scenes or become irritable if your scales are tipped.

Keep the peace by focusing on shared creative or social activities, and be the impartial judge when conflicts arise. You are more equipped than most parents to teach children how the art of compromise and adjustment can bring even the most diverse personalities together. You'll be especially supportive of the child who shows artistic or intellectual ability, providing them with an excellent education suited to their special needs.

The Libra Stepparent

Creating a new family equilibrium is Libra's talent as a stepparent. You are a sharing person who enjoys an extended family. You'll create a calm, accepting, and hospitable atmosphere ready to receive the children as soon as they feel ready. You'll never push them, or be overly demonstrative or insincere. Because you give much consideration to what is right in the situation, you will treat stepchildren fairly and encourage their biological parent to spend time with them, even planning special activities for everyone to enjoy. But if the children are very demanding, you may not take on caregiving responsibilities that are not rightfully yours. Your charm, fairness, and diplomacy will help everyone make this new family situation work.

The Libra Grandparent

Libras are charming, elegant grandparents who remain stylish and beautifully groomed. Libra grandmas are up-to-date on all the latest fashion trends and understand just how to wear them, regardless of age. You'll enjoy sharing your beautiful home and many interests with well-behaved grandchildren. When asked, you'll offer excellent advice and guidance to parents—unless you're asked for spur-of-the-moment babysitting (you may be going out on date yourself!). You'll still have an active social life and will be very occupied with your own interests. Libras treat grandchildren as young companions rather than charges. You'll never take over for Mother, but you will insist that the children be under control. You do not like your hard-earned peace and quiet to be upset by noisy disturbances. But you'll love sharing projects with young friends, perhaps introducing them to new interests or teaching them skills and crafts. You'll teach children that sharing good times knows no age limits!

♎ CHAPTER 18

Libra Style: Using Libra's Special Flair to Enhance Your Life

Are you at home in your house? Does your appearance express your real personality? Why not celebrate being a Libra throughout your life by living with stellar style, inspired by the colors, sounds, fashion, and living environment that suit you best. Showing off the special Libra flair in the way you dress and live could bring more harmony into your life. You'll feel, as the French say, "at home in your skin." Even your vacations might be more fun if you tailor them to your natural Libra inclinations. Try these tips to enhance your lifestyle and express the Libra in you.

The Way You Look

Libra is most creative in packaging yourself beautifully. Your look is always complete from head to toe; you'd never wear the wrong shoes or carry an odd-looking handbag. Your style is extremely feminine, flirty, and sometimes girlish; it's sexy without ever being vulgar.

You're a nonstop shopper who is sure to know the fashion contents of the best stores in town. But before you make a major purchase, you'll be sure it suits your style and complements the contents of your closet. You usually have an extensive wardrobe with plenty of options for every occasion, but such is your fashion flair that you could combine a few basic everyday items with knockout scarves and jewelry to create a stunning outfit. Your natural sense of balance and suitability rarely fails you in any fashion emergency.

Your sun sign usually endows its members with curly hair and well-balanced features. To complement your look, style your hair in a soft and romantic way and use subtle makeup, just enough to give definition to your features.

Libra Colors

Pastels, especially delicate pale shell colors, are usually most becoming to Libra. Pale cosmetic shades are flattering to everyone, promote tranquility and a calm, harmonious feeling. Pink and sky blue are special Libra favorites.

Libra Fashion Role Models

Catherine Zeta-Jones, Naomi Watts, Monica Bellucci, and Gwyneth Paltrow have the classic beauty your sign is famous for. Gwen Stefani and Nicky Hilton have a slightly more dramatic Libra look with flair in every detail. They're style-setting Libras in tune with the latest trends who also design striking accessories.

Libran designers Isaac Mizrahi, Ralph Lauren, and Donna Karan understand your style completely. Like typical Libras, they are known for their total look, including perfume, lingerie, and designs for the home. That way, there's no chance that a single element can be off-balance. They also understand that style knows no budget limitations and create collections for discount outlets and lower-priced chains as well as luxury couture-level boutiques.

Libra Home Makeover Tips

Libra is the sign of good taste. You have a natural eye for proportion, color harmony, and furniture arrangement.

Generally, you prefer a classic look, with carefully coordinated furniture, color, and fabrics. Effects that are jarring, too avant-garde, too dramatic are not for you. You probably have a collection of objets d'art, which you display skillfully in lovely still-life settings. Lighting in your rooms is unobtrusive and flattering to your guests.

Libra loves to decorate and usually has definite ideas. Any discordant note can upset your equilibrium, so assert your preferences when decorating or renovation is done by others.

Create a dreamy serene paradise using delicate shades of pink and airy blues. A little (or a lot of) pink makes everyone look good and uplifts the general mood of a room, promoting a graceful, social atmosphere. Pale colors also serve as a complementary background for your artworks and antiques. Ultrafeminine bedrooms with ruffles, fabric flourishes, extravagant bed linens, and perhaps a canopy bed are a Libra specialty.

There are Libra designers whose visions might suit you. Ralph Lauren's brand of classical home furnishings has conservative flair, enabling you to re-create the look of the country club lifestyle. Donna Karan's home furnishings express a more modern vision, with the coordinated, beautifully balanced Libra flair. Ty Pennington of *Extreme Home Makeover* knows how to create a personal paradise.

Since you are one of the zodiac's great hosts, you'll want elegant table settings and well-chosen background music. You will serve food that is as beautiful to look at as it is delicious.

Libra Sounds

Romantic music makes your heart sing. Libra artists Luciano Pavarotti, Yo-Yo Ma, Julio Iglesias, and Johnny Mathis strike the right notes. Verdi, Liszt, and John Lennon wrote your kind of music. In the right mood, you can rock with Bruce Springsteen, Jerry Lee Lewis, Patti LaBelle, and Sting.

Libra Getaways

Vacations should appeal to Libra aesthetic and social tastes. Libras usually prefer to stay close to civilization rather than explore the wilderness. Beautiful surroundings, good company, excellent food, and wonderful shopping make Libra happy.

Libra loves to do things with a partner, so take a favorite companion along on your trips. You'll enjoy a vacation in elegant surroundings (no camping out, please), where you can dress up and socialize with other well-mannered people. With pleasant company, you could unwind on a trip through the castles of the Loire Valley; spend a weekend at an aristocratic English country house; waltz in Vienna; float through the vale of Kashmir; breathe the clear, clean air of the Swiss Alps or Tibet. Lacking a partner, tour with a special-interest group, perhaps one devoted to exploring the antique markets, museums, and design centers of Europe.

You'll enjoy getting the royal treatment in a gorgeous grand hotel or cruise ship, and especially dressing up for dinner.

Romantic weekends with the one you love are perfect Libra escapes. Keep a list of beautiful bed-and-breakfasts in the country or resorts that cater to lovers. Rent an exotic car for the trip (or a bicycle built for two when you get there). If you're single, plan trips with kindred souls around interests you all share, such as visiting antiques fairs, art shows, music festivals, or historic homes.

Since you're one of the great shoppers of the zodiac, be sure to go somewhere with a selection of stores. Of course, you will take along an empty bag to stash your treasures.

CHAPTER 19

Libra Health and Longevity Secrets

Astrology has many ideas for keeping Libra healthy and happy. Each sign is associated with a part of the body, which could become vulnerable in later years, and within the personality of a sign are other clues for having a long and productive life.

Resist Sweet Temptations

Dr. Robert Atkins, one of the most famous diet doctors, was a Libra. A well-spoken gentleman with a liking for sweets, he fit your sign's profile. At first, the low-carbohydrate diet he advocated was vilified by nutritional "experts." However, in recent years, the effectiveness of the Atkins Diet has been proven, though it has been modified to suit our current lifestyles. It could be the perfect diet for Libras who often put on too much weight from indulging their famous sweet tooth. Because your sign rules the kidneys, it's no surprise that this diet advocates drinking plenty of water to cleanse the system as you reduce.

Since you are one of the most social signs, you may entertain or be entertained often. If possible, plan your food choices before you go out so you'll know exactly what to order and will be more likely to resist sweet temptations. Dieting with your mate or group of friends could provide the support you need and keep you on track when you go out to dinner.

Stay in Balance

Restoring and maintaining equilibrium is the Libra key to health. Balance in all things should be your mantra. If you have been working too hard or taking life too seriously, a dose of art, music, or perhaps some social activity will balance your scales. Make time to entertain friends, be romantic with the one you love, and enjoy the cultural life of your city.

Since Libra is associated with the kidneys and lower back, watch these areas for misalignment or health problems. Consider yoga, spinal adjustments, or a detoxification program if your body is out of balance.

Make Exercise a Social Occasion

Working out in a no-frills gym might be unappealing to an aesthetic Libra, so choose one that is well-designed. Attractive instructors or sociable exercise buddies could make a big difference in your motivation. Treat yourself to some good-looking exercise clothing as well.

Since yours is the sign of relationships, you may prefer exercising with a partner or with loved ones in a more imaginative and aesthetic way. Take morning walks in a beautiful local park or weekend hikes in the mountains with your family. Take a romantic bicycle tour, ending with a picnic in the autumn countryside.

Libra is also the sign of grace, so any kind of dancing may appeal to you. Dancing combines art, music, romance, relaxation, graceful movement, social contact, and exercise. Ballroom dancing would be the perfect way to exercise while flirting with your partner and showing off your dazzling evening wardrobe.

Put more beauty in all areas of your life, and you'll be healthier and happier.

Stay Forever Young

Libra's key to youth is to keep the social, familial, mental, and physical areas of your life in balance. Strengthen your body with balancing exercises like tai chi and yoga or artistic and social exercises in a friendly group. Your back and kidneys are vulnerable areas to keep in good condition with diet and specific exercises. In later years, Libra has the time to become more involved in intellectual pursuits and arts and crafts, which can add much pleasure to your life. It's also important for your mental well-being to remain active socially. You can do this by throwing parties that bring friends and family together and show off your expert entertaining skills. Cultivate relationships with like-minded friends by joining a club or group with common charitable or intellectual interest, and explore the many opportunities in your community to volunteer your time and expertise.

⚖ CHAPTER 20

Libra's Guide to a Stellar Career: What It Takes to Succeed in 2009

Are You in the Right Career?

The right job for Libra should have you bounding out the door in the morning, ready to take on the day. If corporate culture feels confining or the freelance world is too risk-laden, you may need to rethink your career path. If your boss gets on your nerves, or your coworkers steal your thunder, perhaps you should try a new strategy before you decide to walk out the door. Libra has a special combination of talents and abilities that can make you a natural winner. If you develop and nurture these strengths, you'll be more likely to find a career you truly enjoy—and that's the best definition of success.

Where to Look for Your Perfect Job

Your job should be one that engages your mind, gives you social contacts, and has pleasant surroundings. You'll also be happiest when your work satisfies your ideals in some way. That is why Libras so often choose careers in design, law, diplomacy, labor relations, art, fashion, strategic planning, or education. These are fields where you can work out abstract concepts of beauty and justice.

Your innate feeling for balance might lead you to a health-oriented field where you are especially good at diagnosis, massage, chiropractic work, or nutrition. You work very well with partners or on a team, thriving on the social contact and exchange of ideas. Though you are able to mediate between different groups, getting people to work together toward a common goal, you will be happiest if your immediate surroundings are harmonious. Avoid clashing egos and offices that assault your aesthetic tastes. Difficult working conditions such as these can take a toll on your mental and physical health in the long run.

Live Up to Your Leadership Potential

You are a charming, social boss and you rarely raise your voice or handle anyone harshly. Even when annoyed, you prefer to take a diplomatic approach, solving problems with calm discussion. You bring together a winning team and keep everyone working in harmony. You are extremely fair with subordinates, delegating work so that no one has an excessive workload. You may have problems with direct confrontations. You are much better at smoothing over a difficult situation than coming to grips with it head-on or making a quick turnaround. You may leave the face-off scenes to a partner, while you assume the role of mediator. Your office is always neat and harmonious, since you are very conscious of appearances. You are careful to represent your company in the most elegant ways. You enjoy business entertaining and probably have a generous expense account.

One of the keys to Libra success is to find your own brand of personal style and market it well. Libra designer Ralph Lauren marketed his own classic personal style into a billion-dollar company and one of the most recognizable and consistently popular brands in the world. He sold his style not only in clothing, but followed it through to home furnishings. An astute businessman, he has managed to adapt to consumers' changing needs and the fickle fashion world, yet retain the elegant, classic image of his brand. That's quite a Libra balancing act! Probably everyone reading this chapter has at least one item—whether it's a polo shirt, an evening gown, a dinner plate, or even a towel—bearing his name.

How to Work with Others

Libra thrives when working with others, though you avoid getting too personally involved. You prefer to be the peacemaker, the one in the middle who brings opposing factions together. You have a charming telephone manner and work well in a spot where you meet the public directly or indirectly. Your workspace is always harmonious and well organized, and you've probably given it some aesthetic touches because your work may suffer in an ugly or disorderly environment. You are a hard worker, but not a workaholic, sensing that you must balance your work life with play and exercise. Your good looks, personal style, and natural diplomacy make you a good advertisement for your company in a public position.

The Libra Way to Get Ahead

As a Libra, you bring some important assets to the table, such as your sense of style, your social skills, and your analytical ability. It's up to you to decide how to best utilize your talents and abilities to bring you the very highest return on the investment of your time and energy. Choose a job in an aesthetically pleasing environment where you deal with the public or with idealistic issues. Play up these Libra characteristics:

- Intelligence
- Sense of fairness

- Grace under pressure
- Balanced judgment
- Artistic talent
- Social skills
- Elegant taste

CHAPTER 21

Famous Libra Sign Mates

Over the past decade, our culture has become more fascinated than ever with the lives of celebrities. And you know how much fun it is when you find a famous person who shares your sun sign—and even your birthday! Maybe it's your favorite actor or someone you've long admired.

Guessing upcoming headline makers in the Libra roster is another fun activity. Who will be your sign's "It Girl" of 2009? She might be a trendy Libra who rocks the fashion world, like Chelsy Davy, Gwyneth Paltrow, or Catherine Zeta-Jones have done. Who will be the Libra role models? Will there be a scandalous politician, a crusader for human rights, or a controversial talk-show host in your sign's rich and powerful contenders?

As you scope your sign for the tabloid stars, why not take advantage of the fringe benefits to be gained from studying your sun-sign mates? Celebrities who capture the media's attention will reflect the planetary influences of a given time, as well as the unique star quality of his or her sun sign. You can learn from these stellar spotlight stealers what the public is responding to and what this says about our current values.

If someone intrigues you, explore his personality further by looking up his other planets, using the tables in this book. Then apply the effects of Venus, Mars, Saturn, and Jupiter to his sun-sign traits. It's a way to get up close and personal with your famous friend, and maybe learn some secrets not revealed to the public.

You're sure to have lots in common with your famous sign mates. Consider how Ralph Lauren, Donna Karan, and

Isaac Mizrahi have interpreted fashion this season. Do you appreciate the extreme home makeovers of Ty Pennington? Do you enjoy the sounds of Avril Lavigne, Sting, and Paul Simon?

Then why not move on from the red carpet to world leaders and current newsmakers? You can find accurate data online at Internet sites, such as www.Stariq.com or www.astrodatabank.com, which have the charts of world events and headline makers. You can compare notes with other fans, including many professional astrologers who frequent the forums on these sites, and add your own insight and opinions.

Libra Celebrities

Ray Charles (9/23/32)
Bruce Springsteen (9/23/49)
F. Scott Fitzgerald (9/24/1896)
Anthony Newley (9/24/31)
Jim Henson (9/24/36)
Linda McCartney (9/24/41)
Barbara Walters (9/25/31)
Juliet Prowse (9/25/37)
Michael Douglas (9/25/44)
Mark Hamill (9/25/51)
Christopher Reeve (9/25/52)
Heather Locklear (9/25/61)
Will Smith (9/25/68)
Catherine Zeta-Jones (9/25/69)
Jack LaLanne (9/26/14)
Julio Iglesias (9/26/43)
Olivia Newton-John (9/26/48)
James Caviezel (9/26/68)
Serena Williams (9/26/81)
Louis Auchincloss (9/27/17)
Misha Dichter (9/27/45)
Cheryl Tiegs (9/27/47)

Avril Lavigne (9/27/84)
Peter Finch (9/28/16)
Marcello Mastroianni (9/28/24)
Brigitte Bardot (9/28/34)
Mira Sorvino (9/28/67)
Naomi Watts (9/28/68)
Carre Otis (9/28/68)
Gwyneth Paltrow (9/28/72)
Hilary Duff (9/28/87)
Gene Autry (9/29/10)
Trevor Howard (9/29/16)
Anita Ekberg (9/29/31)
Jerry Lee Lewis (9/29/37)
Bryant Gumbel (9/29/48)
Deborah Kerr (9/30/21)
Robert Duvall (9/30/29)
Angie Dickinson (9/30/31)
Truman Capote (9/30/34)
Johnny Mathis (9/30/37)
Victoria Tennant (9/30/50)
Fran Drescher (9/30/57)
Jenna Elfman (9/30/71)
Monica Bellucci (9/30/68)
Jimmy Carter (10/1/27)
Walter Matthau (10/1/30)
George Peppard (10/1/30)
Richard Harris (10/1/32)
Julie Andrews (10/1/37)
Mary McFadden (10/1/38)
Randy Quaid (10/1/50)
Groucho Marx (10/2/1890)
Rex Reed (10/2/40)
Don McLean (10/2/45)
Donna Karan (10/2/48)
Sting (10/2/51)
Lorraine Bracco (10/2/54)
Kelly Ripa (10/2/69)
Tiffany (10/2/71)
Gore Vidal (10/3/25)
Chubby Checker (10/3/41)

Dave Winfield (10/3/51)
Al Sharpton (10/3/54)
Tommy Lee (10/3/62)
Gwen Stefani (10/3/69)
Neve Campbell (10/3/73)
Ashlee Simpson (10/3/84)
Charlton Heston (10/4/23)
Anne Rice (10/4/41)
Patti LaBelle (10/4/44)
Susan Sarandon (10/4/45)
Armand Assante (10/4/49)
Alicia Silverstone (10/4/76)
Ray Kroc (10/5/1892)
Vaclav Havel (10/5/36)
Karen Allen (10/5/51)
Kate Winslet (10/5/75)
Carole Lombard (10/6/1908)
Stephanie Zimbalist (10/6/56)
Elizabeth Shue (10/6/63)
June Allison (10/7/23)
Yo-Yo Ma (10/7/55)
Simon Cowell (10/7/59)
Paul Hogan (10/8/36)
David Carradine (10/8/40)
Jesse Jackson (10/8/41)
Sigourney Weaver (10/8/49)
Matt Damon (10/8/70)
John Lennon (10/9/40)
Sean Lennon (10/9/75)
Helen Hayes (10/10/1900)
Tanya Tucker (10/10/58)
Bai Ling (10/10/70)
Eleanor Roosevelt (10/11/1884)
Mackenzie Phillips (10/11/59)
Joan Cusack (10/11/62)
Michelle Trachtenberg (10/11/85)
Dick Gregory (10/12/32)
Luciano Pavarotti (10/12/35)
Susan Anton (10/12/51)
Hugh Jackman (10/12/68)

Lillian Gish (10/13/1896)
Yves Montand (10/13/21)
Paul Simon (10/13/41)
Marie Osmond (10/13/59)
Kelly Preston (10/13/62)
Chelsy Davy (10/13/85)
Ralph Lauren (10/14/39)
Isaac Mizrahi (10/14/61)
Usher (10/14/78)
Penny Marshall (10/15/42)
Roger Moore (10/15/42)
Sarah Ferguson (10/15/59)
Angela Lansbury (10/16/25)
Suzanne Somers (10/16/46)
Tim Robbins (10/16/58)
Rita Hayworth (10/17/18)
Montgomery Clift (10/17/20)
Dr. Robert Atkins (10/17/30)
Eminem (10/18/74)
Melina Mercouri (10/18/25)
George C. Scott (10/18/27)
Peter Boyle (10/18/35)
Pam Dawber (10/18/51)
Martina Navratilova (10/18/56)
John Lithgow (10/19/45)
Evander Holyfield (10/19/62)
Ty Pennington (10/19/65)
Bela Lugosi (10/20/1882)
Ellery Queen (10/20/1905)
Mickey Mantle (10/20/31)
Snoop Dogg (10/20/72)
Dizzy Gillespie (10/21/17)
Michael Landon (10/21/37)
Patti Davis (1/21/52)
Carrie Fisher (10/21/56)
Joan Fontaine (10/22/17)
Catherine Deneuve (10/22/43)
Jeff Goldblum (10/22/53)
Brian Boitano (10/22/63)

☖ CHAPTER 22

Libra Match-Up and Mating Guide

Is your partner on your same wavelength, or do you some-times wonder if you both are living on separate planets? Did the hot chemistry of an online romance fizzle when you met in person? Relationships are full of contradictions and complexities, especially this year, when there are so many new options for meeting and flirting, from speed dating to online matchmaking.

Astrology has no magic formula for success in love, but it does offer a better understanding of the qualities each person brings to the relationship and how your partner is likely to react to your sun-sign characteristics. Knowing your potential partner's sign and how it relates to yours could give you some clues about what to expect down the line.

There is also the issue of the timing of a new relation-ship. From an astrological perspective, the people you meet at any given time provide the dynamic that you re-quire at the moment. If you're a social Libra, you might benefit from the financial savvy and practical wisdom of a down-to-earth sign like Capricorn or Taurus at a certain time in your life.

The celebrity couples in this chapter can help you visual-ize each sun-sign combination. You'll note that some leg-endary lovers have stood the test of time, while others blazed, then broke up, and still others existed only in the fantasy world of film or television (but still captured our imagination). Is there a magic formula for compatibility?

Traditional astrological wisdom holds that signs of the same element are naturally compatible. For Libra, that would be fellow air signs Gemini and Aquarius. Also favored are signs of complementary elements, such as air signs with fire signs (Aries, Leo, Sagittarius). In these relationships communication supposedly flows easily, and you'll feel most comfortable together.

As you read the following matches, remember that there are no hard-and-fast rules; each combination has perks as well as peeves. So when sparks fly and an irresistible magnetic pull draws you together, when disagreements and challenges fuel intrigue, mystery, passion, and sexy sparring matches, don't rule the relationship out. That person may provide the diversity, excitement, and challenge you need for an unforgettable romance, a stimulating friendship, or a successful business partnership!

Libra/Aries

THE ROMANCE:

This attraction of opposite signs is about sharing (Libra) versus going it alone (Aries), the judge (Libra) versus the crusader (Aries). Libra admires the decision maker in Aries and adores having a true romantic lead. In this combination, Aries supplies the push and energy; Libra, the charm and diplomacy. Libra learns to take a stand; Aries learns to see the opposite point of view.

THE REALITY CHECK:

Libra indecisiveness can make Aries see red. Aries views vacillation as a serious weakness—he who hesitates is lost or last! Aries lack of consideration and pushy manner is a Libra no-no. Aries enjoys a rousing confrontation, while Libra avoids disharmony. Discuss differences frequently and calmly in an elegant setting.

Libra Kelly Ripa and Aries Mark Consuelos

Libra/Taurus

THE ROMANCE:

Both Venus-ruled signs are turned on by beauty and luxury, and enjoy indulging each other. Libra brings intellectual sparkle and social savvy to Taurus. Taurus gives Libra financial stability and adoration. And Libra profits from the strong Taurus sense of direction and decisiveness.

THE REALITY CHECK:

Taurus is possessive and enjoys staying at home. Libra loves social life and flirting. Taurus must watch out for jealousy because Libra flirtations are rarely serious. Libra can be extravagant, while Taurus sticks to a budget, another cause for resentment.

SIGN MATES:

Libra Juan Peron and Taurus Evita Peron

Libra/Gemini

THE ROMANCE:

Air signs Gemini and Libra have both mental and physical rapport. This is an outgoing combination, full of good talk. You'll never be bored. Your Libra good looks and charm, as well as your fine mind, could keep restless Gemini close to home.

THE REALITY CHECK:

Both of you have a low tolerance for the boredom of practical chores. The question of who will provide, do the chores, and clean up can be the subject of many a debate. There could be more talk than action here, leaving you turning elsewhere for substance.

SIGN MATES:

Tiger tamers Libra Roy Horn and Gemini Siegfried

Libra/Cancer

THE ROMANCE:

You'll bring out each other's creativity, as Cancer sensitivity merges with your Libra balanced aesthetic sense. Your Libra innate sense of harmony could create a serenely elegant atmosphere where Cancer flourishes. You'll create an especially beautiful and welcoming home together.

THE REALITY CHECK:

Libra detachment could be mistaken for rejection by Cancer, while Cancer hypersensitivity could throw your Libra scales off balance. Libra avoids emotional confrontations, so Cancer may look elsewhere for sympathy and nurturing.

SIGN MATES:

Libra Heather Locklear and Cancer Richie Sambora
Libra Jenna Elfman and Cancer Bodhi Elfman

Libra/Leo

THE ROMANCE:

Libra is the perfect audience for Leo theatrics. As a Libra, you know how to package Leo for stardom. You both love the best things in life; you both are intelligent, stylish, and social. Since you have similar priorities, and stroke each other the right way, you could have a long-lasting relationship.

THE REALITY CHECK:

Getting the financial area of your life under control could be a problem for these two big spenders. Since you both love to make an elegant impression, you may find yourselves perennially living beyond your means. You are both flirts, which is easier for Libra to tolerate than Leo, who could unleash lethal jealousy.

SIGN MATES:

Libra Eric Benet and Leo Halle Berry

Libra/Virgo

THE ROMANCE:

You are intelligent companions with refined tastes, both perfectionists in different ways. Your Libra charm and elegant style work well with Virgo clear-headed decision making. You both listen to reason and treat each other fairly.

THE REALITY CHECK:

Libra responds to admiration, but will turn off to criticism or too much negativity. Virgo must use diplomacy to keep your Libra scales in balance. Virgo values function as well as form, and sticks to a carefully thought-out budget. Extravagant Libra spends for beauty alone.

SIGN MATES:

Libra Will Smith and Virgo Jada Pinkett Smith

Libra/Libra

THE ROMANCE:

Two Libras are a double dose of charm and style. You'll understand each other's need for beautiful, harmonious surroundings. And you'll be each other's perfect social escort. It's the light, lively, elegant romance seen in Hollywood films of the 1940s.

THE REALITY CHECK:

This couple is long on glamour, short on practicality. Someone has to make the decisions, balance the budget, and handle the chores. Who will it be? Discuss matters gracefully and objectively; then delegate fairly.

SIGN MATES:

Libras Catherine Zeta-Jones and Michael Douglas
Libras Susan Sarandon and Tim Robbins
Libras Naomi Watts and Liev Schreiber

Libra/Scorpio

THE ROMANCE:

The interplay of Scorpio intensity and Libra objectivity makes an exciting cat-and-mouse game. Your Libra intellect and flair will balance the powerful Scorpio charisma.

Scorpio will add warmth and substance to your cool Libra demeanor.

THE REALITY CHECK:

Libra must learn to handle Scorpio sensitive feelings with velvet gloves. When not taken seriously, Scorpio retaliates with a force that could send your Libra scales swinging off balance. On the other hand, Scorpio must give Libra room to exercise his or her mental and social skills.

SIGN MATES:

Libra Gwen Stefani and Scorpio Gavin Rossdale

Libra/Sagittarius

THE ROMANCE:

Libra charm smooths the rough spots, while Sagittarius provides lofty goals and a spirit of adventure. This can be a blazing romance, full of action and fun on the town together. Neither of you likes to stay at home.

THE REALITY CHECK:

Libra vacillation and Sagittarius wanderlust could keep you from making a firm commitment. You both need to find a solid launchpad (either mutual interests or career goals) to give this relationship structure. Libra needs a partner, but Sagittarius, who travels fastest alone, resents being pinned down in any way.

SIGN MATES:

Libra Teresa Heinz Kerry and Sagittarius John Kerry

Libra/Capricorn

THE ROMANCE:

Capricorn is quick to spot Libra potential as a social asset, as well as a romantic partner. Libra loves the Capricorn dignified demeanor and elegant taste. You can climb the heights together, helping each other get the lifestyle you both want.

THE REALITY CHECK:

Capricorn is a loner and a home lover, while Libra is a party person who likes to do things in tandem. Your expensive Libra tastes could create tension with frugal Capricorn. Libra must learn to watch the budget.

SIGN MATES:

Libra Marcello Mastroianni and Capricorn Faye Dunaway

Libra/Aquarius

THE ROMANCE:

Shared interests and common causes are the keys to keeping this relationship on track. You'll have excellent communication, which blends friendship with romantic chemistry. You both understand how to be there for each other without making demands and how to mix public with private life.

THE REALITY CHECK:

Libra needs flattery and romance, which Aquarius is too busy to provide. Aquarius must remember to send Libra valentines as well as never forget your birthday, ever. Aquarius needs freedom (too much togetherness is confining). Libra, remember to let this sign fly solo occasionally.

Libra John Lennon and Aquarius Yoko Ono
Libra Kelly Preston and Aquarius John Travolta

Libra/Pisces

THE ROMANCE:

You're one of the most creative couples. Libra keeps the delicate Pisces ego on an even keel, while Pisces provides the romance and attention Libra craves. You are ideal collaborators. Pisces appreciates your Libra aesthetic judgment. Libra refines Pisces ideas without dampening their creative spirit or deflating their ego.

THE REALITY CHECK:

Pisces swims in emotional waters where Libra gets seasick. Fluctuating moods rock the boat here, unless you find a way to give each other stability and support. Turn to calm reason, avoiding emotional scenes, to solve problems.

SIGN MATES:

Libra Sarah "Fergie" Ferguson and Pisces Prince Andrew
Libra Gwyneth Paltrow and Pisces Chris Martin of Coldplay
Libra Chelsy Davy and Pisces Prince Harry

CHAPTER 23

The Big Picture for Libra in 2009

Welcome to 2009! If you're in the mood for romance, Libra, then this is your year. It all starts on January 5, when expansive Jupiter enters Aquarius and your fifth house. This transit lasts all year and will expand your options if you're not involved with anyone special. If you're already in a committed relationship, then this transit could bring children. Since the fifth house also deals with creativity, Jupiter here attracts a widening base of possibilities where your creative endeavors are concerned. So if you work in the arts, expect major progress.

Saturn, the karmic timekeeper, spends most of the year in Virgo, your twelfth house. This is nothing new for you. It's been happening since the fall of 2007, so you should have a pretty clear idea what it means. Here are some possibilities: Hospitals and nursing homes have been part of your experiences since 2007; you have been exploring your own motives and unconscious mind; you are ridding yourself of habits and attitudes that may be holding you back in some way. On October 29, Saturn enters your sign for the first time in thirty years and spends about two and a half years there. This transit can be as difficult or easy as you make it. You may have to shoulder more than your share of responsibility, but you'll discover in your life new structures that will help you achieve your personal and professional goals. Saturn may delay certain things in your personal life or restrict your freedom of movement in some way, but it forces you to focus on the areas that need your full concentration. And the payoff comes once Saturn leaves your sign.

Uranus, the planet that symbolizes sudden, unexpected change, continues its transit of Pisces and your sixth house. Some possible manifestations: a new job, a different fitness regimen, or a change in your daily work environment and association with coworkers or employees. Uranus's job is to shake up the status quo, to toss you out of your routines, thus forcing you to find new ways to live.

Pluto's demotion as a planet doesn't diminish its impact in astrology. It entered Capricorn and your fourth house, transforming your home and family life. This transformation, though, will happen so slowly that you probably won't notice that the change is profound and permanent. Pluto won't leave Capricorn until 2024! To really fine-tune Pluto's transit, look at your natal chart to see which house is being impacted.

Neptune continues its long transit through Aquarius in your fourth house and this year is joined by Jupiter. Neptune's impact is far more subtle than Jupiter's because it moves more slowly and has been in this sign since 1998. However, over the course of these years, you have gradually integrated your ideals and spirituality into your creativity and into what you're looking for (or have found) in a romantic partner. These characteristics also are playing more readily into what you do for fun and pleasure.

Best Time for Romance

Look for a pleasurable time from November 20 to October 14, when Venus, your ruler, is in your sign. Your love life will improve, and so will every other area of your life. Your artistic sensibilities will be strong then, too, so dive into your creative projects. If you're not involved with anyone special at the beginning of this transit, you probably will be by the time it ends. And if you're not, Venus will be attracting other positive people and experiences into your life.

Great backup dates for romance begin on January 5, with Jupiter's transit into your fifth house, and extend all year. This is a terrific transit to have on your side!

Another date to watch for is January 25, a solar eclipse (and new moon) in your fifth house.

Best Time for Career Decisions

On your calendar, mark the dates from July 31 to August 26, when Venus transits Cancer and your tenth house of career. This period should be absolutely great for your career and all professional activities.

Mercury Retrograde

Every year, Mercury, the planet of communication and travel, turns retrograde three times. During these periods, it's wisest not to negotiate or sign contracts, travel, submit manuscripts, or make major decisions. Granted, we can't live our lives entirely by Mercury retrogrades! However, if you have to travel during the periods listed below, then expect changes in your schedule. If you have to sign a contract, expect to revisit it. Communications are bumpy; it's easy to be misunderstood. It's a good time to revise, review, and rewrite.

During these periods, it's a wise idea to back up computer files before Mercury turns retrograde. Quite often, computers and other communication devices act up. Be sure your virus software is up-to-date, too. Pay special attention to the house in which Mercury retrograde falls in your birth chart. It will tell you the area of your life most likely to be impacted. The periods to watch for in 2009 are:

January 11–February 1: retrograde in Aquarius, your fifth house of romance.

May 6–30: retrograde in Gemini, in your ninth house.

This impacts publishing, education, overseas travel, foreign countries, and your worldview.

September 6–29: retrograde in Libra. This is the retrograde to prepare for. You may be revisiting issues you thought were resolved.

Eclipses

Every year, there are four eclipses, two solar and two lunar. This year, there are six.

Solar eclipses trigger external events that allow us to see something that eluded us before. When an eclipse hits one of your natal planets, it's especially important. Take note of the sign and house placement. Lunar eclipses bring up emotional issues related to the sign and house into which they fall. If you have your birth chart, check to see if the eclipses hit any natal planets. If they do, pay special attention to events that occur for up to six months after the eclipse.

Here are the dates to watch for:

January 26: solar eclipse at six degrees Aquarius, in your fifth house of romance and creativity.

February 9: lunar eclipse at 21 degrees Leo, in your eleventh house of friends.

July 7: lunar eclipse at 15 degrees Capricorn, in your fourth house, family and home.

July 22: solar eclipse, 29 degrees Cancer, in your tenth house of career.

August 6: lunar eclipse in Aquarius, in your fifth house of health and work.

December 31: lunar eclipse in Cancer, in your tenth house of career.

Luckiest Days in 2009

Every year, Jupiter forms a beneficial angle with the sun, usually a conjunction, when both planets are in the same sign. In 2009 it happens early in the year—between January 23 and 25, with the exact conjunction on January 24. Since it occurs in your fifth house of romance, look to that area for a major stroke of luck.

Now let's take a look at what 2009 has in store for you, day by day.

♎ CHAPTER 24

Eighteen Months of Day-by-Day Predictions: July 2008 to December 2009

Moon sign times are calculated for Eastern Standard Time and Eastern Daylight Time. Please adjust for your local time zone.

JULY 2008

Tuesday, July 1 (Moon in Gemini)   Mars goes into your twelfth house. There's a lot of energy involved in secret work. Your imagination is highlighted. You do well in an artistic or creative endeavor, especially if it's related to a humanitarian activity. Work on your own.

Wednesday, July 2 (Moon in Gemini to Cancer 3:54 a.m.)   It's a number 8 day. It's your power day. You attract financial success. Buy a Lotto ticket or two. Expect a windfall. Be courageous.

Thursday, July 3 (Moon in Cancer)   The moon is in your tenth house. Professional matters play a central role; things work to your benefit. You gain a boost in prestige, possibly a raise. You get along well with coworkers. Your life is more in public view.

Friday, July 4 (Moon in Cancer to Leo 4:16 a.m.)   It's a number 1 day. That means you're at the top of your cycle. Be bold and forceful. Take the initiative to start something new. Don't be deterred by naysayers. Trust your hunches. Take the lead and be independent.

Saturday, July 5 (Moon in Leo)   The moon is in your eleventh house. You connect well with friends, especially with members of a group, and you benefit from your friendships. Follow your wishes and dreams; make sure that they remain an expression of who you are. You could be involved in a project that aims to improve social awareness.

Sunday, July 6 (Moon in Leo to Virgo 7:04 a.m.)   It's a number 3 day. That means you communicate well. Just enjoy connecting with people; don't worry about tomorrow. Enjoy the harmony, beauty, and pleasures of life. Your attitude determines everything.

Monday, July 7 (Moon in Virgo)   The moon is in your twelfth house. Work behind the scenes and avoid confrontations, especially with women. You could do well exploring mystical and spiritual matters. Take time for meditation.

Tuesday, July 8 (Moon in Virgo to Libra 1:32 p.m.)   It's a number 5 day. That means you're open to change and want to loosen restrictions. Take a risk and experiment. Variety is the spice of life.

Wednesday, July 9 (Moon in Libra)   The moon is in your first house. Your feelings could be extremely sensitive. You easily change your mind now. You're restless and uncertain what to do. You are responsive regarding the needs of others, so you are easily influenced by those around you.

Thursday, July 10 (Moon in Libra to Scorpio 11:35 p.m.)   Mercury moves into your tenth house. You can expect that you'll be using your communication skills to the fullest in your career. That could include writing or speaking. Or travel could be called for related to your profession.

Friday, July 11 (Moon in Scorpio)   The moon is in your second house. Deal with your finances. You find emotional security in your assets and material goods. It's the memories and feelings related to the belongings, not the objects themselves, that are important.

Saturday, July 12 (Moon in Scorpio)   Venus moves into your eleventh house. There are harmony and warmth in relationships with friends, particularly those whom you know through a group setting. A romance could develop with a particular person in the group.

Sunday, July 13 (Moon in Scorpio to Sagittarius 11:50 a.m.)   It's a number 1 day. That means you're at the top of your cycle. You get a fresh start. Make sure that you take the initiative while the time is right to start a new project. In romance, make room for a new love, if that's what you want now.

Monday, July 14 (Moon in Sagittarius)   The moon is in your third house. Your communications with others are subjective. Take what you know and share it with others. However, keep conscious control of your emotions when communicating with relatives and neighbors. Your thinking is unduly influenced by the past.

Tuesday, July 15 (Moon in Sagittarius)   It's a number 3 day. Your charm and wit are appreciated. You're curious and inventive. Relax and get your batteries recharged. In romance, you feel loyal to your partner.

Wednesday, July 16 (Moon in Sagittarius to Capricorn 12:20 a.m.)   Your responsibilities increase. You try to keep everything in balance around you. You're concerned that you may be overlooking needs in your home. Self-discipline and a firm structure to your day are important.

Thursday, July 17 (Moon in Capricorn)   The moon is in your fourth house. If at all possible, stick close to home and tend to family matters. Retreat to a private place for quiet reflection on everything that's been going on. Do something to beautify your home.

Friday, July 18 (Moon in Capricorn to Aquarius 11:41 a.m.)   It's a number 6 day. Service to others is emphasized. Whether you're in the home or office, you tend to nurture and care for those around you. You offer advice and support. Like yesterday, your heart is in your home and home life.

Saturday, July 19 (Moon in Aquarius)   The moon is in your fifth house. You're emotionally in touch with your creative side. You're easily impressed, so make sure that you don't allow anyone to influence you on a speculative matter. Don't take any risks. Best to tend to children and loved ones. There's a lot of emotion in a romantic relationship.

Sunday, July 20 (Moon in Aquarius to Pisces 9:09 p.m.)   It's a number 8 day. It's your power day. You're ambitious and goal-oriented. You can go far with your plans and achieve financial success. Take action. You can achieve recognition and fame. Avoid being negative or manipulative. Don't neglect the needs of others.

Monday, July 21 (Moon in Pisces)   The moon is in your sixth house. You're busy helping others in your daily work. You offer suggestions for improvements. You're helpful and service-oriented but also restless. Take care of any health issues.

Tuesday, July 22 (Moon in Pisces)   Yesterday's energy continues. You're compassionate and sensitive. You inspire others. It's all about deep healing. Follow your heart. Pay attention to your dreams and intuitive hunches. You seek universal knowledge, eternal truths, and deep spirituality.

Wednesday, July 23 (Moon in Pisces to Aries 4:23 a.m.)   It's a number 2 day. Cooperation and partnerships are highlighted. You're diplomatic and capable of fixing whatever has gone wrong. As usual, you're concerned about keeping everything in balance. You excel in working with a group. You play the role of the visionary. Be honest and open.

Thursday, July 24 (Moon in Aries) The moon is in your seventh house. Yesterday's energy continues. Personal relationships, especially a partnership, play a dominant role. Your partner might be moody and sensitive. You want to be accepted for who you are, but it's difficult to remain detached and objective.

Friday, July 25 (Moon in Aries to Taurus 9:15 a.m.) It's a number 4 day. Stick to practical matters. You're seen as trustworthy and down to earth by others. Stick with this energy and avoid trying to please everyone, and you can gain recognition, success, and fame for your hard work.

Saturday, July 26 (Moon in Taurus) Mercury moves into your eleventh house. There's a lot of communication with friends, especially in a group setting. You help the group, and your friends assist you in achieving your wishes and dreams.

Sunday, July 27 (Moon in Taurus to Gemini 11:56 a.m.) It's a number 6 day. Service to others is the theme. Do a good deed for someone. Visit someone who is ill or someone in need of help. Focus on making people happy. Be sympathetic, kind, and compassionate.

Monday, July 28 (Moon in Gemini) The moon is in your ninth house. You're a dreamer and a thinker who yearns for something new, whether it's long-distance travel or taking a seminar on a subject that grabs your interest. Your beliefs are strong and sincere but changeable.

Tuesday, July 29 (Moon in Gemini to Cancer 1:12 p.m.) It's a number 8 day. It's your power day. You have an opportunity to succeed in whatever you're pursuing. Financial success is at hand. Open your mind to a new approach that could bring in big bucks. But don't do anything that could hurt others.

Wednesday, July 30 (Moon in Cancer)   The moon is in your tenth house. You're in the public eye. You have a chance for recognition, if you're ready for it. It's a good day for sales and dealing with the public. You're responsive to the needs of those around you in the workplace as well as the public in general.

Thursday, July 31 (Moon in Cancer to Leo 2:22 p.m.)   It's a number 1 day. You take a leadership role. You get a fresh start. Stress your independence. Don't let naysayers and close-minded people influence you. Explore, discover, and create.

AUGUST 2008

Friday, August 1 (Moon in Leo)   There's a solar eclipse in your eleventh house. That means that some external events that will help you clarify a friendship or some issue concerning a group to which you belong are likely to occur.

Saturday, August 2 (Moon in Leo to Virgo 4:59 p.m.)   It's a number 9 day. Complete a project. Clear up odds and ends. Make room for something new. Apply the finishing touches, reflect on what you've accomplished, and envision how you can expand.

Sunday, August 3 (Moon in Virgo)   The moon is in your twelfth house. You can be overly self-critical and may need to bolster your confidence. Work behind the scenes and avoid conflict. Confide your deepest thoughts to a confidant.

Monday, August 4 (Moon in Virgo to Libra 10:28 p.m.)   It's a number 2 day. Use your intuition to get a sense of your day. Cooperation is highlighted. Be kind and understanding. Don't make waves; just let things develop. There could be discussions about a marriage or a partnership.

Tuesday, August 5 (Moon in Libra)   Venus moves into your twelfth house. You're introspective and in need of time alone, especially if you must recover from a frustrating romance. Your emotions are strong and controlled deep in your subconscious. Some childhood issues could surface.

Wednesday, August 6 (Moon in Libra)   The moon is in your first house. You're sensitive to other people's feelings, but you're also moody. You're concerned about your appearance.

Thursday, August 7 (Moon in Libra to Scorpio 7:27 a.m.)   It's a number 5 day. You look for a new perspective. You're versatile and changeable, but be careful not to overcommit yourself. Stay focused as best you can. Take risks; experiment. Pursue a new idea. Freedom of thought and action is key.

Friday, August 8 (Moon in Scorpio)   The moon is in your second house. You feel comfortable close to home. You identify emotionally with your belongings, particularly with the memories you associate with them. Your values are important.

Saturday, August 9 (Moon in Scorpio to Sagittarius 7:11 p.m.)   It's a number 7 day. You become aware of confidential information and secret meetings. You investigate like a detective solving a mystery. Gather information, but don't act on what you learn until tomorrow.

Sunday, August 10 (Moon in Sagittarius)   Mercury moves into your twelfth house. Some of your decisions and tendencies are based on subconscious influences. Feelings rather than logic prevail. Express your thoughts to a close friend, but avoid airing your concerns in public.

Monday, August 11 (Moon in Sagittarius)   The moon is in your third house. You have an emotional need to pursue your studies of ideas and subjects that interest you. Your intellectual curiosity requires continued nurturing and growth.

Tuesday, August 12 (Moon in Sagittarius to Capricorn 7:43 a.m.)   It's a number 1 day. Be independent and creative. Get out and meet new people and have new experiences. Explore, discover, and create. In romance, make room for a new love. A flirtation turns serious.

Wednesday, August 13 (Moon in Capricorn)   The moon is in your fourth house. Stay close to home and spend time with family and loved ones. Do something to beautify your home. Reflect on everything that has been happening in your life. Focus on recalling your dreams.

Thursday, August 14 (Moon in Capricorn to Aquarius 6:57 p.m.)   It's a number 3 day. You communicate well. You're receptive to what others tell you. Enjoy the harmony, beauty, and pleasures of life. Remain flexible, curious, and inventive.

Friday, August 15 (Moon in Aquarius)   The moon is in your fifth house. You're emotionally in touch with your creative side. Be yourself and emotionally honest. There's great emotional depth in a relationship. However, you could be somewhat overpossessive of loved ones, especially children.

Saturday, August 16 (Moon in Aquarius)   There's a lunar eclipse in your fifth house. Change any bad habits that are blocking your creativity or interfering with a romantic relationship. You can break an addiction. Start from within and change your life for the better.

Sunday, August 17 (Moon in Aquarius to Pisces 3:47 a.m.)   It's a number 6 day. Service to others is the theme. Offer advice and support to those around you. Remember to be diplomatic, not aggressive or argumentative. Diplomacy wins the way. Do a good deed; make someone happy.

Monday, August 18 (Moon in Pisces)   The moon is in your sixth house. Yesterday's service-oriented energy continues. Others rely on you for help. You're the go-to person to improve, edit, or refine what others are working on. Just make sure that others don't take advantage of your willingness to help. Know when to say enough is enough.

Tuesday, August 19 (Moon in Pisces to Aries 10:11 a.m.) Mars moves into your first house. You're assertive, outgoing, and energetic, especially regarding a partnership or marriage. You'll remain that way for the next couple months. You appeal to the public; relations with the opposite sex are great.

Wednesday, August 20 (Moon in Aries)   The moon is in your seventh house. Partnerships are highlighted. You work well with others and feel secure. You may want to push someone who lags behind, but it's best not to make waves.

Thursday, August 21 (Moon in Aries to Taurus 2:38 p.m.) It's a number 1 day. Be independent and creative. Don't follow others. Just play your hunches and don't be afraid to follow a new path. Your individuality is stressed. Get out and meet new people and have new experiences.

Friday, August 22 (Moon in Taurus)   The moon is in your eighth house. Security issues arise; you feel best when you're out of debt. You may be in a position to control the assets of a partner. You tend to have a strong sense of duty and obligation, so it's natural for you to look out for the interest of all parties. You could be involved in a project to help a large number of people.

Saturday, August 23 (Moon in Taurus to Gemini 5:49 p.m.) It's a number 3 day. You communicate well.

You're warm and receptive to what others say. Your attitude determines everything. Remain flexible. Pay attention to your hunches. Others are impressed by your wit and charm.

Sunday, August 24 (Moon in Gemini)   The moon is in your ninth house. You yearn for new experiences. Break with your usual routine. You're a dreamer and a thinker. Plan a long trip to a foreign land or pursue a subject that interests you, and see where it leads.

Monday, August 25 (Moon in Gemini to Cancer 8:19 p.m.)   It's a number 5 day. Yesterday's energy continues. Freedom of thought and action is key. Promote new ideas; follow your curiosity. A change in perspective works to your advantage. Approach the day with an unconventional mind-set.

Tuesday, August 26 (Moon in Cancer)   The moon is in your tenth house. Professional concerns are highlighted. You're responsive to the needs and moods of a group and of the public in general. You're warm and emotional toward fellow workers, but don't blur the boundaries between your professional and personal lives.

Wednesday, August 27 (Moon in Cancer to Leo 10:51 p.m.)   It's a number 7 day. You could delve into a mystery that involves confidential information. Knowledge is essential for success. Dig deep for answers, but maintain your emotional balance. Don't make any snap decisions on what you find out.

Thursday, August 28 (Moon in Leo)   Mercury joins Mars in your first house. You're in the public and very talkative. You express yourself well. You make connections that you hadn't realized existed. You adapt quickly to changing circumstances.

Friday, August 29 (Moon in Leo)   The moon is in your eleventh house. You work well in a group setting, especially if you're promoting a cause that helps others. You're responsive to the feelings of others. Friends play an important role. Follow your wishes and dreams.

Saturday, August 30 (Moon in Leo to Virgo 2:19 a.m.)
Venus joins Mercury and Mars in your first house. Relations with the opposite sex go well. You're recharged for the month ahead and feel physically vital.

Sunday, August 31 (Moon in Virgo) The moon is in your twelfth house. After all the high energy and romance yesterday, you feel a need to work behind the scenes. You're somewhat moody; avoid confrontations. Keep your feelings secret. Be aware that matters from the past can rise to the surface.

SEPTEMBER 2008

Monday, September 1 (Moon in Virgo to Libra 7:45 a.m.) It's a number 9 day. Kick off the month by wrapping up a project and preparing for something new. Reflect on everything that's been taking place. Look for a way to expand your horizons, but don't start anything new.

Tuesday, September 2 (Moon in Libra) The moon is in your first house along with Mercury, Mars, and Venus. It's a powerful time for you. Your self-awareness is keen. You deal with the person you are becoming. Your feelings and thoughts are aligned.

Wednesday, September 3 (Moon in Libra to Scorpio 4:03 p.m.) It's a number 2 day. You can easily make use of and enhance your native ability to cooperate and work with others. You seek harmony with those around you. Tensions could flare late in the afternoon, but you have the talent to keep everything on an even keel.

Thursday, September 4 (Moon in Scorpio) The moon is in your second house. Take care of payments and collections. Deal with financial matters. Your assets are important to you. They satisfy your need for a sense of well-being.

Friday, September 5 (Moon in Scorpio)   You're passionate. Your sexuality is heightened. It's a day of tense emotional experiences. Investigate a secret matter, and be aware of possible deception. Forgive and forget.

Saturday, September 6 (Moon in Scorpio to Sagittarius 3:12 a.m.)   It's a number 5 day. Variety is the spice of life. Promote new ideas; follow your curiosity. You're versatile and changeable, but be careful not to spread out and diversify too much.

Sunday, September 7 (Moon in Sagittarius)   Jupiter goes direct in your fourth house. Make decisions that will affect you for the coming year. That's especially true regarding matters related to your home life. You could decide to make renovations or to move. You could decide how you and your partner and loved ones can expand on your home life.

Monday, September 8 (Moon in Sagittarius to Capricorn 3:46 p.m.)   It's a number 7 day. Secrets, intrigue, and confidential information play a role. Knowledge is essential to success. Gather information, but don't make any absolute decisions until tomorrow. Go with the flow. Maintain your emotional balance.

Tuesday, September 9 (Moon in Capricorn)   The moon is in your fourth house. Stay close to home, if possible. Meditate and reflect on everything that has been going on. Spend time with your family and work on that home-maintenance project. Get rest and recharged for what's coming tomorrow.

Wednesday, September 10 (Moon in Capricorn)   Your ambition and drive to succeed are highlighted. Your responsibilities increase. Self-discipline and structure are key.

You may feel stressed and overworked. Authority figures, banks, and institutions may play a role, so do a Taurus and a Virgo.

Thursday, September 11 (Moon in Capricorn to Aquarius 3:20 a.m.)   It's a number 1 day. Get out and meet new people and have new experiences. Refuse to deal with people who have closed minds. In romance, make room for a new love. A flirtation turns more serious.

Friday, September 12 (Moon in Aquarius)   The moon is in your fifth house. Your creativity flourishes. You can delve deep into your subconscious for inspiration. In romance, there's great emotional depth. You're nurturing and protective of children in your life.

Saturday, September 13 (Moon in Aquarius to Pisces 12:05 p.m.)   It's a number 3 day. This is your number. Enjoy the harmony, beauty, and pleasures of life. Remain flexible. Intuition is highlighted. You get your ideas across. Your popularity is on the rise.

Sunday, September 14 (Moon in Pisces)   The moon is in your sixth house. Keep your resolutions about exercise; watch your diet. Attend to details related to your health. Make a doctor or dentist appointment. Your personal health occupies your attention.

Monday, September 15 (Moon in Pisces to Aries 5:39 p.m.)   It's a number 5 day. Change your perspective. Approach the day with an unconventional mind-set. Let go of old structures; get a new point of view. You overcome obstacles with ease.

Tuesday, September 16 (Moon in Aries)   The moon is in your seventh house. The focus turns to relationships, business and personal ones. The opposite sex plays a prominent role. You focus on how the public relates to you. Be careful that others don't manipulate you.

Wednesday, September 17 (Moon in Aries to Taurus 8:57 p.m.) It's a number 7 day. A confidential matter comes to your attention. Gather information, but don't make any absolute decisions until tomorrow. Sort out what is real and what is not. Go with the flow. Express your desires, but recognize your limitations. A Virgo and a Pisces play distinctive roles.

Thursday, September 18 (Moon in Taurus) The moon is in your eighth house. Your interest in metaphysics plays a role. So do issues related to sex, death, and rebirth. Your experiences are intense, especially related to a partner. You may take an interest in controlling someone's assets.

Friday, September 19 (Moon in Taurus to Gemini 11:17 p.m.) It's a number 9 day. Finish up a project. Straighten up your desk and get ready for something new. Visualize the future, set your goals, and get to work.

Saturday, September 20 (Moon in Gemini) The moon is in your eighth house. Your emphasis is on creating a secure future for yourself and others. You could get a fresh start on a project that works to uplift large numbers of people. Best of luck!

Sunday, September 21 (Moon in Gemini) You're mentally agile, but you feel restless. Check your e-mail for a special message. Publicize what you're doing. Work on a writing project, especially revising and rewriting.

Monday, September 22 (Moon in Gemini to Cancer 1:49 a.m.) It's a number 3 day. Enjoy the harmony, beauty, and pleasures of life. Remain flexible. You communicate well. You're warm and receptive to what others say. Spread your good news.

Tuesday, September 23 (Moon in Cancer) Venus moves into your second house. Your financial situation is going quite well. You tend to have a love of spending and buying new things. Be careful not to overspend. If you're involved in the arts, make money on your creative efforts.

Wednesday, September 24 (Moon in Cancer to Leo 5:14 a.m.) Mercury goes retrograde in your first house. That means you can expect some delays and glitches in communication, especially related to your health, self-awareness, or personal appearance.

Thursday, September 25 (Moon in Leo) The moon is in your eleventh house. Focus on your wishes and dreams. Examine your overall goals. Make sure these goals are still an expression of who you are. Friends and groups play an important role. You help the goals of a group, which in turn supports your interests.

Friday, September 26 (Moon in Leo to Virgo 9:53 a.m.) It's a number 7 day. After yesterday's camaraderie, you're best being on your own. You investigate, analyze, or observe what's going on from a distance. You quickly come to a conclusion and wonder why others don't see what you see. You detect deception and recognize insincerity with ease.

Saturday, September 27 (Moon in Virgo) The moon is in your twelfth house. Stay out of public view for now. Work behind the scenes. Difficult issues from the past might surface. Confide your thoughts and feelings to a close friend or confidant. Relations with the opposite sex can be difficult.

Sunday, September 28 (Moon in Virgo to Libra 4:06 p.m.) It's a number 9 day. As the month comes to an end, work on wrapping up a project. Look to the future for ways to expand. Clear up odds and ends. Reflect on everything that's been going on, but don't start anything new.

Monday, September 29 (Moon in Libra) The moon is in your first house. You're sensitive to other people's feel-

231

ings. You may feel moody. It's all about your emotional self. You're restless and uncertain what to do. Be aware that you can be easily influenced by others.

Tuesday, September 30 (Moon in Libra)   It's a number 2 day. Partnerships and cooperation are highlighted. Use your intuition to get a sense of your day, especially as it relates to a partner. Be kind and understanding. Don't make waves or show resentment. Go with the flow.

OCTOBER 2008

Wednesday, October 1 (Moon in Libra to Scorpio 12:27 a.m.)   The moon is in your second house. Your values are important. Financial matters occupy your thoughts. Deal with investments. Your assets give you a sense of security and confidence. But watch your spending.

Thursday, October 2 (Moon in Scorpio)   Money issues arise again; you could get defensive about recent purchases. Investigate any secret activities. Control issues might arise. Forgive and forget. You're passionate; your sexuality is heightened now.

Friday, October 3 (Moon in Scorpio to Sagittarius 11:15 a.m.)   Mars moves into your second house. You feel very strongly about your values. You're competitive in business or financial matters and feel compelled to earn as much money as you can. You're not afraid of taking a risk now.

Saturday, October 4 (Moon in Sagittarius)   The moon is in your third house. You deal with the everyday world. You want to get a message out. Accept an invitation. You could have contact with neighbors or siblings.

Sunday, October 5 (Moon in Sagittarius to Capricorn 11:49 p.m.)   It's a number 5 day. Prepare for the changes coming your way. Let go of old structures; find a new point of view. Approach the day in an unconventional way. Experiment, promote new ideas, and take chances. Variety is the spice of life.

Monday, October 6 (Moon in Capricorn)   The moon is in your fourth house. You deal with your home life and the foundations of who you are. Spend time at home with family and loved ones. Take the day off, if possible, or work at home. Spend some time in meditation.

Tuesday, October 7 (Moon in Capricorn)   Stick with the structure. Don't experiment. Stay inside the box. Self-discipline is emphasized. Your ambition and drive to succeed are highlighted. Your responsibilities increase.

Wednesday, October 8 (Moon in Capricorn to Aquarius 12:03 p.m.)   It's a number 8 day. Focus on a power play. You can go far with your plans and achieve financial success. Expect a windfall. Business discussions go well. Be courageous.

Thursday, October 9 (Moon in Aquarius)   The moon is in your fifth house. There's great depth in a romantic relationship. Be emotionally honest. You're in touch with your creative side. Children play a role in your day. So do pets.

Friday, October 10 (Moon in Aquarius to Pisces 9:31 p.m.)   It's a number 1 day. You get a fresh start. Stress your individuality; take the lead in a new project. Creativity is emphasized. Intuition is highlighted. Explore, discover, and create. In romance, make room for a new love, if that's what you want.

Saturday, October 11 (Moon in Pisces)   The moon is in your sixth house. It's a service-oriented day. Help others, but don't deny your own needs. Take care of any health issues. Don't let your fears hold you back.

Sunday, October 12 (Moon in Pisces) Your imagination is highlighted. Pay attention to your dreams. Follow your hunches. Watch for synchronicities. You're sensitive and compassionate. Universal knowledge, eternal truths, and deep spirituality play a role in your day.

Monday, October 13 (Moon in Pisces to Aries 3:07 a.m.) It's a number 4 day. Your organizational skills come into play. Stay focused; emphasize quality. Be methodical and thorough. There could be a tendency to be stubborn.

Tuesday, October 14 (Moon in Aries) The moon is in your seventh house. A contract binding two people is on the table. Partnerships are emphasized. The opposite sex plays a prominent role. It's difficult to remain detached and objective.

Wednesday, October 15 (Moon in Aries to Taurus 5:31 a.m.) Mercury goes direct in your first house. Communication goes smoothly, and those personal issues that surfaced fade into the past as misunderstandings are resolved. Any health concerns are clarified.

Thursday, October 16 (Moon in Taurus) The moon is in your eighth house. Your experiences are intense and could relate to control issues about shared belongings. You could deal with taxes, insurance, or investments. Focus on your sense of stability.

Friday, October 17 (Moon in Taurus to Gemini 6:26 a.m.) It's a number 8 day. You have a chance to gain recognition, fame, and power. Open your mind to a new approach that could bring in big bucks. Be courageous. You deal with power, so make sure that you don't hurt others.

Saturday, October 18 (Moon in Gemini) Venus moves into your third house. Try to avoid any arguments and keep everything in balance. You get along well with family members and communicate your thoughts and feelings. Work on a writing project. You make your point with creative flair.

Sunday, October 19 (Moon in Gemini to Cancer 7:41 a.m.) It's a number 1 day. You're at the top of your cycle. Get out and meet new people and have new experiences. You make connections that others overlook. You're determined and courageous.

Monday, October 20 (Moon in Cancer) The moon is in your tenth house. Business and professional dealings are highlighted. Your hard work pays off. You get along well with coworkers. Your life is public, but make sure you keep your emotions under control while in the public eye.

Tuesday, October 21 (Moon in Cancer to Leo 10:36 a.m.) It's a number 3 day. You communicate well. Like yesterday, you're warm and receptive to what others say. Enjoy the harmony, beauty, and pleasures of life. Remain flexible.

Wednesday, October 22 (Moon in Leo) The moon is in your eleventh house. You join a group of friends or like-minded individuals in pursuit of a common goal. You help the group, and you gain from the group's energy. Follow your wishes and dreams, and make sure that they are still an expression of who you are.

Thursday, October 23 (Moon in Leo to Virgo 3:41 p.m.) It's a number 5 day. Key words are change, variety, and freedom. Don't be limited by self-imposed restrictions. Take risks; experiment. Change your perspective.

Friday, October 24 (Moon in Virgo) The moon is in your twelfth house. Withdraw and stay out of the public eye. Avoid confrontations, especially with the opposite sex. Your past could play a role. Unconscious attitudes can be difficult. You communicate your deepest feelings to a friend.

Saturday, October 25 (Moon in Virgo to Libra 10:48 p.m.) It's a number 7 day. Some of yesterday's energy continues. You work best on your own today. Secrets, intrigue, and confidential information play a role. Gather information, but don't make any absolute decisions until tomorrow. Avoid confusion and conflicts.

Sunday, October 26 (Moon in Libra) The moon is in your first house. You're sensitive to other people's feelings. You're malleable and easily influenced. Your self-awareness and appearance are important to you. You deal with the person you are becoming. Your thoughts and feelings are aligned.

Monday, October 27 (Moon in Libra) With the moon on your ascendant, your face is in front of the public. You're recharged for the month ahead. You feel physically vital and appeal to the public. Relations with the opposite sex go well.

Tuesday, October 28 (Moon in Libra to Scorpio 7:48 a.m.) It's a number 1 day. You get a fresh start. Stress your individuality; don't be afraid to turn in a new direction. Trust your hunches. Be independent and creative; refuse to be discouraged by naysayers. In romance, a flirtation could turn more serious.

Wednesday, October 29 (Moon in Scorpio) The moon is in your second house. You feel best when surrounded by familiar objects. You equate your financial assets with security. Pay attention to how you are spending your income.

Thursday, October 30 (Moon in Scorpio to Sagittarius 6:41 p.m.) It's a number 3 day. You communicate well. You're curious and inventive. Spread your good news, but listen to others. Ease up on your routine. Remain flexible.

Friday, October 31 (Moon in Sagittarius) The moon is in your third house. Take what you know and share it with

236

others. Stay in conscious control of your emotions when making your point, especially when dealing with relatives and neighbors. Express your deepest feelings in a journal.

NOVEMBER 2008

Saturday, November 1 (Moon in Sagittarius)   Neptune goes direct in your fifth house. Your love life takes off. There's an idealistic turn to whatever you do for pleasure. It's a great time for a creative project, especially fiction writing.

Sunday, November 2—Daylight Saving Time Ends (Moon in Sagittarius to Capricorn 6:13 a.m.)   It's a number 3 day. You get your ideas across smoothly and easily. Others appreciate your wit and charm. Foster generosity. You're warm and receptive to what others say. Relax and enjoy yourself.

Monday, November 3 (Moon in Capricorn)   The moon moves into your fourth house. You feel somewhat conflicted between your career and home life. You work hard at your profession, but you feel an urge to spend more time at home with your family. Follow that urge.

Tuesday, November 4 (Moon in Capricorn to Aquarius 7:02 p.m.)   Mercury moves into your second house. There is a lot of discussion related to your finances. You think quick, especially in terms of finances. Your values relate to material wealth rather than to intellectual ideas.

Wednesday, November 5 (Moon in Aquarius)   The moon is in your fifth house. Your creativity is enhanced. You're involved in the creative aspect of your life. You have the ability to go deep into your subconscious for inspiration. In romance, there's great emotional depth.

Thursday, November 6 (Moon in Aquarius)   Friends play an important role. Groups and social events are highlighted. Help others, but dance to your own tune. You have a great sense of freedom as you explore new ideas and look at new options. Find a new perspective.

Friday, November 7 (Moon in Aquarius to Pisces 5:44 a.m.)   It's a number 8 day. It's your power day. Focus on a power play. Financial gain is at hand. Business dealings go well. Be courageous. Fear of failure or fear that you won't measure up will attract tangible experiences that reinforce the feeling.

Saturday, November 8 (Moon in Pisces)   The moon is in your sixth house. Others rely on you for help. You're the go-to person to improve, edit, or refine what others are working on. You're compassionate and sensitive. You think deeply about whatever you're involved in. Keep your resolutions about exercise; watch your diet.

Sunday, November 9 (Moon in Pisces to Aries 12:27 p.m.)   It's a number 1 day. Stress your individuality as you get a fresh start. You creativity is emphasized. Don't be afraid to turn in a new direction. Refuse to deal with people who have closed minds.

Monday, November 10 (Moon in Aries)   The moon moves into your seventh house. You launch a new idea or project that involves a partner. You and your partner could sign a contract. You get off to a quick start. Be careful that others don't manipulate your feelings.

Tuesday, November 11 (Moon in Aries to Taurus 3:06 p.m.)   It's a number 3 day. Your attitude determines everything. You communicate well. Remain flexible. Intuition is highlighted. You're warm and receptive to what others say.

Wednesday, November 12 (Moon in Taurus)   Venus moves into your fourth house. You're loving and affectionate toward your family. You take special care in dealing

238

with a parent. You're happy being home and handling domestic duties. Work on a project to beautify your home.

Thursday, November 13 (Moon in Taurus to Gemini 3:13 p.m.)   It's a number 5 day. Freedom of thought and action is at the center of your day. Promote new ideas; follow your curiosity. A change of scenery will do you good. Get a new perspective. You're versatile and changeable, but be careful not to spread out and diversify too much.

Friday, November 14 (Moon in Gemini)   The moon is in your ninth house. You dream of your future. You've got big ideas. They could involve a long journey to a foreign country. You're intent on breaking out of the everyday routine, but you could change your mind.

Saturday, November 15 (Moon in Gemini to Cancer 2:53 p.m.)   It's a number 7 day. You could launch a journey into the unknown. Secrets, intrigue, and confidential information could play a role. Go with the flow. Keep any secrets entrusted to you. Gather information, but don't make any quick decisions today. Avoid confusion and conflict.

Sunday, November 16 (Moon in Cancer)   Mars moves into your third house. Write in a journal. Be careful not to get too emotional when talking with relatives or neighbors.

Monday, November 17 (Moon in Cancer to Leo 4:08 p.m.)   It's a number 9 day. Finish a project and get ready for something new. Relax and reflect on everything that's been taking place, and look for ways to expand and move beyond any perceived limitations.

Tuesday, November 18 (Moon in Leo)   The moon is in your tenth house. You're at center stage in your professional life. You get a boost in prestige. You get along well with coworkers. You're more in the public, right where you're supposed to be.

Wednesday, November 19 (Moon in Leo to Virgo 8:13 p.m.)   It's a number 2 day. The emphasis turns to cooperation, working with others. Go with the flow. Use your intuition, especially concerning a partnership. But don't forget your own needs. Focus on your direction.

Thursday, November 20 (Moon in Virgo)   The moon is in your twelfth house. Stick close to home and stay out of the public view. Reflect and meditate. Matters from your past may haunt you. You can communicate your deepest feelings to another person.

Friday, November 21 (Moon in Virgo)   Like yesterday, it's best to stay close to home. Take time to write in a journal. Dig deep for information. Take care of details, especially related to your health.

Saturday, November 22 (Moon in Virgo to Libra 3:20 a.m.)   It's a number 5 day. Variety is the spice of life. Change your perspective. Approach the day with an unconventional mind-set. Release old structures; get a new point of view. You can overcome obstacles with ease.

Sunday, November 23 (Moon in Libra)   Mercury moves into your third house. Share what you know with others. However, keep conscious control of your emotions when communicating. Your thinking could be unduly influenced by the past.

Monday, November 24 (Moon in Libra to Scorpio 12:54 p.m.)   It's a number 7 day. You explore a mystery. Dig deep for information. Don't reveal a secret, especially if you've promised to remain quiet. You work best on your own. Maintain your emotional balance.

Tuesday, November 25 (Moon in Scorpio)   The moon is in your second house. You feel intensely emotional related to certain possessions. It's not the objects themselves that are so important as much as the feelings and memories you associate with them. Watch your spending. There's plenty of time before the holidays.

Wednesday, November 26 (Moon in Scorpio)   Pluto moves into your fourth house. You could undergo profound change regarding your family and where you live. But it's a slow process.

Thursday, November 27 (Moon in Scorpio to Sagittarius 12:14 a.m.)   Uranus goes direct in your sixth house. Look for sudden unexpected changes dealing with your work or coworkers. You may have been thinking your job isn't right for you, and the universe may bring one that is. Happy Thanksgiving!

Friday, November 28 (Moon in Sagittarius)   The moon is in your third house. Get your ideas across as you go about your everyday activities. You may be involved in a number of short trips. Stay in conscious control of your emotions. Matters from the past could arise in discussions with relatives.

Saturday, November 29 (Moon in Sagittarius to Capricorn 12:48 p.m.)   It's a number 3 day. Think positive; stay optimistic. Others look to you for inspiration and guidance. You can influence people with your upbeat attitude. In business dealings, diversify. Insist on all the information, not just bits and pieces.

Sunday, November 30 (Moon in Capricorn)   The moon is in your fourth house. You could initiate a romance with someone at work. You feel warmth and compassion regarding a relative. You communicate your feelings well.

DECEMBER 2008

Monday, December 1 (Moon in Capricorn)   With the moon in your fourth house, there's good energy in your home life. Stay home and work on a project to repair or beautify your house. Spend some time in quiet meditation. Recall your dreams.

Tuesday, December 2 (Moon in Capricorn to Aquarius 1:45 a.m.)   It's a number 4 day. Persevere to get things done. Your organizational skills come into play. Tear down the old in order to rebuild. Be methodical and thorough; don't get sloppy. You build foundations for your future.

Wednesday, December 3 (Moon in Aquarius)   With the moon in your fifth house, your emotions tend to overpower your intellect. Be yourself. In love, there's great emotional depth to a relationship.

Thursday, December 4 (Moon in Aquarius to Pisces 1:24 p.m.)   It's a number 6 day. Diplomacy wins the way. Focus on making people happy. Be generous and tolerant. Do a good deed for someone. Visit someone who is ill or in need of help.

Friday, December 5 (Moon in Pisces)   The moon is in your sixth house. Yesterday's energy continues. Others look to your creative touch. Help others, but don't deny your own needs. Take care of your health needs.

Saturday, December 6 (Moon in Pisces to Aries 9:45 p.m.)   It's a number 8 day. It's your power day. Business discussions go well, especially if you open your mind to a new approach. Be courageous. You attract financial success, but be careful not to hurt others.

Sunday, December 7 (Moon in Aries)   Venus moves into your fifth house. You feel vital and attractive to the opposite sex. You get along well with others, especially young people and children. Your popularity is on the rise. Pursue a creative project.

Monday, December 8 (Moon in Aries)   The moon is in your seventh house. You could negotiate or sign a contract. You take the initiative with your partner; emotions could get volatile. It's difficult to maintain an objective and detached point of view. Be careful not to let others manipulate your feelings.

Tuesday, December 9 (Moon in Aries to Taurus 1:53 a.m.)   It's a number 2 day. That means partnerships are highlighted. Cooperation is the key word. Don't make waves. Don't rush or show resentment. Let things develop. Use your intuition regarding a relationship.

Wednesday, December 10 (Moon in Taurus)   The moon is in your eighth house. Your experiences are intense. The issue at hand could be a joint project or possessions that you share. Try not to manipulate or control the matter. Your actions, for better or worse, could attract the attention of powerful people.

Thursday, December 11 (Moon in Taurus to Gemini 2:34 a.m.)   It's a number 4 day. Take care of your obligations. Persevere to get things done. Control your impulses to wander. Be methodical and thorough. Tear down in order to rebuild. Be practical with money.

Friday, December 12 (Moon in Gemini)   As Mercury moves into your fourth house, you feel emotionally attached to your home environment. The domestic scene rules. Redecorate a room. You feel close to your parents. Domestic purchases are highlighted today and tomorrow.

Saturday, December 13 (Moon in Gemini to Cancer 1:41 a.m.)   It's a number 6 day. Diplomacy wins the way. Be sympathetic, kind, and compassionate. Do a good deed for someone. Attend to someone who is ill or in need of your help. A domestic adjustment works out for the best.

Sunday, December 14 (Moon in Cancer)   The moon is in your tenth house, and even though it's Sunday, you focus on a professional matter. You've got homework or you could visit coworkers at a holiday gathering. You're warm and receptive. Your prestige is enhanced.

Monday, December 15 (Moon in Cancer to Leo 1:23 a.m.) It's a number 8 day. Back to work on a power day. Business deals swing your way. You're in the driver's seat. You feel the power. Be especially careful not to run over others as you strive for your financial goals.

Tuesday, December 16 (Moon in Leo) With the moon in your eleventh house, friends play a significant role. They embolden you to pursue your wishes and dreams. You do exceedingly well working with a group, especially if you're involved in a project that emphasizes raising social consciousness.

Wednesday, December 17 (Moon in Leo to Virgo 3:36 a.m.) It's a number 1 day. You're at the top of your cycle. It's a new beginning. Your intuition is highlighted. You make connections that others overlook. Get out and meet new people. You attract creative individuals. Explore and discover.

Thursday, December 18 (Moon in Virgo) The moon is in your twelfth house. Withdraw and work behind the scenes. Don't worry about getting out in public. You could deal with some issues from your past. A long talk with a close friend or confidant helps resolve a matter.

Friday, December 19 (Moon in Virgo to Libra 9:23 a.m.) It's a number 3 day. Your attitude determines everything. Spread your good news. Ease up on routines. Your popularity is on the rise. Your imagination is keen. Remain flexible.

Saturday, December 20 (Moon in Libra) With the moon in your first house, the focus is on self-awareness. You're sensitive to the needs of others and therefore influenced easily. You may feel moody. It's all about your emotional self.

Sunday, December 21 (Moon in Libra to Scorpio 6:37 p.m.) It's a number 5 day. Promote new ideas; follow your curiosity. Freedom of thought and action is key. A change of scenery lifts your spirits. You're versatile and changeable. But be careful not to spread out and diversify too much.

Monday, December 22 (Moon in Scorpio)   The moon is in your second house. Handle finances. Pay your bills and collect what's owed to you. Investments pay off. But watch your spending.

Tuesday, December 23 (Moon in Scorpio)   Your experiences are emotional. You feel best when you're surrounded by your possessions. Investigate, research, and be aware of possible deception.

Wednesday, December 24 (Moon in Scorpio to Sagittarius 6:14 a.m.)   It's a number 8 day. It's your power day. You can go far with your plans and achieve financial success. You play with power, so be careful not to hurt others.

Thursday, December 25 (Moon in Sagittarius)   The moon is in your third house. You communicate well with relatives and neighbors. Spiritual values surface. You get your message across, but don't overdo it. Merry Christmas!

Friday, December 26 (Moon in Sagittarius to Capricorn 6:57 p.m.)   It's a number 1 day. You find yourself back at the top of your cycle. You get a fresh start. Make room for a new love. Get out and do something that you've never done before. You're determined and courageous.

Saturday, December 27 (Moon in Capricorn)   Mars moves into your fourth house. Dig in and work on a home-repair project. There's a lot of energy directed toward the domestic scene. Parents could play a role.

Sunday, December 28 (Moon in Capricorn)   Your ambition and drive to succeed are highlighted. Your responsibilities in the home increase. Your parents again could enter the picture. Maintain your emotional balance. A Taurus and a Virgo play a prominent role.

Monday, December 29 (Moon in Capricorn to Aquarius 7:44 a.m.)   It's a number 4 day. Get caught up on your work before the upcoming holiday. Tear down the old in order to build the new. You can overcome bureaucratic red tape. There could be a tendency to be stubborn, but you can overcome obstacles.

Tuesday, December 30 (Moon in Aquarius)   The moon is in your fifth house. Your emotions tend to overpower your intellect. You're in touch with your creative side. You could be somewhat possessive of loved ones, especially children. In romance, you feel a deep connection.

Wednesday, December 31 (Moon in Aquarius)   Saturn turns retrograde in your twelfth house. Your New Year's plans could get disrupted. Be aware that someone in your party could drink excessively. Don't allow that person to drive.

HAPPY NEW YEAR!

JANUARY 2009

Thursday, January 1 (Moon in Aquarius to Pisces 4:05 a.m.)   Mercury moves into your fifth house. Drama is highlighted. It's a good day for pursuing your artistic interests, especially a writing project, or writing in a journal. By writing out your thoughts, you can solve a problem that's been bothering you.

Friday, January 2 (Moon in Pisces)   The moon is in your sixth house. People look to you for help. You can improve whatever others are working on. Keep your resolutions about exercise and watch your diet. Attend to details related to your health. Make a doctor or a dentist appointment.

Saturday, January 3 (Moon in Pisces to Aries 4:50 a.m.)
Venus moves into your sixth house. You get along well with others. Your marriage and friendships are important to you. You're good at mediating any disputes.

Sunday, January 4 (Moon in Aries) The moon is in your seventh house. The focus continues on relationships, business and personal ones. You get along well with others, and you fit in just about anywhere. Loved ones and partners are more important than usual.

Monday, January 5 (Moon in Aries to Taurus 10:46 a.m.)
Jupiter moves into your fifth house. It's a great day to expand on any creative endeavor. A budding love interest might just blossom. Children and animals play a large role.

Tuesday, January 6 (Moon in Taurus) The moon is in your eighth house. Your experiences are more intense than usual. You have a strong sense of duty and feel obligated to fulfill your promises. Security is an important issue with you. It's a good time to deal with mortgage, insurance, or investment matters. You could also be taking a greater interest in a metaphysical subject, such as life after death.

Wednesday, January 7 (Moon in Taurus to Gemini 1:12 p.m.) It's a number 8 day. It's your power day. Unexpected money arrives. You attract financial success. Be aware that you're playing with power, so try not to hurt anyone.

Thursday, January 8 (Moon in Gemini) The moon is in your ninth house. You're a dreamer and a thinker. You may feel a need to get away. You yearn for a new experience. Plan a long trip. Sign up for a workshop or seminar. A foreign person or land could play a role.

Friday, January 9 (Moon in Gemini to Cancer 1:14 p.m.) You're at the top of your cycle. Be independent and creative; refuse to be discouraged by naysayers. Don't be afraid to turn in a new direction. Take the lead and trust your hunches.

Saturday, January 10 (Moon in Cancer)   There's a full moon in your tenth house. Reap what you've sown related to your career or profession. You gain an elevation in prestige. Business is highlighted. You're in the public eye. Avoid any excessive emotional displays.

Sunday, January 11 (Moon in Cancer to Leo 12:41 p.m.)   Mercury goes retrograde in your fifth house. Over the next three weeks, expect some confusion in your communication with your spouse or lover. You and your partner could get into a spat or a misunderstanding. Expect delays in your daily activities, especially related to a creative project.

Monday, January 12 (Moon in Leo)   The moon is in your eleventh house. Friendships are important to you. You could join a group of like-minded people to pursue a project, especially one in which social awareness plays a role. You work for the common good, but keep an eye on your own wishes and dreams.

Tuesday, January 13 (Moon in Leo to Virgo 1:33 p.m.)   It's a number five day. Think outside the box. Promote new ideas and follow your curiosity. Let go of old structures. Get a new point of view. Freedom of thought and action is key.

Wednesday, January 14 (Moon in Virgo)   The moon is in your twelfth house. Think carefully before you act. There's a tendency to undo all the positive actions you've taken. Avoid any self-destructive tendencies, especially during Mercury retrograde. Be aware of hidden enemies. You might feel a need to withdraw and work behind the scenes.

Thursday, January 15 (Moon in Virgo to Libra 5:31 p.m.)   It's a number 7 day. Secrets, intrigue, and confidential information play a role in your day. You investigate, analyze, or simply observe what's going on now. You quickly come to a conclusion and wonder why others don't see what you see. You can detect deception and recognize insincerity with ease.

Friday, January 16 (Moon in Libra)   The moon is in your first house. Your self-awareness or appearance is important. You're dealing with the person you are becoming. You may feel moody, withdrawn one moment, happy the next, then sad. It's all about your emotional self. Your feelings and thoughts are aligned.

Saturday, January 17 (Moon in Libra)   With the moon in your sign, romance is highlighted. Relationship issues figure prominently in your day. You're looking for harmony and peace. It's a good day for pursuing the creative arts. Attend a concert, a play, or a gallery opening.

Sunday, January 18 (Moon in Libra to Scorpio 1:21 a.m.)   You're at the top of your cycle again. Stress originality in whatever you pursue. You make connections that others overlook. You're determined and courageous. In romance, something new is developing.

Monday, January 19 (Moon in Scorpio)   The moon is in your second house. You feel strongly about a money issue. Finances and material goods are important to you and give you a sense of security. You identify emotionally with your possessions or whatever you value.

Tuesday, January 20 (Moon in Scorpio to Sagittarius 12:31 p.m.)   It's a number 3 day. You're innovative and creative; you communicate well. Your imagination is keen; your popularity is on the rise. Your attitude determines everything. Ease up on routines. Spread your good news.

Wednesday, January 21 (Moon in Sagittarius)   The moon is in your third house. Your communications with others are subjective. Take what you know and share it with others. However, keep conscious control of your emotions when getting your ideas across. Your thinking can be unduly influenced by the past.

Thursday, January 22 (Moon in Sagittarius)   You're restless, impulsive, and inquisitive today. Don't limit yourself. Attend a sporting event. Make use of your sense of humor. Look to the big picture, not just the details.

Friday, January 23 (Moon in Sagittarius to Capricorn 1:19 a.m.)   It's a number 6 day. Service to others is the theme of the day. You offer advice and support. Be sympathetic, kind, generous, and tolerant. Diplomacy wins the way.

Saturday, January 24 (Moon in Capricorn)   The moon is in your fourth house. Spend time with your family and loved ones. Stick close to home. You're dealing with the foundations of who you are and who you are becoming. A parent plays a role.

Sunday, January 25 (Moon in Capricorn to Aquarius 1:57 p.m.)   It's a number 8 day. Play it your way. Open your mind to a new approach, and you can attract financial success. You have a chance to gain recognition, fame, and power.

Monday, January 26 (Moon in Aquarius)   There's a new moon in your fifth house. That means it's a great time for a new love affair or pursuing a new project. Your creative juices are flowing. A door opens or a door shuts behind you as you move on.

Tuesday, January 27 (Moon in Aquarius)   Group and social events are highlighted. Play your hunches. Look beyond the immediate. You have a greater sense of freedom. You're looking at new options. Stress your originality. Find a new perspective.

Wednesday, January 28 (Moon in Aquarius to Pisces 1:13 a.m.)   It's a number 2 day. Don't make waves. Don't rush or show resentment. Let things develop. Cooperation is highlighted. Use your intuition to get a sense of your day. Be kind and understanding.

Thursday, January 29 (Moon in Pisces)   The moon is in your sixth house. It's a service day. Others rely on you. Help others, but don't deny your own needs. Keep your resolutions about exercise; watch your diet.

Friday, January 30 (Moon in Pisces to Aries 10:25 a.m.)   It's a number 4 day. Your organizational skills are highlighted. Stay focused. Control your impulses to wander off task. You're building foundations for an outlet for your creativity, so emphasize quality.

Saturday, January 31 (Moon in Aries)   The moon is in your seventh house. The focus turns to relationships, business and personal ones. You get along well with others, and you can fit in just about anywhere. Loved ones and partners are more important than usual. A legal matter could come to your attention.

FEBRUARY 2009

Sunday, February 1 (Moon in Aries to Taurus 5:09 p.m.)   Mercury goes direct in your fifth house. That means any confusion, miscommunication, and delays that you've been experiencing, especially related to a creative project, children, or a love interest, recede into the past.

Monday, February 2 (Moon in Taurus)   Venus moves into your seventh house. It's a great day for romance with your partner. Personal and business-related relationships work well.

Tuesday, February 3 (Moon in Taurus to Gemini 9:15 p.m.)   It's a number 5 day. Try a new approach. Get a new point of view. Change and variety are highlighted. You're versatile, but be careful not to spread out and diversify too much.

Wednesday, February 4 (Moon in Gemini)   Mars moves into your fifth house. You're highly competitive related to a creative project. You're also aggressively seeking sex for pleasure. Your sexual drive is strong; you're willing to take a chance. Alternately, you could be putting in lots of energy in your dealings with children.

Thursday, February 5 (Moon in Gemini to Cancer 11:06 p.m.)   It's a number 7 day. You could be actively investigating a matter of importance to you. There could be secret dealing involved. Knowledge is essential to success. Gather information, but don't make any absolute decisions until tomorrow.

Friday, February 6 (Moon in Cancer)   The moon is in your tenth house. Professional concerns and business dealings are highlighted. You gain an elevation of prestige for all your hard work. Your life is more public. You're emotional and warm toward coworkers.

Saturday, February 7 (Moon in Cancer to Leo 11:44 p.m.)   It's a number 9 day. Finish what you started. Visualize the future, set your goals, and get to work. Look beyond the immediate. Make room for something new.

Sunday, February 8 (Moon in Leo)   The moon is in your eleventh house. Friends play an important role. You find strength in numbers, especially if you're working for a good cause. You make new connections; you can expect them to be deep and meaningful. Superficial friendships tend to fade.

Monday, February 9 (Moon in Leo)   There's a lunar eclipse in your eleventh house. Yesterday's energy related to friendships flows on. You can expect to experience a strong emotional reaction to an event related to a group or friends. Social consciousness plays a role.

Tuesday, February 10 (Moon in Leo to Virgo 12:39 a.m.)   It's a number 3 day. Enjoy the harmony, beauty, and pleasures of life. Beautify your home. Remain flexible. Your imagination is keen. Your intuition is highlighted. You communicate well; you're warm and receptive to what others say.

Wednesday, February 11 (Moon in Virgo)   The moon is in your twelfth house. Work behind the scenes. You're sensitive to what others say or do. Think carefully before you act. There's a tendency to undo all the positive actions you've taken. Avoid any self-destructive tendencies; be aware of hidden enemies.

Thursday, February 12 (Moon in Virgo to Libra 3:34 a.m.)   It's a number 5 day. Change is highlighted. Take risks. You're versatile and changeable, but be careful not to diversify too much.

Friday, February 13 (Moon in Libra)   The moon is on your ascendant. That means the way you see yourself is the way others see you. You're recharged for the month ahead; this makes you more appealing to the public. You're physically vital; you can expect relations with the opposite sex to go well.

Saturday, February 14 (Moon in Libra to Scorpio 9:52 a.m.)   It's a number 7 day. You work best on your own today. Knowledge is essential to success. Gather information, but don't make any absolute decisions until tomorrow. Go with the flow. Secrets or intrigue could play a role. You investigate, analyze, or simply observe what's going on.

Sunday, February 15 (Moon in Scorpio)   The moon is in your second house. Expect emotional experiences related to money. Money and material goods are important to you and give you a sense of security. You identify emotionally with your possessions or whatever you value. Watch your spending.

Monday, February 16 (Moon in Scorpio to Sagittarius 7:54 p.m.)   It's a number 9 day. It's a favorable time to complete a project. Clear up odds and ends. Make room for something new. Take an inventory on where things are going in your life. Make a donation to a worthy cause.

Tuesday, February 17 (Moon in Sagittarius)   The moon is in your third house. You write from a deep place. Work on a writing project. Be aware that your thinking could be unduly influenced by matters from the past. A female relative plays a role.

Wednesday, February 18 (Moon in Sagittarius)   Today you see the big picture, not just the details. Worldviews are emphasized. If you're involved in a publishing project, look for good news. You're feeling restless, impulsive, and inquisitive. Think abundance and prosperity.

Thursday, February 19 (Moon in Sagittarius to Capricorn 8:26 a.m.)   It's a number three day. You're innovative and creative; you communicate well. Enjoy the harmony, beauty, and pleasures of life. Beautify your home. Remain flexible.

Friday, February 20 (Moon in Capricorn)   The moon is in your fourth house. Spend time with your family and loved ones. You feel close to your roots. Stick close to home, if possible. A parent plays a role. Work on a home-repair project.

Saturday, February 21 (Moon in Capricorn to Aquarius 9:06 p.m.)   It's a number 5 day. Think freedom, no restrictions. Take risks; experiment. Release old structures; get a new point of view.

Sunday, February 22 (Moon in Aquarius)   The moon is in your fifth house. There could be more involvement

254

with kids. You feel strongly attached to loved ones, particularly children. You're more protective and nurturing, but eventually you need to let go. You're emotionally in touch with your creative side.

Monday, February 23 (Moon in Aquarius)   Play your hunches. Look beyond the immediate. Help others, but dance to your own tune. Your wishes and dreams come true. You have a greater sense of freedom as you come up with new options. You find a new perspective.

Tuesday, February 24 (Moon in Aquarius to Pisces 8:00 a.m.)   It's a new moon and a number 8 day. That means there are opportunities related to money matters. A doorway opens. It's your power day.

Wednesday, February 25 (Moon in Pisces)   The moon is in your sixth house. It's a service day. Others rely on you for help. You're the one others go to for help. You improve, edit, and refine the work of others. Help others, but don't deny your own needs, and don't let your fears hold you back.

Thursday, February 26 (Moon in Pisces to Aries 4:24 p.m.)   It's a number 1 day. Be independent and creative; refuse to be discouraged by naysayers. You get a fresh start. You can take the lead on a new project. You're determined and courageous.

Friday, February 27 (Moon in Aries)   The moon is in your seventh house. You get along well with others. You can fit in just about anywhere. Loved ones and partners are more important than usual. Take time to consider how others see you. You're in the public eye.

Saturday, February 28 (Moon in Aries to Taurus 10:34 p.m.)   It's a number 3 day. You get your ideas across. You're curious and inventive. Your attitude determines everything. Spread your good news. Ease up on routines.

MARCH 2009

Sunday, March 1 (Moon in Taurus)   The moon is in your eighth house of shared resources and investments. Your experiences are more intense than usual. You have a strong sense of duty; you feel obligated to fulfill your promises. Security is an important issue with you. Deal with mortgages, insurance, and investments.

Monday, March 2 (Moon in Taurus)   You could be feeling somewhat stubborn and fixed in your opinions. You're highly sensual. Exercise and deal with any health issues. Be practical with money. Think carefully before making a major purchase.

Tuesday, March 3 (Moon in Taurus to Gemini 3:00 a.m.)   It's a number 6 day. Service to others is the theme of the day. You offer advice and support. Diplomacy wins the way. Focus on making people happy. You'll be glad you did.

Wednesday, March 4 (Moon in Gemini)   The moon is in your ninth house. You're a dreamer and a thinker. You may feel a need to get away. You yearn for a new experience. Plan a long trip or sign up for a workshop or seminar.

Thursday, March 5 (Moon in Gemini to Cancer 6:08 a.m.)   It's a number 8 day. It's your power day. Unexpected money arrives. Focus on a power play, but be aware that you're playing with power, so try not to hurt anyone.

Friday, March 6 (Moon in Cancer)   Venus goes retrograde in your seventh house. There could be some confusion and mixups in any intimate relationship. Don't make any important decisions regarding a relationship until Venus goes direct on April 17. It's not a very good time to get married. Expect delays related to relationships.

Saturday, March 7 (Moon in Cancer to Leo 8:26 a.m.)   It's a number 1 day. You make connections that

256

others overlook. You're determined and courageous. Trust your hunches. Intuition is highlighted. You get a fresh start. In romance, something new is developing, but make sure your read yesterday's daily horoscope.

Sunday, March 8—Daylight Saving Time Begins (Moon in Leo)   Mercury moves into your sixth house. You do very well handling any paperwork, especially if it deals with a service issue. You're very adept at handling details. Avoid worrying too much, watch your diet, and take care of your health.

Monday, March 9 (Moon in Leo to Virgo 11:35 a.m.)   It's a number 3 day. Your charm and wit are appreciated today. Your imagination is keen; you communicate well. You're warm and receptive to what others say. Your popularity is definitely on the rise.

Tuesday, March 10 (Moon in Virgo)   There's a full moon in your twelfth house. You reap what you've sown related to deep emotional issues. Whatever you've been doing behind the scenes comes to fruition. Your intuition is heightened.

Wednesday, March 11 (Moon in Virgo to Libra 2:47 p.m.)   It's a number 5 day. You're versatile and changeable, but be careful not to spread yourself too thin. Release old structures; get a new point of view. Approach the day with an unconventional mind-set.

Thursday, March 12 (Moon in Libra)   The moon is in your first house. You're dealing with the person you're becoming. Your self-awareness and appearance take on new meaning. It's all about your emotional self and health. Your moods can shift from ebullient to sad and then back again in a short time.

Friday, March 13 (Moon in Libra to Scorpio 8:23 p.m.)   It's a number 7 day. Secrets, intrigue, and confidential information play a role. You work best on your own. Knowledge is essential to success. Gather information, but don't make any absolute decisions until tomorrow. Go with the flow.

Saturday, March 14 (Moon in Scorpio)   Mars moves into your sixth house. You're working hard and feeling energetic. You're probably doing something you like, and you want perfection. But be aware that your aggressive activities can cause others around you to feel neglected. Don't overlook the big picture.

Sunday, March 15 (Moon in Scorpio)   The moon is in your second house. There could be some emotional discussions related to money. Watch your spending. You feel a sense of security by surrounding yourself with the things that have meaning to you. It's not the objects themselves that are important, but the feelings and memories you associate with them.

Monday, March 16 (Moon in Scorpio to Sagittarius 5:22 a.m.)   It's a number 1 day. You're at the top of your cycle. Take the lead in a new project. You get a fresh start. Stress originality. In romance, something new is developing. Get out and meet people; have new experiences.

Tuesday, March 17 (Moon in Sagittarius)   The moon is in your third house. You're dealing with your everyday world, but you're thinking about the big picture. You get your ideas across, but you could be overinfluenced by past events. Stay in control of your emotions when talking with others, especially family members.

Wednesday, March 18 (Moon in Sagittarius to Capricorn 5:19 p.m.)   It's a number 3 day. Take time to relax, enjoy yourself, and recharge your batteries. You can influence people with your upbeat attitude. In business dealings, diversify. Insist on all the information, not just bits and pieces.

Thursday, March 19 (Moon in Capricorn)   Your ambition and drive to succeed are highlighted. Your responsibilities increase, but you might feel overworked. Self-discipline and structure are key. Maintain emotional balance. Sorry, it's not a particularly good day for pursuing romance.

Friday, March 20 (Moon in Capricorn)   The moon is in your fourth house. Spend time with your family and loved ones. Stick close to home, if possible. You're dealing with the foundations of who you are and who you are becoming. A parent might play a role.

Saturday, March 21 (Moon in Capricorn to Aquarius 6:07 a.m.)   It's a number 6 day. Do a good deed for someone. You offer advice and support. Be sympathetic, kind, and compassionate, but avoid scattering your energies. Be understanding and avoid confrontations. Diplomacy wins the way.

Sunday, March 22 (Moon in Aquarius)   The moon is in your fifth house. In love, there's greater emotional depth to a relationship. Spend time with children and pets. Work on a creative project.

Monday, March 23 (Moon in Aquarius to Pisces 5:08 p.m.)   It's a number 8 day. It's your power day, so focus on a power play. You attract financial success. You have a chance to gain recognition, fame, and power.

Tuesday, March 24 (Moon in Pisces)   The moon is in your sixth house. Keep your resolutions about exercise; watch your diet. Attend to details related to your health. Make a doctor or a dentist appointment. Help others, but don't deny your own needs.

Wednesday, March 25 (Moon in Pisces)   Mercury moves into your seventh house of partnerships. You tend to gravitate toward bright, articulate people. You communicate well; you're in a good position to bring two sides in a dispute together. You counsel and they listen!

Thursday, March 26   (Moon in Pisces to Aries 1:03 a.m.)   There's a new moon, and it's a number 2 day. That means that cooperation and partnership are highlighted again. A new opportunity arises. Your intuition focuses on relationships. Don't make waves. Don't rush or show resentment. Let things develop.

Friday, March 27 (Moon in Aries)   The moon joins Mercury in your seventh house as the high energy related to partnerships continues for a third day. You communicate well with a spouse or partner. It's all about working together. It could also relate to your communication with an unknown person, a contract, or a lawsuit.

Saturday, March 28   (Moon in Aries to Taurus 6:10 a.m.)   It's a number 4 day. Your organizational skills are highlighted, but try not to wander off task. Emphasize quality. You're building a creative foundation for your future. Tear down the old in order to rebuild. Be methodical and thorough.

Sunday, March 29 (Moon in Taurus)   The moon is in your eighth house. Security is an important issue with you. You want to feel firmly grounded. Be aware that your efforts could result in intense emotional experiences. An interest in metaphysics plays a role.

Monday, March 30   (Moon in Taurus to Gemini 9:37 a.m.)   It's a number 6 day. Do a good deed for someone. Visit someone who is ill or in need of help. Focus on making people happy. Be diplomatic, understanding, and generous with your time.

Tuesday, March 31 (Moon in Gemini)   The moon is in your ninth house. Your mind is active; you yearn for new experiences. You can create positive change through your ideas. A publishing project takes off. Publicity and advertising are emphasized.

Wednesday, April 1 (Moon in Gemini to Cancer, 12:31 p.m.)   It's a number 5 day. Get ready for change. Experiment and let go of old structures. Approach the day with an unconventional mind-set.

Thursday, April 2 (Moon in Cancer)   The moon is in your tenth house. Focus on your professional concerns. You could be dealing with bosses and others in power. You can be more responsive to the needs and moods of others around you. An office romance could be dangerous.

Friday, April 3 (Moon in Cancer to Leo 3:33 p.m.)   It's a number 7 day. You could be dealing with confidential information and intrigue. Dig deep for information. Express your desires, but avoid self-deception. Make sure that you see things as they are, not as you wish them to be.

Saturday, April 4 (Moon in Leo)   Pluto goes retrograde in your sixth house. Any efforts to improve your situation at work are on hold. You might want to change jobs, but it's best to hold off. Watch out for upset or delayed plans. You may need to back off from a situation before it's too late.

Sunday, April 5 (Moon in Leo to Virgo 7:02 p.m.)   It's a number 9 day. Finish what you started, and get ready for something new. But don't start anything. Look beyond the immediate. Visualize the future, set your goals, and get to work.

Monday, April 6 (Moon in Virgo)   The moon is in your eighth house. You could be dealing with inherited money, taxes, and investments. Whatever it is affects your feelings about shared income or possessions. Control your emotions.

Tuesday, April 7 (Moon in Virgo to Libra 11:23 p.m.)   It's a number 2 day. Use your intuition to get a sense of your day. Be kind and understanding. The spotlight is on relationships. Don't make waves. Don't rush or show resentment. Let things develop. Help comes through friends or a partner.

Wednesday, April 8 (Moon in Libra)   The moon is in your first house. You get your batteries recharged for the month ahead. You're feeling physically vital; you get along well with the opposite sex. Your feelings and thoughts are aligned.

Thursday, April 9 (Moon in Libra)   Mercury moves into your eighth house, and the moon is full. You investigate and get to the bottom of a mystery. You're seeking the truth. You could be pursuing a metaphysical subject, such as the connection between science and spirit. You can gain considerable knowledge through your intuition rather than through books. Joint resources play a role in your day.

Friday, April 10 (Moon in Libra to Scorpio 5:23 a.m.)   It's a number 5 day. Promote new ideas; follow your curiosity. Freedom of thought and action is key. It's a good day for a change of scenery. You could be planning a move to a new location. You can overcome obstacles with ease.

Saturday, April 11 (Moon in Scorpio)   The moon is in your second house. Financial matters take priority. You seek both financial and domestic security. You feel best surrounded by familiar objects. It's not the objects that are important but the feelings you associate with them.

Sunday, April 12 (Moon in Scorpio to Sagittarius 2:01 p.m.)   It's a number 7 day. You look into a mystery. Gather information, but don't make any absolute decisions until tomorrow. Go with the flow. Maintain emotional balance; avoid confusion and conflict.

Monday, April 13 (Moon in Sagittarius)   The moon is in your third house. Get your ideas across as you go about your everyday activities. Take what you've learned recently and tell others about it. But avoid getting overemotional, especially when dealing with neighbors or relatives.

Tuesday, April 14 (Moon in Sagittarius)   You see the big picture, not just the details. But you're feeling restless and impulsive. You're looking for something new. Plan a trip or sign up for a workshop. There's passion in relationships.

Wednesday, April 15 (Moon in Sagittarius to Capricorn 1:28 a.m.)   It's a number 1 day. You're at the top of your cycle. Trust your hunches. You're inventive. You're determined and courageous. A flirtation turns more serious.

Thursday, April 16 (Moon in Capricorn)   The moon is in your fourth house. Make an effort to spend more time at home with loved ones. Beautify your surroundings with a home-repair or redecoration project. Retreat to a private place for meditation.

Friday, April 17 (Moon in Capricorn to Aquarius 2:20 p.m.)   Venus goes direct in your seventh house. Create a new partnership or enhance an old one, whether it's personal or business-oriented. You're friendly and affectionate with loved ones.

Saturday, April 18 (Moon in Aquarius)   The moon is in your fifth house. Follow your heart on a creative project. You can tap deeply into the collective unconscious for inspiration. In love, there's greater emotional depth than usual. However, make an effort to avoid being overpossessive with a loved one, even though that's your tendency.

Sunday, April 19 (Moon in Aquarius)   Group and social events are highlighted. Help others, but dance to your own tune. Your individuality is stressed. Your visionary abilities are heightened. Look beyond the immediate.

Monday, April 20 (Moon in Aquarius to Pisces 1:56 a.m.) It's a number 6 day. It's all about service. Do a good deed for someone. Visit a sick family member. Focus on making people happy. A domestic adjustment works out for the best.

Tuesday, April 21 (Moon in Pisces) The moon is in your sixth house. Yesterday's energy flows on. It's another service day. Attend to daily details and be of service. Help your coworkers, but don't overlook your own needs. Make appointments that you've been putting off.

Wednesday, April 22 (Moon in Pisces to Aries 10:10 a.m.) Mars joins Venus in your seventh house. You exert new energy now in a partnership. You take the lead. However, you can create problems by being overaggressive in a relationship. Be sure to use tact in all your dealings.

Thursday, April 23 (Moon in Aries) The moon joins Mars and Venus in your seventh house. Partnerships once again play a key role. You have a strong desire to be accepted. You can fit in just about anywhere.

Friday, April 24 (Moon in Aries to Taurus 2:47 p.m.) There's a new moon in your eighth house. Opportunities related to shared resources arise. Deal with mortgages, insurance, and investments. Alternately, a doorway related to an interest in a metaphysical subject, such as life after death or past lives, could open.

Saturday, April 25 (Moon in Taurus) Tend to money matters, but set aside time for outdoor activities. Your health and physical stamina are highlighted. Go hiking or biking, or have a picnic. Get out in nature.

Sunday, April 26 (Moon in Taurus to Gemini 5:03 p.m.) It's a number 3 day. Your attitude determines everything. Spread your good news. Ease up on routines. Make time to listen to others. Your charm and wit are appreciated. In romance, you're an ardent lover and loyal.

Monday, April 27 (Moon in Gemini)   The moon is in your ninth house. You're probably feeling restless and looking beyond the everyday scope of your life. Ideas, philosophies, and worldviews catch your interest. You could be preparing for or planning a long trip to a foreign country now. Alternately, it's a good time to sign up for a workshop or seminar.

Tuesday, April 28   (Moon in Gemini to Cancer 6:39 p.m.)   It's a number 5 day. The emphasis is on freedom of thought and movement. Get ready for a change of scenery or a possible relocation. Experiment and find a new outlook.

Wednesday, April 29 (Moon in Cancer)   The moon is in your tenth house. Business dealings are highlighted. It's a good day for sales and dealing with the public. You get along well with fellow workers. Avoid any emotional displays in public.

Thursday, April 30   (Moon in Cancer to Leo 8:56 p.m.)   Mercury moves into your ninth house. Any interest in philosophy, religion, law, or publishing is highlighted. You have lot of ideas and beliefs, and you readily express them. Your curiosity about foreign cultures and travel expands.

MAY 2009

Friday, May 1 (Moon in Leo)   The moon is in your eleventh house. Friends play an important role, especially a Gemini and an Aquarius. You find meaning through friends and groups, especially a group of like-minded people working for the common good.

Saturday, May 2 (Moon in Leo)   It's a number 7 day. You investigate, analyze, or simply observe what's going on. You quickly come to a conclusion and wonder why others don't see what you see. You detect deception and recognize insincerity with ease. You work best on your own. Knowledge is essential to success.

Sunday, May 3 (Moon in Leo to Virgo 12:37 a.m.) The moon is in your twelfth house. Think carefully before you act or speak. If you're not careful, there's a tendency to undo all the positive actions you've taken. You might feel a need to withdraw. Take time to reflect and meditate.

Monday, May 4 (Moon in Leo to Virgo 12:37 a.m.) Take care of details related to your health. Start exercising; watch your diet. Stop fretting. You seek perfection, but don't get so compulsive about it. Stick close to home, focus on tidying up the house, and attend to tying up loose ends.

Tuesday, May 5 (Moon in Virgo to Libra 5:52 a.m.) It's a number 1 day. Don't be afraid to turn in a new direction. Trust your hunches. Get out and meet people; have new experiences. Creativity is highlighted. Express your opinions dynamically.

Wednesday, May 6 (Moon in Libra) Mercury goes retrograde in your ninth house. That means you can expect some delays and glitches in communication over the next three weeks, especially related to education or long-distance travel. If you're traveling to a class or workshop, leave plenty of time for traffic congestion.

Thursday, May 7 (Moon in Libra to Scorpio 12:48 p.m.) It's a number 3 day. Enjoy the harmony, beauty, and pleasures of life. Your attitude determines everything. Like yesterday, you communicate well. You're warm and receptive to what others say. You're curious and inventive.

Friday, May 8 (Moon in Scorpio) The moon is in your second house. Money and material goods are important and give you a sense of security. You identify emotionally with your possessions or whatever you value. You may be dealing with payments and collecting what's owed to you. Look at your priorities in handling your income.

Saturday, May 9 (Moon in Scorpio to Sagittarius 9:50 p.m.) There's a full moon in your second house. It's a time of completion related to money issues. You reap what you've sown. You equate your financial assets with emotional security.

Sunday, May 10 (Moon in Sagittarius) The moon is in your third house. You write from a deep place. Be aware that your thinking might be unduly influenced by the past. Take what you know and share it with others. However, keep conscious control of your emotions when communicating.

Monday, May 11 (Moon in Sagittarius) You're restless, impulsive, and inquisitive. See the big picture, not just the details. Education, workshops, publishing, seminars, or travel influence your day. The law, the justice system, or jury duty might play a role. Spiritual values arise. Worldviews are emphasized.

Tuesday, May 12 (Moon in Sagittarius to Capricorn 9:10 a.m.) It's a number 8 day. It's your power day. Open your mind to a new approach. Unexpected resources arrive. You can go far with your plans and achieve financial success.

Wednesday, May 13 (Moon in Capricorn) The moon is in your fourth house. You're dealing with the foundations of who you are and who you are becoming. Work at home, if possible. Retreat to a private place to spend some time in meditation. But come out of hiding and do something with family members. Make an effort to beautify your home.

Thursday, May 14 (Moon in Capricorn to Aquarius 10:03 p.m.) It's a number 1 day. You're at the top of your cycle again. Follow any intuitive leads. Be independent; refuse to be discouraged by naysayers. You get a fresh start.

Don't be afraid to turn in a new direction. Trust your hunches.

Friday, May 15 (Moon in Aquarius)   The moon is in your fifth house. Your emotions tend to overpower your intellect. You're in touch with your creative side. You feel strongly attached to loved ones, particularly children. But eventually you need to let go.

Saturday, May 16 (Moon in Aquarius)   Saturn goes direct in your twelfth house. Unconscious attitudes can be difficult. So can relations with women. You feel best working behind the scenes and keeping your feelings to yourself. Follow your intuition and work on your self-confidence.

Sunday, May 17 (Moon in Aquarius to Pisces 10:18 a.m.)   It's a number 4 day. Your organizational skills are highlighted. Control your impulses. Take care of your obligations. You're building foundations for an outlet for your creativity.

Monday, May 18 (Moon in Pisces)   The moon is in your sixth house. It's a service-oriented day. You improve, edit, and refine the work of others. Don't let your fears hold you back.

Tuesday, May 19   (Moon in Pisces to Aries 7:31 p.m.)   It's a number 6 day. It's another service day. Diplomacy wins the way. Do a good deed for someone. Focus on making people happy. Be sympathetic, kind, and compassionate, but avoid scattering your energies.

Wednesday, May 20 (Moon in Aries)   The moon is in your seventh house. The focus turns to personal relationships, business and personal ones. You get along well with others. You comprehend the nuance of a situation, but it's difficult to go with the flow. It's a challenge to remain detached and objective.

Thursday, May 21 (Moon in Aries)   It's a number 8 day. It's your power day again. You attract financial success. Focus on a power play. But be aware that you're playing with power, so try not to hurt anyone. You have a chance to gain recognition, fame, and power.

Friday, May 22 (Moon in Aries to Taurus 12:41 a.m.)   The moon is in your eighth house. After your success yesterday, you could attract the attention of powerful people. Your experiences could be more intense than usual, especially if they deal with shared belongings. A metaphysical subject, such as life after death or astrology, catches your attention.

Saturday, May 23 (Moon in Taurus)   Health and physical activity are highlighted. It's a good day for gardening, cultivating ideas, doing practical things, or handling money matters. Get out in nature. Your senses are heightened.

Sunday, May 24 (Moon in Taurus to Gemini 2:34 a.m.)   There's a new moon in your ninth house. A door opens for a long journey to a foreign country. Alternately, you take new interest in worldviews, ideas, philosophy, and mythology. Sign up for a workshop or seminar. Follow whatever opportunity opens for you.

Monday, May 25 (Moon in Gemini)   Yesterday's energy flows on. You're a dreamer and a thinker. You may feel a need to get away. Your mind is active; you yearn for a new experience. Worldviews are emphasized. A publishing project goes well.

Tuesday, May 26 (Moon in Gemini to Cancer 2:58 a.m.)   It's a number 3 day. Think positive; stay optimistic. Others look to you for inspiration. You can influence people with your upbeat attitude. In business dealings, diversify. Insist on all the information, not just bits and pieces.

Wednesday, May 27 (Moon in Cancer) The moon is in your tenth house. Professional concerns are the focus. You gain an elevation in prestige. Your life is more public. You feel close to coworkers, but don't blur the boundaries between your private and professional lives.

Thursday, May 28 (Moon in Cancer to Leo 3:45 a.m.) Neptune goes retrograde in your ninth house. You could encounter delays and miscommunication related to a long journey. Alternately, you could be confused about religion and spirituality. Remember that what's true and real for one person might not make sense to someone else.

Friday, May 29 (Moon in Leo) The moon is in your eleventh house. You get along better with friends and associates. Your sense of security is tied to your relationships and to your friends. Your interests are so diverse that others might think you lack depth. Work for the common good, but keep an eye on your own wishes and dreams.

Saturday, May 30 (Moon in Leo to Virgo 6:18 a.m.) Mercury goes direct in your eighth house. Any delays related to tax issues, insurance, or investments come to an end. Everything works better, including computers and other electronic equipment.

Sunday, May 31 (Moon in Virgo) Mars moves into your eighth house. You make use of any specialized knowledge or skills you have. You investigate a matter thoroughly. It's a great day for problem solving and attending to details. Your sexual desires are strong; you're very grounded with the one you love.

JUNE 2009

Monday, June 1 (Moon in Virgo to Libra 12:17 p.m.) It's a number 7 day. You work best on your own. You investigate, analyze, or simply observe what's going on. Knowledge is essential to success. Gather information, but don't make any absolute decisions until tomorrow.

Tuesday, June 2 (Moon in Libra)   The moon is in your first house. It's all about your health and emotional self. You're sensitive and responsive regarding the needs of others. You easily change your mind. You're restless and uncertain what to do.

Wednesday, June 3 (Moon in Libra to Scorpio 7:45 p.m.)   It's a number 9 day. Finish what you started. Visualize the future, set your goals, and get to work. Look beyond the immediate. Get ready for something new. Strive for universal appeal.

Thursday, June 4 (Moon in Scorpio)   The moon is in your second house. You identify emotionally with your possessions or whatever you value. Money and material goods are important to you and give you a sense of security. However, watch your spending. Put off making any major purchases.

Friday, June 5 (Moon in Scorpio)   Investigate, research, and dig deep. Be aware of things happening in secret and of possible deception. Forgive and forget; try to avoid going to extremes. Control issue might arise.

Saturday, June 6 (Moon in Scorpio to Sagittarius 5:25 a.m.)   Venus moves into your eighth house. You can gain financially through a marriage or any type of partnership. Things might seem easy, but don't just lie back. Get motivated.

Sunday, June 7 (Moon in Sagittarius)   There's a full moon in your third house. You communicate well; as a result, you reap what you've sown. Whatever you've been doing in your daily life or with neighbors or relatives pays off generously—unless you've acted in a negative way.

Monday, June 8 (Moon in Sagittarius to Capricorn 5:01 p.m.)   It's a number 5 day. Change your perspective. Approach the day with an unconventional mind-set. Release old structures; get a new point of view. Remain positive. Promote new ideas. Be careful not to spread out and diversify too much.

Tuesday, June 9 (Moon in Capricorn)   The moon is in your fourth house. You're dealing with the foundations of who you are and who you are becoming. Retreat to a private place for meditation. It's a good day for dream recall. Change a bad habit. A parent plays a role.

Wednesday, June 10 (Moon in Capricorn)   Your ambition and drive to succeed are highlighted. You're feeling financially flush. With your success comes new responsibilities. You may feel overworked. Don't ignore your exercise routine.

Thursday, June 11 (Moon in Capricorn to Aquarius 5:53 a.m.)   It's a number 8 day. It's your power day again. Be courageous. Open you mind to a new approach. You attract financial success.

Friday, June 12 (Moon in Aquarius)   The moon is in your fifth house. Just try to be yourself. There's greater quality in a relationship. You might be possessive of loved ones. You're protective and nurturing toward children.

Saturday, June 13 (Moon in Aquarius to Pisces 5:33 p.m.)   It's a number 1 day. You're at the top of your cycle again. Stress originality. In romance, something new is developing. Refuse to deal with people who have closed minds.

Sunday, June 14 (Moon in Pisces)   The moon is in your sixth house. It's a service day. Help others where you can. Visit someone who is ill, but don't deny your own needs, especially if it's related to your own health. Keep your resolutions about exercise; watch your diet. Emotional repression is likely.

Monday, June 15 (Moon in Pisces)   Jupiter goes retrograde in your fifth house. Your creative life is expanding. A romance takes on new dimensions. Think abundance. Whatever you're pursuing related to a creative project, a love interest, or children goes well on a large scale.

Tuesday, June 16 (Moon in Pisces to Aries 4:52 a.m.)   It's a number 4 day. Organizational skills are highlighted. You're building foundations for the future. Persevere to get things done. Emphasize quality. Be bold and courageous. You're developing outlets for your creativity.

Wednesday, June 17 (Moon in Aries)   The moon is in your seventh house. The focus is on partnerships, both personal and professional. Like yesterday, be careful how you deal with disagreements. Any conflict will be more emotional than usual. It's difficult to remain detached and objective.

Thursday, June 18 (Moon in Aries to Taurus 11:21 a.m.)   It's a number 6 day. Focus on making people happy. Diplomacy wins the way. Be sympathetic, kind, generous, and tolerant. Be understanding and avoid confrontations. Dance to your own tune.

Friday, June 19 (Moon in Taurus)   The moon is in your eighth house. Take care of any matters related to taxes, insurance, or investments. Be aware that emotions can get intense, especially when dealing with shared resources. Metaphysics could play a role.

Saturday, June 20 (Moon in Taurus to Gemini 2:01 p.m.)   It's a number 8 day. It's your power day. Expect a financial windfall or a gift that comes out of the blue. You attract financial success.

Sunday, June 21 (Moon in Gemini)   The moon is in your ninth house. You're feeling as if you need to get away. Plan a trip or sign up for a seminar or workshop. A foreign country or person of foreign birth could play a role.

Monday, June 22 (Moon in Gemini to Cancer 2:12 p.m.)   There's a new moon in your tenth house. Opportunities come your way in the workplace. You're more responsive to the needs and moods of a group and of the public in general. It's a good day for sales and dealing with the public.

Tuesday, June 23 (Moon in Cancer)   The moon is in your tenth house. You communicate well with coworkers. You're bold and dramatic, but also more responsive to the needs of a group.

Wednesday, June 24 (Moon in Cancer to Leo 1:51 a.m.)   It's a number 3 day. Your popularity is on the rise. Spread your good news. Ease up on routines. You're curious and inventive. You communicate well. You're warm and receptive to what others say.

Thursday, June 25 (Moon in Leo)   The moon is in your eleventh house. You get along better with friends and associates. Focus on your wishes and dreams. Examine your overall goals.

Friday, June 26 (Moon in Leo to Virgo 2:47 p.m.)   It's a number 5 day. Get ready for adjustments that could include a possible move or relocation. You're versatile and changeable. Get a new point of view. Experiment.

Saturday, June 27 (Moon in Virgo)   The moon is in your twelfth house. Think carefully before you act. There's a tendency to undo all the positive actions you've taken. Avoid any self-destructiveness. Be aware of hidden enemies. You feel best working behind the scenes.

Sunday, June 28 (Moon in Virgo to Libra 6:25 p.m.) It's a number 7 day. Dig deep into a mystery. You're pursuing the unknown. You could be dealing with confidential information, secrets, and intrigue. Gather information, but don't make any immediate decisions based on what you learn.

Monday, June 29 (Moon in Libra) The moon is in your first house today. Everything you do is filtered through your sense of self. Your self-awareness and appearance are highlighted. Your feelings and thoughts are aligned. You get recharged for the month ahead.

Tuesday, June 30 (Moon in Libra) Romance is highlighted. Relationship issues figure prominently in your day. You're seeking harmony and peace as you try to keep everyone in balance around you. You arbitrate any disputes that come up.

JULY 2009

Wednesday, July 1 (Moon in Libra to Scorpio 1:20 a.m.) Uranus goes retrograde in your sixth house. Things could get erratic related to your daily work or health. You're originality can get you in trouble with a boss. You tend to experiment with alternative health methods.

Thursday, July 2 (Moon in Scorpio) The moon is in your second house. Deal with your finances; plan how to spend your income. You feel emotionally tied to certain possessions that make you feel secure. Alternately, you discuss your values openly.

Friday, July 3 (Moon in Scorpio to Sagittarius 11:12 a.m.) Mercury moves into your tenth house. You can use your speaking and writing abilities to move ahead in your profession. You get along well with others at work, but you don't feel any strong emotional attachments at this time. Work out a new strategy to advance your career.

Saturday, July 4 (Moon in Sagittarius)   The moon is in your third house. Take what you know and share it with others. However, keep conscious control of your emotions when communicating. Your thinking is unduly influenced by things of the past. You take a few short trips handling your everyday chores.

Sunday, July 5 (Moon in Sagittarius to Capricorn 11:08 p.m.)   Venus moves into your ninth house. You have a love of travel, philosophy, and art. You appreciate the finer things in life. Plan a long journey.

Monday, July 6 (Moon in Capricorn)   The moon is in your fourth house. Family matters play a big part. You're dealing with the foundations of who you are. Spend time with family and loved ones; make an effort to beautify your home. Your surroundings are a reflection of your personality.

Tuesday, July 7 (Moon in Capricorn)   There's a lunar eclipse in your fourth house. You have a strong emotional reaction to something going on at home. You could be dealing with parents. You feel close to your roots.

Wednesday, July 8 (Moon in Capricorn to Aquarius 12:04 p.m.)   It's a number 6 day. It's another service day. Be sympathetic, kind, generous, and tolerant. Focus on making people happy. Be understanding and avoid confrontations. Dance to your own tune.

Thursday, July 9 (Moon in Aquarius)   The moon is in your fifth house. Your emotions tend to overpower your intellect. You're feeling in touch with your creative side. Be emotionally honest. Look for greater emotional depth in a relationship.

Friday, July 10 (Moon in Aquarius) It's a number 8 day. Focus on a power play. Business dealings go well, especially if you try a new approach. Unexpected money arrives. Keep in mind that you're playing with power, so be careful not to hurt others.

Saturday, July 11 (Moon in Aquarius to Pisces 12:44 a.m.) Mars moves into your ninth house. You're interested in travel, especially related to sports. You're aggressive in your pursuit of knowledge. You can be combative in defending your beliefs.

Sunday, July 12 (Moon in Pisces) The moon is in your sixth house. It's a service-oriented day. Help others, but don't deny your own needs. Visit someone who is sick, but attend to your own health concerns.

Monday, July 13 (Moon in Pisces to Aries 11:40 a.m.) It's a number 2 day. Cooperation is highlighted. Use your intuition to get a sense of the day. A partnership plays an important role. Be kind and understanding. Don't make waves. Go with the flow.

Tuesday, July 14 (Moon in Aries) The moon is in your seventh house. Yesterday's energy flows on. Personal relations are highlighted. You're dealing with partnerships, personal and business. Loved ones play an important role. Be careful that others don't manipulate your feelings. A legal matter comes to your attention.

Wednesday, July 15 (Moon in Aries to Taurus 6:30 p.m.) It's a number 4 day. Persevere to get things done. Don't get sloppy. Tear down the old in order to rebuild. Be methodical and thorough. You're building a creative base for your future. You may feel somewhat inhibited in showing affection.

Thursday, July 16 (Moon in Taurus) The moon is in your eighth house. You pursue an interest in a metaphysical subject, such as life after death, or past lives. Your experiences related to these matters are more intense than usual. Alternately, matters related to your belongings as well as things that you share take on added importance. You could be dealing with inheritances, insurance, and investments.

Friday, July 17 (Moon in Taurus to Gemini 11:42 p.m.) Mercury moves into your eleventh house. You get along well with others, exchanging thoughts and ideas. You work well with a group, even though you're not emotionally tied with these people. You're using your mental agility to pursue your wishes and dreams.

Saturday, July 18 (Moon in Gemini) The moon is in your ninth house. After all your hard work, you may feel you need a break from your usual routines. Your beliefs are strong and sincere, but changeable. You pursue an interest in new philosophy. Foreign travel is on your radar.

Sunday, July 19 (Moon in Gemini) It's a number 8 day. It's another power day. You have a chance to gain recognition, fame, and power, especially if you open your mind to a new approach. Be courageous, but be yourself. You're dealing with power, so don't do anything that hurts others.

Monday, July 20 (Moon in Gemini to Cancer 12:52 a.m.) The moon is in your tenth house. You're pushing ahead in your career. You've got your eye on a promotion. Aim high!

Tuesday, July 21 (Moon in Cancer) There's a solar eclipse in your tenth house. Events in your professional life that are out of your control work to your advantage. You could be ending a job or beginning a new one, especially one that has eluded you.

Wednesday, July 22 (Moon in Cancer to Leo 12:28 p.m.) The moon is in your eleventh house. Group activities work in your favor. You help the group, and the group provides you with a sense of security. Friends also play an important role. Focus on your wishes and dreams, but make sure that your goals remain an expression of who you really are.

Thursday, July 23 (Moon in Leo)   It's a number 3 day. Play your hunches. Have fun in preparation for tomorrow's discipline and focus. Make time to listen to others. You can influence people with your upbeat attitude. Take time to relax, enjoy yourself, and recharge your batteries.

Friday, July 24 (Moon in Leo to Virgo 12:24 a.m.)   The moon is in your twelfth house. You might feel a need to withdraw and work behind the scenes. The past could play a role. Take time to reflect and meditate. Communicate your deepest feelings to another person.

Saturday, July 25 (Moon in Virgo)   Stick close to home, and focus on tidying up the house. Take care of details, especially related to your health. Start exercising; watch your diet. Stop fretting.

Sunday, July 26 (Moon in Virgo to Libra 2:26 a.m.)   It's a number 6 day. Service to others is the theme of the day. You offer advice and support. Be diplomatic toward someone who is giving you a hard time. Be generous and tolerant, but know when to say enough is enough. Make time to dance to your own tune.

Monday, July 27 (Moon in Libra)   The moon is in your first house. You are sensitive and responsive regarding the needs of others, so you are easily influenced by those around you. The way you see yourself is the way others see you. You may feel moody, withdrawn one moment, happy the next, then sad. It's all about your emotional self.

Tuesday, July 28 (Moon in Libra to Scorpio 7:57 a.m.)   It's a number 8 day. Focus on a power play. Business discussions go well. You can go far with your plans and achieve financial success. Unexpected money arrives.

Wednesday, July 29 (Moon in Scorpio)   The moon is in your second house. Yesterday's energy flows on. Money and material goods are important to you now and give you a sense of security. You identify emotionally with your possessions or whatever you value. Watch your spending.

Thursday, July 30 (Moon in Scorpio to Sagittarius 5:10 p.m.)   It's a number 1 day. Take the lead; get a fresh start. Don't be afraid to turn in a new direction. Trust your hunches. Intuition is highlighted. You make connections that others overlook.

Friday, July 31 (Moon in Sagittarius)   Venus moves into your third house. You're socially active; you follow artistic pursuits. You get along famously with others. You see the big picture and find ways to expand your creative base. Good experiences from your past work to your benefit.

AUGUST 2009

Saturday, August 1 (Moon in Sagittarius)   The moon is in your third house. Your mental abilities are strong; you have an emotional need to reinvigorate your studies, especially regarding the past. You're attracted to historical or archaeological studies. You could be dealing with siblings or neighbors. Stay in control of your emotions when making your point.

Sunday, August 2 (Moon in Sagittarius to Capricorn 5:09 a.m.)   Mercury moves into your twelfth house. Any decisions you make are probably based on feelings rather than logic. Matters from the past affect your thinking. You tend to keep your thoughts to yourself.

Monday, August 3 (Moon in Capricorn)   The moon is in your fourth house. Get organized. You're dealing with the very foundations of who you are and who you are becoming. Make an effort to change a bad habit. It's best to work on your own and stay focused.

Tuesday, August 4 (Moon in Capricorn to Aquarius 6:08 p.m.)   It's a number 3 day. Your optimism and positive point of view are appreciated. You express yourself well and share your creative talents. Make time to listen to others. Relax and enjoy yourself.

Wednesday, August 5 (Moon in Aquarius)   There's a lunar eclipse in your fifth house. You react with strong emotions to an incident related to your love life, to a child, or to your creativity. You're possessive of loved ones and protective and nurturing toward children.

Thursday, August 6 (Moon in Aquarius)   The moon is in your fifth house. Yesterday's emotion flows on. Be aware that your emotions tend to overpower your intellect. If it feels right, take a chance. Sex for pleasure is emphasized.

Friday, August 7 (Moon in Aquarius to Pisces 6:35 a.m.)   It's a number 6 day. Diplomacy wins the way. Be generous, tolerant, and understanding. Do a good deed for someone. Focus on making people around you happy. A domestic adjustment works out for the best.

Saturday, August 8 (Moon in Pisces)   The moon is in your sixth house. Yesterday's energy related to service flows on. You're busy helping others in your daily work. You offer suggestions for improvements; then you move on to the next person. Take care of any health issues.

Sunday, August 9 (Moon in Pisces to Aries 5:24 p.m.)   It's a number 8 day. It's your power day again. You can go far with your plans and achieve financial success. You have an opportunity to succeed in whatever you're pursuing. Open your mind to a new approach, but don't do anything that could hurt others.

Monday, August 10 (Moon in Aries)   The moon is in your seventh house. A contract is on the table. Partnerships are emphasized. Women play a prominent role, but it's difficult to remain detached and objective.

Tuesday, August 11 (Moon in Aries)   It's a great time for initiating projects, launching new ideas, brainstorming. Be aware that emotions can be volatile. You're extremely persuasive and passionate about whatever you're doing, but you're also impatient. Avoid acting recklessly.

Wednesday, August 12 (Moon in Aries to Taurus 1:51 a.m.)   It's a number 2 day. Cooperation is highlighted. After yesterday's high energy, it's best to back off. Don't make waves. Focus on your direction and motivation. Where are you going and why? Your intuition focuses on relationships.

Thursday, August 13 (Moon in Taurus)   The moon is in your eighth house. You could attract the attention of powerful people. Your experiences could be more intense than usual. Matters related to shared belongings, investments, taxes, or insurance could play a role.

Friday, August 14 (Moon in Taurus to Gemini 7:27 a.m.)   It's a number 4 day. Tear down in order to rebuild. Revise and rewrite. Persevere to get things done, but emphasize quality. You're building a creative base for the future.

Saturday, August 15 (Moon in Gemini)   The moon is in your ninth house. You're probably feeling restless today and looking beyond the everyday scope of your life. Ideas, philosophies, and worldviews catch your interest. Sign up for a workshop or seminar on a subject that interests you, or plan a long journey to a foreign land.

Sunday, August 16 (Moon in Gemini to Cancer 10:14 a.m.)   It's a number 6 day. Service to others is the theme. You offer advice and support. Be diplomatic to anyone complaining or criticizing. Try to make people happy. Be sympathetic, kind, and compassionate. But avoid scattering your energies.

Monday, August 17 (Moon in Cancer)   The moon is in your tenth house. Your life is more public. You gain an elevation in prestige related to your profession and career. You get along better with coworkers, but don't blur the boundaries between your professional and personal lives.

Tuesday, August 18 (Moon in Cancer to Leo 10:57 a.m.)   It's a number 8 day. Unexpected money arrives as business discussions go well. You have a chance to gain recognition, fame, and power. You attract financial success. But remember that you're playing with power. Be careful not to hurt others.

Wednesday, August 19 (Moon in Leo)   The moon is in your eleventh house. You have deeper contact with friends. Focus on your wishes and dreams. You could get help in realizing them by joining a group of like-minded individuals.

Thursday, August 20 (Moon in Leo to Virgo 11:01 a.m.)   There's a new moon in your eleventh house. Yesterday's energy flows on, with opportunities arising. A doorway opens with the help of friends.

Friday, August 21 (Moon in Virgo)   The moon is in your twelfth house. Withdraw from the action and keep to yourself. Work on a solo project. Keep your feelings secret. Be aware that relations with women can be difficult. Things affecting you from the past could surface.

Saturday, August 22 (Moon in Virgo to Libra 12:12 p.m.)   It's a number 3 day. You're innovative and creative. Spread your good news; listen to others. Your attitude determines everything. Enjoy the harmony, beauty, and pleasures of life.

Sunday, August 23 (Moon in Libra)   The moon is in your first house. It's all about the emotional self. You tend to focus on your appearance and self-awareness. You also could be feeling strongly about a personal health issue or about details that you've overlooked regarding a matter of importance.

Monday, August 24 (Moon in Libra to Scorpio 4:17 p.m.)   It's a number 5 day. Get ready for changes in your life, along with a new point of view. Take a chance. Follow your curiosity. You can overcome obstacles with ease.

Tuesday, August 25 (Moon in Scorpio)   Mars moves into your tenth house as Mercury moves into your first house. You're putting a lot of energy into your personal life. You're in the public eye and making your ideas known. You're recharged and appealing to the public. The way you see yourself is the way others see you.

Wednesday, August 26 (Moon in Scorpio)   Venus moves into your eleventh house. Your friends and social contacts are impressed with whatever you're doing. Your popularity is on the rise. Your vitality and positive attitude are appreciated. You help others, and they help you pursue your wishes and dreams.

Thursday, August 27 (Moon in Scorpio to Sagittarius 12:16 a.m.)   The moon is in your third house. Express yourself through writing. Take what you know and share it with others. As you go about your everyday life, look to the big picture. Expect an invitation to a social event.

Friday, August 28 (Moon in Sagittarius)   You see the big picture, not just the details. You're restless, impulsive, and inquisitive. Don't limit yourself. Spiritual values arise. Worldviews are emphasized. In romance, there's more passion in a relationship.

Saturday, August 29 (Moon in Sagittarius to Capricorn 11:45 a.m.)   It's a number 1 day. Take the lead now. You get a new beginning. Don't be afraid to turn in a different direction. Trust your hunches. Stress originality. In romance, something is developing.

Sunday, August 30 (Moon in Capricorn)   The moon is in your fourth house. Spend time with your family and loved ones. Stick close to home. You're dealing with the foundations of who you are and who you are becoming. A parent plays a role. You feel a close tie to your roots.

Monday, August 31 (Moon in Capricorn)   It's a number 3 day. Some of yesterday's energy flows on. Enjoy the harmony, beauty, and pleasures of life. Beautify your home. Your attitude determines everything. Spread your good news; make time to listen to others.

SEPTEMBER 2009

Tuesday, September 1 (Moon in Capricorn to Aquarius 12:43 a.m.)   The moon is in your fifth house. There's greater depth in a relationship. But make sure that you're emotionally honest. It's a good creative time. You have the ability to tap deeply into the collective unconscious for inspiration.

Wednesday, September 2 (Moon in Aquarius)   Groups and social events are highlighted. Help others, but dance to your own tune. Your wishes and dreams come true. You have a greater sense of freedom. You're dealing with new ideas. You get a different perspective.

Thursday, September 3 (Moon in Aquarius to Pisces 12:59 p.m.)   It's a number 3 day. You're innovative; you communicate well. Remain flexible. Your intuition is highlighted. You're warm and receptive to what others say. Your attitude determines everything.

Friday, September 4 (Moon in Pisces)   There's a full moon in your sixth house. You reap what you've sown related to your daily work. Be of service to others, but don't limit yourself or let your fears hold you back. Get ready to move ahead, but take care of any health issues.

Saturday, September 5, (Moon in Pisces to Aries 11:15 p.m.)   It's a number 5 day. Approach the day with an unconventional mind-set. Freedom of thought and action is highlighted. Experiment. Be careful not to spread yourself too thin. Slow down and enjoy the day!

Sunday, September 6 (Moon in Aries)   Mercury goes retrograde in your first house for the next three weeks. There could be delays and confusion related to your health or other personal matters. You're restless and uncertain what to do. As a result, others might misunderstand you. Make sure you read the fine print on any contracts.

Monday, September 7 (Moon in Aries)   The moon is in your seventh house. The focus is on partnerships, both personal and professional. Be aware that any conflict will be more emotional than usual. It's difficult to stay detached and objective.

Tuesday, September 8 (Moon in Aries to Taurus 7:19 a.m.)   It's a number 8 day. It's your power day! Open your mind to a new approach to attain financial success. Be courageous, and be aware that you're being watched by people in power. Business dealings go well.

Wednesday, September 9 (Moon in Taurus)   The moon is in your eighth house. You attract power people. Your energy is more intense than usual. Your emotions could affect your feelings about shared belongings. An interest in metaphysics could play a role.

Thursday, September 10 (Moon in Taurus to Gemini 1:18 p.m.)   It's a number 1 day. You're at the top of your cycle again. Initiate a new project. Get out and meet people; have new experiences. You get a fresh start. Don't be afraid to turn in a new direction. Creative people play an important role.

Friday, September 11 (Moon in Gemini)   Pluto goes direct in your fourth house. You could experience some disruption in the home. There could be a power struggle among family members. You have a strong attachment to your home and property. You're not willing to give up without a fight.

Saturday, September 12 (Moon in Gemini to Cancer 5:20 p.m.)   It's a number 3 day. After all the tension yesterday, your energy settles down. Your attitude determines everything. Make use of your charm and wit. Others are impressed. Remain flexible. Be happy, positive, and upbeat. Relax and enjoy yourself.

Sunday, September 13 (Moon in Cancer)   The moon is in your tenth house. It's a good day for sales and dealing with the public. You get along well with coworkers. You're good at problem solving.

Monday, September 14 (Moon in Cancer to Leo 7:40 p.m.)   It's a number 5 day. Get a new point of view. Approach the day with an unconventional mind-set. Promote new ideas. Get ready for change. Experiment. You can overcome obstacles with ease.

Tuesday, September 15 (Moon in Leo)   The moon is in your eleventh house. You're very busy with friends. You put a lot of energy into group activities, and it should pay off, especially if you're involved in a project for the common good. All in all, you're moving closer to obtaining your wishes and dreams.

Wednesday, September 16 (Moon in Leo to Virgo 8:56 p.m.)   It's a number 7 day. Pursue the mystery. You're setting out on a journey into the unknown. Be aware of intrigue and confidential information. Dig deep for information, but don't make any absolute decisions until tomorrow. Stay emotionally balanced.

Thursday, September 17 (Moon in Virgo)　　The moon is in your twelfth house. You could have emotional dealings with institutions such as a hospital, a court, or a prison. Communicate your deepest feelings with a trusted ally or friend.

Friday, September 18 (Moon in Virgo to Libra 10:26 p.m.)　　There's a new moon in your twelfth house. By stepping away from the action and working behind the scenes you get a chance to start over. You might also gain an opportunity through contact with a large institution, such as a hospital, a government office, or a corporation.

Saturday, September 19 (Moon in Libra)　　The moon is on your ascendant. The way you see yourself is the way others see you. You're recharged for the month ahead; this makes you more appealing to the public. You're physically vital; relations with the opposite sex go well. You're sensitive to other people's feelings.

Sunday, September 20 (Moon in Libra)　　Venus moves into your twelfth house. It feels good to get away from all the activity and spend some quiet time alone. You keep your thoughts and emotions to yourself and tend to be somewhat secretive.

Monday, September 21 (Moon in Libra to Scorpio 1:52 a.m.)　　It's a number 3 day. People appreciate your sense of optimism and your upbeat point of view. You express yourself well and share your good news. Make time to listen to others. Relax and enjoy yourself.

Tuesday, September 22 (Moon in Scorpio)　　The moon is in your second house. It's a good day for finances and all money matters. Consider your priorities in handling your income. Collect what's owed you and make payments. Put off any big purchases for another few days. Your values play an important role.

Wednesday, September 23 (Moon in Scorpio to Sagittarius 8:44 a.m.)   It's a number 5 day. Freedom of thought and action is key. Approach the day with an unconventional mind-set. Promote new ideas. You're feeling versatile, but be careful not to diversify too much. You'll be in a hurry, so watch your step.

Thursday, September 24 (Moon in Sagittarius)   The moon is in your third house. You're probably taking care of your everyday needs. Take your cell phone with you. Get in touch with others, especially relatives. You'll have a message to pass on. A neighbor could play a surprising role.

Friday, September 25 (Moon in Sagittarius to Capricorn 7:19 p.m.)   It's a number 7 day. It's all about mystery, as you launch a journey into the unknown. Secrets, intrigue, and confidential information are at the heart of the matter. Knowledge is essential to success. Maintain emotional balance, and avoid making any important decisions for a couple days.

Saturday, September 26 (Moon in Capricorn)   Your ambition and drive to succeed are highlighted. Your responsibilities increase with your success. You could be feeling stressed. Self-discipline and structure are key. Your domestic scene needs attention.

Sunday, September 27 (Moon in Caprocorn)   The moon is in your fourth house. Spend time with your family. You feel emotionally secure in your home setting. The home is both a mental construct and a physical place. It's your sanctuary.

Monday, September 28 (Moon in Capricorn to Aquarius 8:07 a.m.)   It's a number 1 day. You get a fresh start. Don't be afraid to turn in a new direction. Trust your hunches. Stress originality. You're inventive; you make connections that others overlook. You're determined and courageous.

Tuesday, September 29 (Moon in Aquarius)   Mercury goes direct in your twelfth house. Your interest in the occult, the mystical, and the mysteries of the unknown plays a role. You communicate your ideas well to someone with similar interests. Misunderstandings are resolved, but it's still best to pursue your interests behind the scenes.

Wednesday, September 30 (Moon in Aquarius to Pisces 8:27 p.m.)   It's a number 3 day. Stay optimistic and remain flexible. Attitude determines everything. Listen to any intuitive nudges. Make time to listen to others. Your charm and wit are appreciated.

OCTOBER 2009

Thursday, October 1 (Moon in Pisces)   The moon is in your sixth house. It's a service-oriented day. Help others. Visit someone who is sick or in need of your help. But also tend to your own health concerns. Make a doctor or a dentist appointment.

Friday, October 2 (Moon in Pisces)   Your imagination is highlighted. Watch for psychic events. You feel inspired. Keep track of your dreams. Your ideas are ripe. You're compassionate and more sensitive to others. It's a day for deep healing.

Saturday, October 3 (Moon in Pisces to Aries 6:21 a.m.)   It's a number 4 day. Your organizational skills are highlighted. Control your impulses. Take care of obligations. Make an effort to avoid wandering off-task. Tear down the old in order to rebuild. Clean out a closet, the attic, or your garage.

Sunday, October 4 (Moon in Aries)   There's a full moon in your seventh house. You reap what you've sown related to a relationship. You harvest your rewards; you can aggressively assert yourself. A partnership works to your benefit.

Monday, October 5 (Moon in Aries to Taurus 1:34 p.m.)   It's a number 6 day. It's another service day. Focus on making people happy. Do a good deed for someone, but avoid scattering your energies. Be sympathetic, kind, generous, and tolerant.

Tuesday, October 6 (Moon in Taurus)   The moon is in your eighth house. Your sense of duty and obligation can affect your feelings about your belongings, as well as things that you share with others. Security is an important issue with you. Matters of sex, death, rebirth, rituals, and relationships emerge now. Your feelings are more intense than usual.

Wednesday, October 7 (Moon in Taurus to Gemini 6:47 p.m.)   It's a number 8 day. You attract financial success. You're playing with power, so be careful not to hurt others. You can go far with your plans and achieve financial success. Business discussions go well.

Thursday, October 8 (Moon in Gemini)   The moon is in your ninth house. You can create positive change through your ideas. Your mind is active; you yearn for new experiences. You can guide others in their intellectual development. A publishing project goes well.

Friday, October 9 (Moon in Gemini to Cancer 10:48 p.m.)   It's a number 1 day. Be independent and creative; refuse to be discouraged by naysayers. Stress originality. Refuse to deal with people who have closed minds. In romance, something new is developing.

Saturday, October 10 (Moon in Cancer)   The moon is in your tenth house. Professional concerns are the focus of the day, even though it's a weekend. You're more responsive to the needs and moods of a group and of the public in general. You're emotional and warm toward coworkers, but don't blur the boundary between your personal and professional lives.

Sunday, October 11 (Moon in Cancer)   You're sensitive to other people's moods. Tend to loved ones, do something with your children, or snuggle up to your sweetheart. Beautify your home. Take care of home repairs.

Monday, October 12 (Moon in Cancer to Leo 2:03 a.m.) Jupiter goes direct in your fifth house. Take a chance, and expand your horizons. You can move ahead on any creative project. Meanwhile, a personal relationship grows deeper and takes on new meaning. A family could be expanding.

Tuesday, October 13 (Moon in Leo)   The moon is in your eleventh house. You get along better with friends and associates. But your interests could be so diverse that others might think you lack depth. You work for the common good, but keep an eye on your own wishes and dreams.

Wednesday, October 14 (Moon in Leo to Virgo 4:46 a.m.) Venus moves into your first house. Your personal life is going well. You appear attractive to other people. There's also more involvement with the arts and women.

Thursday, October 15 (Moon in Virgo)   The moon is in your twelfth house. Unconscious attitudes can be difficult. Best to keep your feelings secret, especially in dealings with women. You communicate your deepest feelings with a confidant. It's a great day for a mystical or spiritual discipline. Your intuition is heightened.

Friday, October 16 (Moon in Virgo to Libra 7:30 a.m.) Mars moves into your eleventh house. You put out a lot of energy for a good cause. You work well with a group to achieve your goals. You organize and initiate. You arouse people's enthusiasm for the common good.

Saturday, October 17 (Moon in Libra)   The moon is in your first house. You may feel happy one moment and sad the next. You're sensitive to other people's feelings. The way you see yourself is the way others see you. There's greater focus on your self-awareness and health.

Sunday, October 18 (Moon in Libra to Scorpio 11:23 a.m.)   There's a new moon in your first house. New opportunities related to public appearances arise. You're recharged for the month ahead; this makes you more appealing to the public. You're physically vital; relations with the opposite sex go well.

Monday, October 19 (Moon in Scorpio)   The moon is in your second house. Expect emotional experiences related to money. You may be dealing with payments and collecting what's owed to you. You equate your financial assets with emotional security. Look at your priorities in handling your income.

Tuesday, October 20 (Moon in Scorpio to Sagittarius 5:50 p.m.)   It's a number 3 day. Think positive; stay optimistic. Others are impressed with your upbeat attitude. In business dealings, diversify. Insist on all the information, not just bits and pieces.

Wednesday, October 21 (Moon in Sagittarius)   The moon is in your third house. Your mental abilities are strong; you have an emotional need to reinvigorate your studies, especially regarding the past. You're attracted to historical or archaeological studies. Get in touch with a relative and offer your opinion on a matter.

Thursday, October 22 (Moon in Sagittarius)   You're restless, impulsive, and inquisitive. Your energy keeps driving you ahead. You're persistent in your search for knowledge as you look for the big picture. You might need to get away to find it.

Friday, October 23 (Moon in Sagittarius to Capricorn 3:40 a.m.)   It's a number 6 day. Focus on keeping everyone happy and in balance around you, but avoid scattering your energies. Some change or adjustment in the home scene works out for the best. Domestic purchases are highlighted. Be generous and tolerant.

Saturday, October 24 (Moon in Capricorn)   The moon is in your fourth house. Spend time at home with family and loved ones on this Saturday. Work on a project to beautify your home. But take time to retreat to a private place and spend some time in meditation.

Sunday, October 25 (Moon in Capricorn to Aquarius 3:08 p.m.)   It's a number 8 day. It's your power day. You have a chance to gain recognition and even fame. Keep in mind that you're playing with power. Be careful not to hurt others.

Monday, October 26 (Moon in Aquarius)   The moon is in your fifth house. You have an opportunity to achieve greater depth in a relationship, but it could take hard work to achieve. Be emotionally honest. It's also a good creative time. You have the ability to tap deeply into the collective unconscious.

Tuesday, October 27 (Moon in Aquarius)   Your visionary abilities are heightened, especially if you're working on a project for the common good. Friends come to your aid. You're dealing with an original approach to a problem. You work well with a group of like-minded people. Your wishes and dreams come true.

Wednesday, October 28 (Moon in Aquarius to Pisces 3:46 a.m.)   Mercury moves into your second house. You communicate your ideas well, especially if it's about ways to make money. You enjoy networking and teaching. Your intellect is keen, and you're focusing your mind on commerce. At the same time, you stick with your values.

Thursday, October 29 (Moon in Pisces)   Saturn moves into your first house. It's an important day. You're very serious and disciplined, but you also might feel moody and depressed. You could be saddled with a lot of responsibilities. If that's the case, your personal life is limited.

Friday, October 30 (Moon in Pisces to Aries 1:57 p.m.)   It's a number 4 day. The emphasis is on your organization skills. In romance, your persistence pays off. You're building a foundation for the future. Control your impulses to wander; take care of obligations. You could find missing papers.

Saturday, October 31 (Moon in Aries)   The moon is in your seventh house. It's all about working together, whether in a personal relationship or business partnership. Stay emotionally balanced. A legal matter or contract could come into play.

NOVEMBER 2009

Sunday, November 1—Daylight Saving Time Ends (Moon in Aries to Taurus 7:45 p.m.)   It's a number 3 day. Your intuition is highlighted. Social activities and spiritual values are stressed. Ease up on your routines. Spread your good news; make time to listen to others.

Monday, November 2 (Moon in Taurus)   There's a full moon in your eighth house. You reap what you've sown. That's especially true related to shared possessions or matters related to insurance, an inheritance, or taxes. If you're exploring a metaphysical subject, you gain illumination.

Tuesday, November 3 (Moon in Taurus to Gemini 11:53 p.m.)   It's a number 5 day. Variety and freedom of restrictions are emphasized. Look for a change of scenery. Take a risk or experiment with a new idea. Approach the day with an unconventional mind-set.

Wednesday, November 4 (Moon in Gemini) Neptune goes direct in your fifth house. Explore any creative project related to film, theater, or television. You could be working on a script or acting in a play. You're a true romantic. You're highly intuitive, and so are any children in your life.

Thursday, November 5 (Moon in Gemini) The moon is in your ninth house. You could be feeling restless and looking for something new. Your mind is active; you're curious about philosophy, mythology, or religion. You can create positive change through your ideas.

Friday, November 6 (Moon in Gemini to Cancer 2:43 a.m.) It's a number 8 day. It's a power day. If you play the lottery, buy an extra ticket today. It could be your day! Expect a financial windfall. Open your mind to the possibilities.

Saturday, November 7 (Moon in Cancer) Venus moves into your second house. You love the good things in life. You feel good about your belongings and the memories associated with them. You love the idea of making a lot of money, and you could do so through a creative endeavor.

Sunday, November 8 (Moon in Cancer to Leo 5:23 a.m.) It's a number 1 day. You're at the top of your cycle again. You get a fresh start. Stress originality. Trust your hunches, follow your intuition, and refuse to deal with people who have closed minds. If you're ready, make room for a new love.

Monday, November 9 (Moon in Leo) The moon is in your eleventh house. While yesterday you were taking the lead on something new, today you bring in friends or a group association. You get along well with others. You work for the common good; others support your wishes and dreams.

Tuesday, November 10 (Moon in Leo to Virgo 8:31 a.m.) It's a number 3 day. Stay optimistic. Your attitude determines everything. Your charm and wit are appreciated. You can influence people with your upbeat attitude. In romance, you're an ardent lover.

Wednesday, November 11 (Moon in Virgo) The moon is in your twelfth house. Retreat from public view and work behind the scenes. Unconscious attitudes can be difficult and could relate to the past. Share your deepest feelings with someone you trust.

Thursday, November 12 (Moon in Virgo to Libra 12:23 p.m.) It's a number 5 day. Freedom of thought and action is called for. You're versatile and adaptable. Get ready for change. Find a new perspective. Take a chance.

Friday, November 13 (Moon in Libra) The moon is on your ascendant. The way you see yourself is the way others see you. You're recharged for the month ahead; and this makes you more appealing to the public. You're physically vital; relations with the opposite sex go well.

Saturday, November 14 (Moon in Libra to Scorpio 5:25 p.m.) It's a number 7 day. There's mystery in the air. Something hidden or secretive comes to light. Look beneath the surface for the reasons others are shifting their points of view. But don't make any final decisions on what you uncover until tomorrow.

Sunday, November 15 (Moon in Scorpio) Mercury moves into your third house. You're mind is active and alert. You're adaptable and versatile, especially when dealing with relatives or neighbors. You express your point of view, and you're understood.

Monday, November 16 (Moon in Scorpio) There's a new moon in your second house. New opportunities related to earning money arise. Begin a new project. Work on something that brings value to your life or supports your values. You're seeking comfort, security, money, and prosperity.

Tuesday, November 17 (Moon in Scorpio to Sagittarius 12:23 a.m.)   It's a number 1 day. Explore and discover. Take the lead. Creativity and originality are emphasized. Get out and meet people; have new experiences. In romance, something new is developing.

Wednesday, November 18 (Moon in Sagittarius)   The moon is in your third house. You're interested in getting your ideas across, but you've got your mundane, everyday activities to handle. Siblings and neighbors could play a role.

Thursday, November 19 (Moon in Sagittarius to Capricorn 10:01 a.m.)   It's a number 3 day. You're creative; you communicate well because yesterday's energy continues. Remain flexible, and pay attention to any intuitive nudges. Your imagination is keen. You're curious and inventive. You inspire others with your enthusiasm and willingness to listen.

Friday, November 20 (Moon in Capricorn)   The moon is in your fourth house. Spend time with your family and loved ones. Stick close to home. You're dealing with the foundations of who you are and who you are becoming. A parent could play a role. You're feeling close to your roots. Make an effort to beautify your home.

Saturday, November 21 (Moon in Capricorn to Aquarius 10:11 p.m.)   It's a number 5 day. Variety is the spice of life. It's all about freedom of thought and action. You're versatile and changeable. Let go of old structures; find a new point of view.

Sunday, November 22 (Moon in Aquarius)   The moon is in your fifth house. Work on a creative project. You can delve deeply into your unconscious for inspiration. There's greater depth in a relationship. Children play a role.

Monday, November 23 (Moon in Aquarius)   You and your friends or colleagues get together to brainstorm or discuss plans that concern all of you. Don't hesitate to offer your thoughts. You get support from surprising quarters. Your wishes and dreams come true.

Tuesday, November 24 (Moon in Aquarius to Pisces 11:08 a.m.)   It's a number 8 day. It's another power day, and you get another chance for a big windfall. You pull off a financial coup. Unexpected money arrives. Be careful not to hurt others.

Wednesday, November 25 (Moon in Pisces)   The moon is in your sixth house. Delegate some of your responsibilities. Avoid taking on too much work. Allow others to shoulder some of the burden. Take care of any health issues.

Thursday, November 26 (Moon in Pisces to Aries 10:11 p.m.)   It's a number 1 day. You're at the top of your cycle again. You get a fresh start. Be independent, but work with creative people, while avoiding those with closed minds. In romance, a flirtation could turn more serious.

Friday, November 27 (Moon in Aries)   The moon is in your seventh house. Try not to be overaggressive. There could be some tension with a partner. Be patient and tolerant. You want to move ahead quickly, but a partnership requires cooperation. Take time to listen to your partner's point of view.

Saturday, November 28 (Moon in Aries)   It's a great day for brainstorming or initiating a new project. Be original; imprint your style. Set out on an adventure. A Pisces and a Virgo play extraordinary roles.

Sunday, November 29 (Moon in Aries to Taurus 5:35 a.m.)   It's a number 4 day. Tear down the old in order to rebuild. Be methodical and thorough. Revise; rewrite. You're building foundations for an outlet for your creativity. Emphasize quality.

Monday, November 30 (Moon in Taurus)   The moon is in your eighth house. The Taurus moon helps to keep you grounded, especially in your pursuit of a metaphysical subject or matters dealing with death, taxes, insurance, or inheritance.

DECEMBER 2009

Tuesday, December 1 (Moon in Taurus to Gemini 9:24 a.m.)   You're romantic at heart; with Venus moving into Sagittarius, you see the big picture concerning a romance. Meanwhile, with Uranus going direct in your tenth house, you can expect sudden changes in the workplace. Some chaos and erratic behavior could result.

Wednesday, December 2 (Moon in Gemini)   There's a full moon in your ninth house. Your ideas come to fruition. You are provoking change. Others are finally listening to you. Even though you have a tendency to change your mind, your suggestions are taking root. Plan a getaway.

Thursday, December 3 (Moon in Gemini to Cancer 11:01 a.m.)   It's a number 6 day. Service to others is the theme of the day. You offer advice and support. Be sympathetic, kind, generous, and tolerant, especially toward someone who is hurting. Focus on making people happy.

Friday, December 4 (Moon in Cancer)   The moon is in your tenth house of profession and career. You're warm toward fellow workers; you're responsive to the needs of the public. Emotions run high, so be careful not to blur the boundaries between your personal and professional lives.

Saturday, December 5 (Moon in Cancer to Leo 12:08 p.m.)   Mercury moves into your fourth house. There's a lot of activity related to education in the home. You could be helping a child with homework, considering homeschooling, or looking into colleges for an older child. Things are definitely changing in your home life. Try to take time to relax.

Sunday, December 6 (Moon in Leo)   The moon is in your eleventh house. You find an identity within a group that allows you to move forward with your plans and ideas. Friends inside and outside the group help you achieve your goals, especially if they involve an effort for the common good.

Monday, December 7 (Moon in Leo to Virgo 2:07 p.m.)   It's a number 1 day. You're in a position to take the lead. You make connections that others overlook. You're determined and courageous. Express your opinions dynamically. Get out and meet new people.

Tuesday, December 8 (Moon in Virgo)   The moon is in your twelfth house. You work behind the scenes and keep your thoughts to yourself. You might confide in a close friend, discussing hidden fears and worries. You also could be in contact with institutions, such as hospitals or courts.

Wednesday, December 9 (Moon in Virgo to Libra 5:48 p.m.)   It's a number 3 day. Think positive; stay optimistic. You can influence others with your upbeat attitude. You're definitely the life of the party. In business dealings, diversify. Insist on all the information, not just bits and pieces.

Thursday, December 10 (Moon in Libra)   The moon is in your first house. You get recharged for the month ahead. You're feeling strong and vital. Relations with the opposite sex work well. Your feelings and thoughts are aligned.

Friday, December 11 (Moon in Libra to Scorpio 11:32 p.m.)   It's a number 5 day. You're feeling versatile and changeable, but you have a tendency to diversify too much. You'll be in a hurry all day, so watch your step; you could be accident-prone.

Saturday, December 12 (Moon in Scorpio)   The moon is in your second house. It's a good day for investments, but be practical. You seek financial and domestic security; you feel best surrounded by familiar objects. It's not the objects that are important but the feelings you associate with them.

Sunday, December 13 (Moon in Scorpio)   A new romance is highly passionate. Your connection is both emotional and intuitive. If your love interest is more established, things could get intense. Forgive and forget; try to avoid going to extremes.

Monday, December 14 (Moon in Scorpio to Sagittarius 7:25 a.m.)   It's a number 8 day. It's your power day. Unexpected money comes your way. Be bold. Be aware that fear of failure or fear that you won't measure up might attract exactly that.

Tuesday, December 15 (Moon in Sagittarius)   The moon is in your third house. You express your ideas clearly. But try not to get overemotional, especially when you're dealing with relatives or neighbors. A female relative plays a role in your day, especially a Leo or an Aries.

Wednesday, December 16 (Moon in Sagittarius to Capricorn 5:32 p.m.)   There's a new moon in your third house. Yesterday's energy flows on, and you get a new opportunity related to your ideas, especially those that are connected to the past. Put it all down in writing. You won't regret it!

Thursday, December 17 (Moon in Capricorn)   The moon is in your fourth house. Work at home, if possible. Combine business with personal needs. Decorate your home for the holidays. Wrap those gifts that you've stuffed away. Get everything in order. Spend time with your family and enjoy your quiet time.

Friday, December 18 (Moon in Capricorn)   Your drive to succeed is highlighted. Your responsibilities increase, and you could feel somewhat stressed. Authority figures or elderly people play a role. Self-discipline is key. Maintain emotional balance; don't overlook your exercise routine.

Saturday, December 19 (Moon in Capricorn to Aquarius 5:39 a.m.)   It's a number 4 day. Get organized and restructure. Tear down in order to rebuild. Stay focused. Be methodical and thorough. Emphasize quality. You could feel inhibited in showing affection.

Sunday, December 20 (Moon in Aquarius)   Mars goes retrograde in your eleventh house. You're ready to charge ahead, but it seems that others aren't so willing now. In spite of your high energy, expect a glitch or two, especially related to any high-powered plans with a group. Delays and confusion could involve friends. Hold your temper; be patient. Things will get done.

Monday, December 21 (Moon in Aquarius to Pisces 6:42 p.m.)   It's a number 6 day. It's all about making other people feel good. Get out and finish your holiday shopping, wrap those presents, and prepare your menu for your holiday meals. If you're all caught up, give someone else a hand.

Tuesday, December 22 (Moon in Pisces)   The moon is in your sixth house. Yesterday's energy flows on. It's another service day. Help others where you can. Be generous and tolerant, but don't ignore your own needs. Take care of any health issues.

Wednesday, December 23 (Moon in Pisces)   Your intuition flows like a rapid current of energy that brings you exactly what you're seeking. Remain aware, follow your hunches, and watch for synchronicities.

Thursday, December 24 (Moon in Pisces to Aries 6:40 a.m.)   It's a number 9 day. Complete projects and get ready for something new. Clear up odds and ends. Take an inventory on where things are going in your life. Make a donation to a worthy cause. Look beyond the present.

Friday, December 25 (Moon in Aries)   Venus moves into your fourth house. That means love, happiness, and generosity in the home! Perfect timing. You feel strongly connected to your family and home. The domestic scene flourishes. Merry Christmas!

Saturday, December 26 (Moon in Aries into Taurus 3:27 a.m.)   Mercury goes retrograde in your fourth house. The energy shifts. You can expect some delays regarding your plans and some disruptions in your home life. Group activities can be particularly challenging over the next three weeks.

Sunday, December 27 (Moon in Taurus)   The moon is in your eighth house. Your experiences are more intense than usual. You have a strong sense of duty and feel obligated to fulfill your promises. Security is an important issue with you. Deal with mortgages, insurance, and investments. Managing shared resources takes on new importance.

Monday, December 28 (Moon in Taurus to Gemini 8:15 p.m.)   It's a number 4 day. You're at the right place at the right time. Missing papers or objects are found. You can overcome any bureaucratic red tape. Be practical with your money.

Tuesday, December 29 (Moon in Gemini)   The moon is in your ninth house. As the year is coming to a close, look at the big picture and prepare for 2010. You could map out a long journey or plan a course of study to enhance your education. Focus on your philosophy of life and what you are bringing into the New Year.

Wednesday, December 30 (Moon in Gemini to Cancer 9:46 p.m.)   It's a number 6 day. Diplomacy wins the way. Be sympathetic, kind, generous, and tolerant. Focus on making people happy. Get your New Year's resolutions in order.

Thursday, December 31 (Moon in Cancer) The year ends with a lunar eclipse in your tenth house. You can expect emotional events related to your career or to your home life. It could involve a matter with your fellow workers or your family. Your life is more public, especially if you're going out tonight. Avoid excessive emotional displays.

HAPPY NEW YEAR!

SYDNEY OMARR

Born on August 5, 1926, in Philadelphia, Pennsylvania, Sydney Omarr was the only person ever given full-time duty in the U.S. Army as an astrologer. He is regarded as the most erudite astrologer of our time and the best known, through his syndicated column and his radio and television programs (he was Merv Griffin's "resident astrologer"). Omarr has been called the most "knowledgeable astrologer since Evangeline Adams." His forecasts of Nixon's downfall, the end of World War II in mid-August of 1945, the assassination of John F. Kennedy, Roosevelt's election to a fourth term and his death in office . . . these and many others are on the record and quoted enough to be considered "legendary."

ABOUT THE SERIES

This is one of a series of twelve *Sydney Omarr® Day-by-Day Astrological Guides* for the signs of 2009. For questions and comments about the book, go to www.tjmacgregor.com.